TWENTIETH CENTURY VIEWS

The aim of this series is to present the best in
contemporary critical opinion on major authors,
providing a twentieth century perspective on
their changing status in an era of profound
revaluation.

Maynard Mack, *Series Editor*
Yale University

DICKENS

DICKENS

A COLLECTION OF CRITICAL ESSAYS

Edited by

Martin Price

Prentice-Hall, Inc.  *Englewood Cliffs, N. J.*

A SPECTRUM BOOK

Current printing (last number):

10   9   8   7   6   5

Contents

Introduction

by Martin Price

There is no term that recurs more often in recent Dickens criticism than "Shakespearean," for the comparison is an almost inevitable way of defining some of Dickens' powers: his effortless invention, his brilliant play of language, the scope and density of his imagined world. The comparison serves to identify those powers all would grant; and it helps also to free Dickens' work from false expectations—that he is, or should be, writing the kind of novel George Eliot or Henry James wrote. Throughout English criticism, the example of Shakespeare confounds critical dogmatism. It makes us ask ourselves what we have achieved when we have created a critical system that disables us for reading our greatest writers.

So it is in the case of Dickens. As the nineteenth century novel began to seek the dignity of high art, the pleasures of Dickens did not seem adequately "serious," and his novels became the experience of the nursery. Those who later rejected Victorian sentiment and morality were disdainful of the creator of the Christmas books or the death of Little Nell and overlooked, as best they could, the vehement satirist of Podsnappery and the Circumlocution Office. As best they could: there were always some to take him seriously. Bernard Shaw considered *Little Dorrit* "a more seditious book than *Das Kapital.*" What we are coming belatedly to see is that *Little Dorrit* is seditious in more than a political sense. It requires us to examine most of our conceptions of what the novel should be, and, as we turn back to Dickens from Dostoevsky or Kafka, from Brecht or the theater of the absurd, we are better able to see some of what has been there all the time.

To recover Dickens is not to remake him in the shape of our current literary heroes. It has been too easy to stress the darkness and bitterness of the later Dickens, to turn the long-hidden facts of his affair with Ellen Ternan into the myth of a buried self and of social alienation, to find in the dust-heaps of *Our Mutual Friend* the *frisson* of T. S. Eliot's "waste land." It is important to see these elements of his life

1

and fiction as part of the more puzzling fullness that includes his hard-headed plans for management of Miss Coutts' home for fallen women, his fascinated horror of violence, his reliance upon the teachings of the Gospels, his resolution of social evils in small enclaves of domestic warmth such as he never quite achieved in his own life.

Comparisons with other writers may be helpful so long as they do not claim too much. In *Bleak House,* Jo's death is marked by the narrator's outrage: "Dead, your Majesty. Dead, my lords and gentlemen. Dead, Right Reverends and Wrong Reverends of every order. Dead, men and women, born with Heavenly compassion in your hearts. And dying thus around us every day." The temptation is irresistible to add, from Swift's *A Modest Proposal,* "as fast as can be reasonably expected." For these are both satirists of the "official version," echoing its jargon until specious humanity reveals its full ugliness.

But the confrontation helps us to define differences as well: Dickens is more explicit, more overtly compassionate, insisting always upon the perversions of feeling as well as of thought. His outrage is of the same consistency as his generous celebration, the satirical wit of the same copious extravagance as the comic elaborations. Dickens' world is alive with things that snatch, lurch, teeter, thrust, leer; it is the animate world of Netherlandish genre painting or of Hogarth's prints, where all space is a field of force, where objects vie or intrigue with each other, where every human event spills over into the things that surround it. This may become the typically crowded scene of satire, where persons are reduced to things and things to matter in motion; or it may pulsate with fierce energy and noisy feeling. It is different from Swift; it is the distinctive Dickensian plenitude, which we find again in his verbal play, in his great array of vivid characters, in his massed scenes of feasts or public declamations. It creates rituals as compelling as the resuscitation of Rogue Riderhood, where strangers participate solemnly in the recovery of a spark of life, oblivious for the moment of the unlovely human form it will soon inhabit.

II

To think of Dickens is first of all to remember the great characters: Pickwick, Pecksniff, Micawber, Jaggers, William Dorrit, Madame Defarge. Even in this short list, one can see the range: if all of them are "grand hyperbolic beings," "humanity caught . . . and kept permanent in its highest and extremest mood" (as David Masson wrote in Dickens' lifetime), they vary from comic charm to monstrous hypocrisy, from adroit professionalism to selfish impotence, from fanaticism to honorable limitation. What strikes us about such characters is not simply their unchanging nature, but the fact that this very stability demands resourcefulness; each of them can find, in Mary McCarthy's phrase, "the most unexpected ways of being himself." And while he is always himself, what he means will change from moment to moment. Pecksniff as suitor is a more frightening figure than Pecksniff as father. William Dorrit, absurdly ceremonious as he accepts the gratuities due the Father of Marshalsea, is the exploiter of his daughter and the abject worshiper of Society. Old Turveydrop appears as a selfish parent like Mrs. Jellyby, a preserver of dead forms like Sir Leicester Dedlock, an infantile egocentric like Harold Skimpole. These characters gain their full meaning from the structure of which they are a part; no single character exists without his counterpart or contrast, and none fails to participate at some level in one of those unifying themes that are stated and restated in various keys—comic, pathetic, satiric—throughout a work.

For example, whose "great expectations" concern us most—Pip's dream of gentility, Magwitch's dream of the gentleman he can create, Miss Havisham's dream of revenge upon all men for the shame she has suffered? They are all inextricably connected. Pip's fantasies are tied to the unattainable Estella, whom Miss Havisham has trained in heartlessness. Magwitch succeeds in creating a creature genteel enough to despise him, while his own daughter has become the despair of his artificial gentleman. And presiding over all these ironies is the mysterious Jaggers, himself a victim of his own defenses, hardened by disappointment, still concerned for the savage woman he seems to abuse, foolishly saving her daughter by making her the instrument of Miss Havisham. The simple malevolence of Compeyson or Orlick seems almost refreshingly clear in a world of self-destroying fantasies that range from Pumblechook's snobbery or Wopsle's declamations all the way to the grim self-hatred of Estella, convinced that she cannot love and can only be a curse to the man who wins her. And yet there are other expectations that are rewarded in time: the warm trust of Joe Gargery, the modest ambitions of Herbert Pocket, even Pip's own dreams, as they are freed of the tawdry social pretensions that travesty gentility of spirit. Pip cannot return to the marshes or to the life of a blacksmith or even to Biddy; but his new accent and station need no longer cut him off from the self he has been or from the life he cannot now share. The mature Pip, whose voice we hear throughout the novel, with its saving humor of self-acceptance, can finally see Estella as what she is instead of as the fantasy he has had to make her; and for that reason it seems appropriate that she can return to him in the second and happier ending. Each is a fantasist who has grown into maturity; each is a fantasy that has dwindled into humanity.

Some such pattern—and this version is a highly simplified one—is at work in each of the major novels, and the pattern holds together characters who, by their very nature, must inhabit private worlds and fail to understand each other. All, that is, but the central characters. They are less colorful and obsessive; they are capable of self-awareness and responsibility; they must make decisions and undergo change. They may be fallible: self-centered and resentful like Martin Chuzzlewit or Bella Wilfer; depressed in spirit by the neglect or cruelty of others, damaged unassertive selves like Arthur Clennam or Esther Summerson or Florence Dombey; restless, perhaps cynical men, unconsciously seeking a commitment they can surrender themselves to, like Sydney Carton or Eugene Wrayburn. These central characters are more than the conventional "leads" in romantic plays or simple melodramas. They are observed with remarkable acuteness; the moments which may seem cloying have their explanation in the needs as well as the virtues of these characters. Esther Summerson may jingle her housekeeper's keys too often and simper over Ada, but she has her nightmares, too, and a terrifying sense of unworthiness that she has the strength to turn to service. She may be slow to believe that she can be loved, she may treasure a little coyly the praise she wins; but she provides a contrast to the self-indulgence of Richard Carstone, who is incapable of patient effort and finally enslaved by Chancery, or to the more wilful self-indulgence of Skimpole, who gaily forswears all the responsibility Esther assumes and exploits the goodness of Jarndyce which has also saved Esther.

There is a good instance of the moral contrasts Dickens creates in William Dorrit's two daughters. Amy is wholly selfless, seen in shadows at Mrs. Clennam's house, totally self-effacing. She cannot behave as a woman; not only does she seem like a child, she sees herself as a child. She refuses personality and remains the invisible servant of her family, never embarrassing them with the fact of their dependence upon her, supporting her father's maudlin selfishness, reproached or at best neglected by her family for want of style, clinging to the Marshalsea for its freedom from worse pretension. She can assume maturity only with Maggy, the great child of twenty-seven whose mind stopped at ten, or with her uncle Frederick, childlike and timid as he has become. There are sufficient reasons for her behavior, and we can both admire the tenacity of spirit and deplore the denial of self-assertion. The man she loves, Arthur Clennam, is another such, unloved in childhood, returning at forty from a wasted life abroad, persuaded that he is too old and too unsuccessful to win Pet Meagles' love, retreating gratefully into the shadows as "nobody." Yet both of them are strong in their resistance to the perverse selfishness of their parents. Clennam remains unspoiled by the sour self-righteousness of his mother's Calvinistic religion. Amy escapes the self-pity of her father: "If he had been a man with strength of purpose to face those troubles and fight them, he might have broken the net that held him, or broken his heart; but being what he was, he languidly slipped into this smooth descent, and never more took one step upward." It is their strength that turns them toward life, however obliquely and hesitantly, until Clennam grows younger and Amy older and both become persons at last in "the autumn morning sun's bright rays." To a degree Amy Dorrit suggests something more simple and austere than a person, and she may shade off, as Lionel Trilling has proposed, into an embodiment of a divine principle. But she is, nevertheless, a psychologically convincing person, imperfect, moving reluctantly and unbelievingly toward a sense of self. It is Dickens' power to give us both, to allow us to glimpse the archetype beneath the individual, somewhat as we do in Cordelia, and to contain the allegorical in something more complex and robust.

Fanny Dorrit is one of the most brilliant of Dickens' studies of self-imprisonment in a novel that presents that theme at every level. Bribed, threatened, and scorned by Mrs. Merdle, she devotes her life to winning her revenge. Although she despises Mrs. Merdle's son, Sparkler, she cannot resist marrying him: "I shall make him fetch and carry, my dear, and I shall make him subject to me. And if I don't make his mother subject to me, too, it shall not be my fault" (II, vi). When Amy points to the futility of such a life, Fanny is sadly defiant: "It wouldn't be an unhappy life, Amy. It would be the life I am fitted for. Whether by disposition or circumstances, is no matter; I am better fitted for such a life than for almost any other" (II, xiv). One can detect here the note that Fanny often sounds, in alternate outrage and remorseful weeping, that peculiar compound of self-pity and self-hatred that makes her, like Pope's Atossa, "Sick of herself through very selfishness." When she resolves on the marriage, she responds to Amy's tears with her own. "It was the last time Fanny ever showed that there was any hidden, suppressed, or conquered feeling in her on the matter. From that hour the way she had chosen lay before her, and she trod it with her own imperious self-willed step." We see her shortly after, "completely arrayed for her new part. . . . No longer feeling that want of a defined place and character which had caused her so much trouble . . ." (II, xv). At the close, after the collapse of the Merdle empire, we find Fanny and Mrs. Merdle "inhabiting different floors of the genteel little temple of inconvenience to which the smell of the day before yesterday's soup and coach-horses was as constant as Death to man," arraying themselves "to fight it out in the lists of Society, sworn rivals." Amy is caring for Fanny's neglected children as she once did for Fanny, and Fanny has locked herself into her new "superior sort of Marshalsea."

One more pair of characters may stand for all those vivid grotesques from Alfred Jingle in *The Pickwick Papers* through Silas Wegg in *Our Mutual Friend*. Flora Finching is the girl Arthur Clennam might have married but for his mother's tyranny and his submission. She is now widowed, and in the twenty years since she has seen Clennam she has become a large woman, "diffuse and silly," much given to drink, locked up in a coy and breathless monologue. She has moments of shrewdness that she will not sustain, and she buries them in a torrent of girlish words, constantly testing her charm but afraid to test it too far. One sees the "spoiled and artless" girl buried in the blowsy caricature; her talk is tremendously funny and faintly pathetic. With her comes her inheritance from the brief marriage to Finching, Mr. F.'s Aunt, "an amazing little woman, with a face like a staring wooden doll too cheap for expression." She is locked up, too; her prison is a savage senility, and she emerges from her own dark fantasies only to spit out cryptic abuse, "breathing bitterness and scorn, and staring leagues away" (I, xxiii). She is ludicrous and terrible, voicing all the contempt Arthur Clennam half-expects of the world, raging with more overt insanity than Miss Wade or Rigaud, always coupled with Flora's bland inanities. She has the wonderful comic force of an unnerving hostility that, for once, has no ground or meaning, a rage that is terrible and yet harmless, like those frightening grimaces one watches monkeys enact in their cages.

III

Dickens' characters are remarkable individuals, but they are more than that. It is not upon the special case or the unique specimen that the mind dwells; rather it is the uniquely intense embodiment of the universal. Characters as menacing or grotesque as Fagin, Tulkinghorn, and Orlick are memorable because of all they include, because of all they deny, because of all they overleap and surpass. And this meaning is conferred upon them by the plot structures of which they are a part.

To encompass such figures and give them the many strands of connection—of partial contrast, telling similarity, common motive, and disparate expression—requires plots of bold artifice. Popular literature is always close to the artifice of the formula. We look for the twice-told tale, or the tale told a hundred times, and we are ready to see it worked out anew, the old formula discernible beneath the ingenious variations, the pleasures of recognition as acute as those of discovery. In the variations lie the possibilities of topical reference, of social criticism, of the circumstantiality of life lived here and now. But the formulas invoke the old categories, the traditional metaphors, the shape of the world we framed with the imagination of childhood; bolder, simpler, cruder, and more compelling than the world of adult intelligence.

Scholars have shown how Dickens used the materials of popular literature, from pantomime to romance. Clearly he remained open to the imagination of childhood, but he is remarkable for the weight of mature awareness he could make the old forms of romance, of folk tale and fairy tale, sustain. Some writers reject the familiar forms as too simplistic and too conservative; their object is to extend our sympathies or to submit us to the pain of radically new awareness, and they refuse us the comfort of the old formulas. Others renew those formulas and deliberately use the most rigid and artificial of them as the basis of their fiction. Must Lear have three daughters or Portia three caskets? Can we credit the Duke's disguise or Angelo's sudden toppling from righteousness in *Measure for Measure*? And how shall we support, in the midst of a play where everyone is acting or choosing a part, a company of players who present a play within a play?

If these are foolish questions to raise about Shakespeare, are they wiser applied to Dickens? Clearly his plots, like his characters, are part of a coherent Dickens world: a world in which causality is intensified into a web of coincidence. All novels, however realistic they may seem, hold together careers that would drift apart in real life. We cannot conceive George Eliot's Lydgate without the presence of Dorothea; we cannot understand Anna Karenina without the coexistence of Constantin Levin. If those characters meet only tangentially, with less violence to probability, there is still the control of the author, disposing their lives in a structure which relates them more intimately than mere probability could ever permit. Dickens is flagrant about connecting his characters, and we enter his novels with the expectation that their world permits, in fact demands, such collisions. It is a world of heightened significance, a world of unrelieved and often frightening relevances, a world where crime and disease are not discrete experiences but dimensions of a larger and more oppressive dehumanization. It is a world of doubles and counterparts, of actions that reticulate into a vast mesh of consequences. As W. J. Harvey says, it "expresses our sense that real life blends the casual and the causal, that things are connected and contingent, patterned and random, that we are both free and determined." He speaks of this real world as a "labyrinth of the conditional," where "what seems to us a straight path is nothing but a series of cross-roads."

When the third brother of the fairy tale meets a feeble old man in the woods, we do not expect an accidental encounter; we have seen the old man twice before, perhaps in a different guise, and we are waiting to see the completion of a pattern. We are all familiar with those game-like plots which fall into place like a hand at solitaire. In these plots we ask only that the characters should not distract us from the problems they set; it would hardly do for each chess queen to have a distinct personality. But if the game-like element persists, it can support much more, as the story of Portia's three caskets recalls. If we can submit to the pleasures of the game without too fastidious a demand for real life, we shall find reality that life cannot give us. The more we seek to find meaning in life, the greater our recourse to the type or the model, to the general or universal that lends import to the individual. The characters of fiction are constellations of universal traits; every term we can apply to them, except their proper names, is the name for a common trait. (And in fiction we expect more even of proper names than we do in real life.) But more than that, the characters of fiction have fewer traits, seen in clearer and closer relationship than in the persons of real life, seen in all their congruity and incongruity without the allowances or resentments or confusions we bring to actual encounters.

Just as fiction is built of characters we know more fully than we know most actual persons, its plots, unlike most patterns in actual life, are such as we can follow to their full completion. If there are accidents, they are part of a world that is significantly without significance. It is appropriate that Mrs. Rachael should turn out to be Mrs. Chadband, wedded to that oiliest of false Christians. It is appropriate that Jo's smallpox should disfigure Esther and leave Skimpole untouched except for the money Skimpole gains by turning over Jo to the police. It is appropriate that Eugene Wrayburn should encounter, as he toys with the seduction of Lizzie Hexam, the rivalry of a man like Bradley Headstone, the rigid and repressed schoolmaster. Both of them are indifferent to what Lizzie really is; one is seeking relief from boredom and indolence, the other is bursting out of the respectability he has never allowed himself to question. Wrayburn can be saved by Lizzie because of his difference from Headstone; he can face things in himself that Headstone can only enact.

The coincidences and the artful symmetries of plot have the force of those themes that produce counterparts in character. They connect and relate not as real life does but as those meanings we derive from life do. They operate by the magic that makes the landscape weep with the mourning pastoral lover or thunder with the madness of Lear. We may speak of pathetic fallacy in the idiom of logic, but magic has its own logic of sympathy; and it is a logic we live with most of our unscientific lives. What is surprising about all of this is the reluctance of readers to give in to a logic they admire in other writers. If it clears the air to call Dickens a poet, as George Ford does, this does not seem an undue extension of that term. We must distinguish between the triteness of the stereotyped romance and the vigor of the full meaningfulness of true poetry. We can easily disdain the opiates of wishfulness that seem to restore to us the world we never had. But there are romances, as there are pastorals, that recall things hoped for, as well as things present we cannot deny. We can read them with full consciousness that both elements are present and that the former will govern this imagined world, if only to set it apart from real life and to give us the liberation and discovery of metaphor. The imagined and metaphorical world stands as a model by which to explore the realities of real life; it can provide the most serious of games and the most thoughtful of pleasures.

The typical world of the mature Dickens novels has two main dimensions. There is the lower world of selfishness, of money and power, of exploitation and the reduction of people to interlocking parts of a social system. The system may be embodied in business, as in *Dombey and Son, Hard Times,* and *Little Dorrit;* in legality or inheritance, as in *Bleak House, Great Expectations,* and *Our Mutual Friend.* The two forms overlap. They have in common the fact that they are forms: codes that impoverish experience, displace humane feeling, and generate repetitive cycles of fear and hostility. When Henry Gowan's mother asks Mrs. Merdle for her sanction, as Priestess of Society, of Henry's marriage, the play of forms is most intensely farcical. Mrs. Merdle, knowing "what was expected of her, and perceiving the exact nature of the fiction to be nursed, . . . took it delicately in her arms, and put her required contribution of gloss upon it. . . . And Mrs. Gowan, who of course saw through her own threadbare blind perfectly, and who knew that Society would see through it perfectly, came out of this form, notwithstanding, as she had gone into it, with immense complacency and gravity" (II, xxiii). The forms are no less farcical but more cruelly so as we see Merdle, the object of worship in a commercial society, terrified of his Chief Butler; that noble specter greets the news of Merdle's suicide with, "Sir, Mr. Merdle never was the gentleman, and no ungentlemanly act on Mr. Merdle's part would surprise me." But if the forms are farcically unreal, they are all-powerful, as we see in Chancery or in Pip's gentlemanly rise or in the world of Podsnappery. Each exploiter is sure of being exploited; most sufferers exact suffering in turn, as Miss Wade schools Tattycoram in the satisfactions of paranoid resentment.

Opposed to this world of forms, of selfhood, and of repetition there are the few who hold onto freedom or earn it. They may sustain love and fidelity against odds, helping the disregarded as Esther Summerson does Caddy Jellyby, or refuse to enter the system, as John Harmon does. At their most tortured, like Miss Flite or Betty Higden, they escape into fantasy or vision; and in Jenny Wren we find the mixture of torture, resentment, and a vision of innocence. The girl with a warped body has precocity thrust upon her by a drunken father. She treats him as an unruly child and shows all the parental viciousness that she feels in his failure toward her. Yet she keeps alive a vision of a world that transcends all she endures, and from the curiously pastoral City rooftop where Riah has spread a carpet, she calls down after him, "Come back and be dead." "As he mounted, the call or song began to sound in his ears again, and, looking above, he saw the face of the little creature looking down out of a Glory of her long bright radiant hair, and musically repeating to him, like a vision: 'Come up and be dead! Come up and be dead!' " (II, v). It is Jenny's vision that Wrayburn needs as he returns to life.

The novels are shot through with these intimations of transcendence. The sea in *Dombey and Son* is one instance, as Kathleen Tillotson has shown. In *Little Dorrit,* there is the vision over the river: "The smoke that rose into the sky had lost its dingy hue and taken a brightness upon it. . . . From a radiant centre over the whole length and breadth of the tranquil firmament, great shoots of light streamed among the early stars, like signs of the blessed later covenant of peace and hope that changed the crown of thorns into a glory" (II, xxxi). In the first chapter of that novel we see the division between worlds: "the stars came out in the heavens, and the fire-flies mimicked them in the lower air, as men may feebly imitate the goodness of a better order of beings." One might put beside it the sentence of Dickens' will that urges his children "humbly to try to guide themselves by the teaching of the New Testament in its broad spirit, and to put no faith in any man's narrow construction of its letter here or there." In the last sentence of *Little Dorrit* we can see the mixture of those worlds as the limit of human possibility: "They went quietly down into the roaring streets, inseparable and blessed; and as they passed along in sunshine and shade, the noisy and the eager, and the arrogant and the froward and the vain, fretted, and chafed, and made their usual uproar." Dickens has sometimes been compared with Blake, and in Blake's "London" we can find the most compact version of Dickens' lower world, as in the *Songs of Innocence* we can see something of his vision of transcendence.

IV

The coherence of the Dickens world is in large part the coherence of his language. Steven Marcus has written acutely about the presence of the novelist in his work, "his disciplined, magisterial sensibility, acting as a kind of deity, freely creating and controlling the experience he imposes on his readers." There is no way to read Dickens without submitting to this presence, but to say "submitting" is to imply a reluctance that not many feel. There are critics who resent the frankness of artifice and the overtness of rhetoric, however brilliant. But Dickens never aspires to create a world we can mistake for real life, or a style that is transparent. He has, as George Ford suggests, something of what Keats calls "negative capability" in his creation of characters who are superbly themselves and speak their own remarkable idiom; but he has something also of what Keats calls the "egotistical sublime." All he presents is made part of the Dickensian vision, caught in the peculiar Dickensian play of language, heightened with the same Dickensian extravagance. His style is one that always exhibits pleasure in its own resourcefulness, that rejoices in its power to catch the wonderful logic of the outrageous. "Mr. Podsnap could tolerate taste in a mushroom man who stood in need of that sort of thing, but was far above it himself. Hideous solidity was the characteristic of the Podsnap plate. Everything was made to look as heavy as it could, and to take up as much room as possible." The wit and assurance, the fusion of the plausible and the fatuous, the mixture of emptiness and stuffed fullness—all these give such a passage the force of a controlling sanity observing a world that acts without it. Dickens' verbal control of his world is an important element in our reading of his work; it voices a fuller awareness than his characters usually have, an awareness that stands outside the impositions and tangles of their world, ready to twist its logic tighter and to give it that extravagance that makes it magnificent and absurd.

There is no more splendid parody in Dickens than the speech of the American Transcendentalist literary lady in *Martin Chuzzlewit:*

> "Mind and matter . . . glide swift into the vortex of immensity. Howls the sublime, and softly sleeps the calm Ideal, in the whispering chambers of Imagination. To hear it, sweet it is. But then, outlaughs the stern philosopher, and saith to the Grotesque, 'What, ho! arrest for me that Agency. Go bring it here!' And so the vision fadeth."

Dickens' comic play, illustrated again and again in the essays that follow, gives us the assurance that we gain from the mock-heroic style of a great Augustan satire. The style is itself the touchstone by which we test the falsity or rigidity of what it describes. For the freedom and flexibility, both the openness to fantasy and the saving ironic detachment, make us aware of a guiding intelligence and sensibility. In the great satiric passages, such as the impersonal narrator's view of Tom-all-alone's or the account of the Veneerings' dinners, the figures of speech gain a peculiar boldness. As Hillis Miller points out, the metaphors are suddenly adopted as literal names; the violence of reality outruns the extravagance of fantasy, and in a novel like *Our Mutual Friend* the theme of the predators is caught in the comic monstrosities of Mr. Venus's taxidermy shop, filled with stuffed animals or bits and pieces of "human warious" waiting to be put to new uses.

The style has more than comic range, of course. In a passage like the following, which sets the scene for the murder of Tulkinghorn in *Bleak House,* there is an ironic movement from images of pastoral peace to satirical parody and finally to menacing suspense:

> [London's] steeples and towers, and its one great dome, grow more ethereal; its smoky house-tops lose their grossness, in the pale effulgence; the noises that arise from the streets are fewer and are softened, and the footsteps on the pavements pass more tranquilly away. In these fields of Mr. Tulkinghorn's inhabiting, where the shepherds play on Chancery pipes that have no stop, and keep their sheep in the fold by hook and by crook until they have shorn them exceeding close, every noise is merged, this moonlight night, into a distant ringing hum, as if the city were a vast glass, vibrating.

In stressing the verbal control of Dickens, one must not neglect the hypnotic power his art can achieve. All art allows us both to lose ourselves in what it presents and to preserve a saving distance from it; there is no more contradiction in this than in any complex experience.

As Taylor Stoehr has put it, "the combination of techniques working for and against the artificial verisimilitude produces a strange impression of a world 'supernaturally natural' and true to life as a nightmare seems true to life." He treats the panoramic scene of the breaking of the wine-cask in *A Tale of Two Cities* and shows how "the scene quivers with suppressed fury" caught in the rhetorical structure of the language rather than in a narrator's personality. Things "vibrate with immediacy, as if it were our hallucination and not Dickens'" (*Dickens: The Dreamer's Stance* [Ithaca: Cornell University Press, 1965], Chapter 2). If this overstates the process, it also corrects any tendency to neglect the presentational power of Dickens' rhetoric. His scene, like his characters, is boldly *there*, even while we sense the artistry that is giving it immediacy. For the artistry is a constant; the novels are structures of language, whatever else, and their language prepares us for a mode of imagination that is distinctively Dickensian. It is a mode that takes artifice for granted, that deliberately heightens and intensifies, that exacts from an event all the rage or wonder or pity it can claim.

V

Much has been written about Dickens as a social critic, so much in fact that it has seemed surprising to find him attacking evils that had ceased to be current in his day. It would be ridiculous to undervalue the social criticism, and yet one may be struck much more by a moral criticism that finds its inevitable extension in the vast panorama of a social system. Dickens distrusts most programs for revolutionary change, and one feels a disparity between the fury he may voice and the limited and private solutions he allows. For there seems a strong sense of the irremediable in Dickens' images of society. Ferdinand Barnacle, the frankest and most knowing of the inhabitants of the Circumlocution Office, puts the challenge to Arthur Clennam: "Our place is not a wicked Giant to be charged at full tilt; but only a windmill showing you . . . which way the country wind blows." When Clennam refuses to accept such a "dismal prospect" of universal complicity, Barnacle airily, and not unconvincingly, replies: "We must have humbug, we all like humbug, we couldn't get on without humbug." So, too, in a world of oppression, the most oppressed, the people of Bleeding Heart Yard, are ready to patronize Cavaletto because he is a foreigner. They are helpful and generous, as is Mr. Meagles in his way, but they too have a taint of the Circumlocution Office. They treat Cavaletto like a baby, "laughing immoderately at his lively gestures and his childish

English. . . . They constructed sentences, by way of teaching him the language in its purity, such as were addressed by the savages to Captain Cook, or by Friday to Robinson Crusoe." It is charming and very funny, and hardheadedly unsentimental, too.

The men who seem to command Dickens' admiration are those who work earnestly, as inventors or manufacturers (like Rouncewell the iron-master and Daniel Doyce) rather than as financiers. They share to some degree the selflessness of Dickens' heroines, for they are concerned with their work more than with power or wealth. They are disinterested as someone like Henry Gowan never can become, as he trifles with art and despises others to assuage his own self-contempt. Henry Gowan must persuade himself that the world is a hollow farce lest he face his own failure clearly. Others like Eugene Wrayburn and Mortimer Lightwood are clearly without any devotion to a career pressed upon them by family and society, cultivating bored self-pity rather than seeking an alternative. Dickens shows us how dangerous the boredom of a gifted man can become. But earnestness is scarcely a program for social reform; it is moral counsel for the private man.

Furthermore, Dickens is ready to see the failings of those people whose selflessness he admires. Such figures as Tom Pinch, Betty Higden, or Riah raise problems seen only more tellingly in Little Dorrit herself. Tom Pinch wants to believe in Pecksniff and needs his overweening authority. Riah allows his sense of gratitude and honor to make him an instrument for maligning his people. Betty Higden flees the Good Samaritan of the Poor Laws, determined to accept no charity at the expense of her dignity; but she becomes a victim of her own fears as much as of social institutions. And Little Dorrit keeps her father alive by fostering his selfishness, preserving his delusions, and protecting him from reality. These are all characters for whom we feel great sympathy, but Dickens does not ignore the difficulties of their situation.

What must finally strike one about Dickens' world is its tremendous energy, often misdirected, caught up in compulsion, elaborating forms and systems, but also seeking to uncover old guilts, painfully holding to a vision of goodness, opening into gestures of warmth and love. The energy is as much a part of the crazed goodness of some characters as it is of the ingenious rationalizations and disguises of others. And if it can be seen in the incomparable images of London, whose very stag-nation is a fierce repression of energy, it can be found as well in a scene that might have been imagined by the visionary painter, Samuel Palmer:

So, in the rosy evening, one might watch the ever-widening beauty of the landscape—beyond the newly-released workers wending home—beyond the silver river—beyond the deep green fields of corn, so prospering, that the loiterers in their narrow threads of pathway seemed to float immersed breast-high—beyond the hedgerows and the clumps of trees—beyond the windmills on the ridge—away to where the sky appeared to meet the earth, as if there were no immensity of space between mankind and Heaven.

The primary purpose of this collection is to make available a body of good criticism that concentrates on the art of Dickens' novels. This has meant scanting a few of the lesser novels as well as treatments of Dickens as social critic and journalist. If Dickens is the greatest of English novelists, as many have claimed in recent years, or simply one of the greatest, as most would agree, the novels demand our attention first of all.

A second purpose is to bring together material that has not, for the most part, been reprinted before in a collection of this kind. These essays provide a fair sampling of the best writing on Dickens by critics of our day, and they include a variety of approaches. Other essays, listed in the bibliography, and notably those of G. B. Shaw, George Orwell, Edmund Wilson, and F. R. Leavis, are landmarks of Dickens criticism; they are widely available, and their insight has, happily, been absorbed by much of the recent writing included here. Anyone seriously interested in Dickens will soon reach as well Edgar Johnson's biography, Humphry House's essay on his thought, and J. Hillis Miller's brilliant interpretation of his novels.

The Heroes and Heroines
of Dickens

by Angus Wilson

To examine the heroes and heroines of Dickens is to dwell on his weaknesses and failures. Only a strong conviction of Dickens' extraordinary greatness can make such an examination either worthwhile or decorous; since the literary critic, unlike the reviewer, can always choose his fields and should seek surely to appreciate rather than to disparage. Even in the weak field of his heroes and heroines, Dickens made remarkable advances, for though he matured—or, to use a less evaluating word, changed—late both as a man and as an artist, his immense energy drove him on through the vast field of his natural genius to attempt the conquest of the territory that lay beyond. The development of the heroes and heroines of his novels is indeed a reflection of this change or maturing, and a measure of his success in going beyond the great domain he had so easily mastered. Some of the dilemmas that lay at the root of his difficulties were personal to him; but others were historical, and some perhaps will never be solved by any novelist.

In general, the subject of Dickens' heroes has not received much attention from serious critics. Admirers have preferred to dwell on his excellencies; detractors had found more positive qualities to excite their antipathy. The child heroes and heroines brought tears to the eyes of contemporary readers, and have found equal portions of admiration and dislike in later times. There has been some general recognition that the now highly acclaimed late novels owe something of their declared superior merit to a greater depth in the portrayal of the heroes and the heroines.

I shall not discuss the child heroes and heroines, except to suggest that as Dickens matured he found them inadequate centers for the

"The Heroes and Heroines of Dickens" by Angus Wilson. From *Dickens and the Twentieth Century*, ed. John Gross and Gabriel Pearson (London: Routledge & Kegan Paul, Ltd., 1962; Toronto: University of Toronto Press, 1962). Copyright © 1962 by Routledge & Kegan Paul, Ltd. Reprinted by permission of the publishers.

complex social and moral structures he was trying to compose. The children too gained in realism by being removed from the center. The peripheral Jo has a deeply moving realism that is not there in the necessarily falsely genteel Little Nell or Oliver. It is also perhaps worth noticing as a mark of Dickens' rich genius that he could be prodigal with his gifts, making masterly child portraits of Paul, David, and Pip serve merely as fractions of a large structure. Most post-Jamesian novelists would have exhausted their total energies in such portrayals of the childhood vision.

It is, however, the adult heroes and heroines with whom I am concerned. Let me first suggest the limitations which I believe hampered Dickens in successfully creating central figures in his works, and then, by analysis of the development of the heroes and heroines through his novels, throw some light perhaps upon how far he overcame or could overcome these limitations.

The historical limitations of the Victorian novelists are too well known to be worth more than a mention. The happy ending is an unfortunate distortion in Dickens' work as it is in that of the other great Victorians, but, despite the change made to *Great Expectations,* it goes deeper than a mere capitulation to the whims of readers. With Dickens as with Thackeray, though for different reasons, the contemporary idea of domestic happiness as the resolution of, or perhaps more fairly one should say, the counterpoise to social evil, was a strongly held personal conviction. Even more vital to Dickens was the idea of pure love as the means of redemption of flawed, weak, or sinful men. Neither of these beliefs can properly take the weight that he imposed upon them; though the latter, at any rate, is not such a psychological falsity perhaps as many twentieth century critics have thought. The main destructive effort of this exaggerated view of love as a moral solvent falls upon those characters in the novels who, under any view, could be regarded as heroes and heroines. Closely allied to the popular prejudice in favor of wedding bells and the patter of tiny feet is the contemporary absolute demand for sexual purity. There has been a recent tendency to play down the effects of this on the Victorian novel. True, these effects have so often been discussed as now to be trite, but that does not unfortunately diminish them. This censorship did, in fact, reduce the great Victorian novelists in the sexual sphere to a childish status beside their continental contemporaries. It is surprising how often they can get past the ban by suggestion; it is surprising how often the ban does not matter to an imaginative reader; again, our freedom is only relative and has its own danger of absurdity; all this is true—yet the fact remains that our great Victorian novelists were forced at times to devices that are false, ridiculous, or blurred. And these faults occur too often at the moral heart of their work. In English fashion, and with reason, we may take pride in the degree to which our Victorian novelists achieved greatness in spite of this—but we can't efface it. No characters, of course, suffer so greatly as the heroes and heroines. Once again, however, I would suggest that Dickens had a special personal relationship to this sexual censorship—and that, while it sometimes led him into exceptionally absurd devices, it also produced a characteristically powerful effect. The sexual life of Charles Dickens, like that of most Victorians, has become a shop-soiled subject, but one may briefly say four things of it—he was a strongly sensual man, he had a deep social and emotional need for family life and love, he had a compensating claustrophobic dislike of the domestic scene, and he woke up to these contradictions in his sexual make-up very late. Surely the distressing feature about the famous letter to the press upon the break-up of his marriage is not so much the tasteless publicity, but the tasteless publicity sought by a man of Dickens' years and standing. He acted at best like a young man blinded by new fame. His emotional life, in fact, for all his many children, was by most standards immature. Thackeray, very percipient where his dislike of Dickens was concerned, hit the right note, when he said of Kate, 'the poor matron.' Dickens behaved not as a middle-aged man but as a young fool or as an old fool.

The contemporary censorship, in fact, went along with, rather than against, Dickens' natural inclinations. His submerged, but fierce, sensuality was to run some strange courses from the days of John Chester until it came to light in the diverging streams of Wrayburn and Headstone. Seduction withheld, deferred, foiled—at any rate never accomplished—produced many interesting and complex characters, who would not have been born in a fiction that reflected the real world where men are more resolute and women are weaker.

Perhaps even more important in its effect on his heroes and heroines than the imperfect view of love and the impossible view of sex that Dickens shared with his readers was the ambiguous view of Victorian society that he shared with so many of the artists and intellectuals of his age. Broadly speaking, one could say that the young Dickens aspired to a respectable middle-class radicalism attacking particular social evils, and ended as a middle-aged revolutionary with a peculiar hostility to the middle classes. Such an evolution in a man not given to intellectual self-analysis inevitably produced ambiguities in his portrayal of every social class at one time or another. And in no group of characters is this unconscious evolution with its accompanying contradictions more clearly displayed than in the young men who stand at the heroic center of his books. This uneven course in his social opinions, now veering, now tacking, yet for all its changes moving in one final direction, affected his attitude to the future and to the past, to all classes, to education, to money, to ambition, to work, to play, to conformity, and to rebellion. This strange and complex pattern of life may be observed working out in various ways among his heroes and heroines.

Any account of Dickens must start with *Pickwick Papers*, the novel which announces an age of innocence before the course has begun. Perhaps Dickens never produced so satisfactory a hero as Mr. Pickwick again—a man who, like his author, imperceptibly changes; but not from hope to despair, rather from nullity to positive goodness. None of the problems of Dickens are met in this book: Mr. Pickwick developed in the garden of Eden before the fall, the next step from him was to Oliver and Nell—children, at least, have their measure of original sin. Yet no article on Dickens' heroes should fail to salute the perfection of Mr. Pickwick before it goes on to the real story.

Apart from the children, the first group of heroes may be seen leading up to the self-portrait of David Copperfield. Like Mr. Pickwick, this "walking gentleman," genteel hero group begins in near nullity: one cannot discuss Harry Maylie or Edward Chester, for they are not there. Nicholas and Martin advance us a few steps: they are haters of hypocrisy, cant, and cruelty; sharp-tongued and humorous; hot-tempered; inclined to selfishness; a bit weak and spoilt; pale reflections, with their eye for the absurd, of the unintrospective young Dickens as he saw himself. Martin, with Jonas and Chevy Slyme for his relations, can hardly claim gentility; but Nicholas is a born gentleman of a somewhat ill-defined kind, although his uncle is a money-lender. The young, socially unsure Dickens had need not only of false gentility and of hatred of the aristocracy, he needed also a suffused and vague love of the past—a mark of the genteel. So Nicholas's first act, when he became a rich and prosperous merchant, was to buy his father's "old house . . . none of the old rooms were ever pulled down, no old tree was ever rooted up, nothing with which there was any association of bygone times was ever removed or changed."

It is something of the same undefined traditional gentility which so endears to David Copperfield Dr. Strong's vaguely traditional old school and the aroma of scholarship given off by his improbable dictionary. David is the culmination, in fact, of these purely genteel heroes for whom Pip was later to atone. Of course, being a self-portrait, David has more life, but, after childhood, it is a feeble ray. To begin with, who can believe that he is a novelist? Indeed, although he is said to be a model of hard work, we never have any sense of it except in his learning short-hand. Dickens was far too extrovert in those days to analyse the quali-ties in himself that made for his genius. It is notable that David is no more than "advanced in fame and fortune," where Dickens was ad-vanced in literary skill and imaginative power. It is also notable that after childhood, nothing happened to David himself except the passion of his love for Dora and the shock of her death—and these, which should be poignant, are somehow made less so by being smiled back upon through the tears as part of youth's folly and life's pageant. *David Cop-perfield* is technically a very fine novel of the sentimental education genre, but the mood of mellow, wise reflection is surely too easily held; and, when we think of Dickens' age at the time of its writing, held all too prematurely. "Advanced in fortune and fame," as a result, has inevitably a smug sound, and "my domestic joy was perfect" seems to demand the Nemesis that was to come in real life.

Nor is this smug, genteel, conformist quality of David helped by Agnes. A successful novelist guided by her "deep wisdom" would surely become a smug, insensitive, comfortable old best seller of the worst kind. Agnes, indeed, is the first of the group of heroines who mark the least pleasing, most frumpy, and smug vision of ideal womanhood that he produced. Agnes, in fact, is betrayed by Esther Summerson, when Dickens in his next book so unwisely decided to speak through his heroine's voice. It is not surprising that this wise, womanly, housekeeping, moraliz-ing, self-congratulating, busy little creature should have needed a good dose of childlikeness, a dose of Little Nell to keep her going when she reappears as Little Dorrit. If we cannot believe in the child-woman Little Dorrit, at least we are not worried as we are by Agnes or Esther Summerson about her complete lack of a physical body—a deficiency so great that Esther's smallpox-spoilt face jars us because she has no body upon which a head could rest.

But if nothing happens to David himself after Mr. Murdstone goes off the scene, something does happen in the novel, about which David (Dickens) uses language that suggests that there lies the real drama—as well he may, for with Steerforth's seduction of Em'ly, and indeed with Steerforth himself, we are at the beginning of all those twists and turns by which Dickens eventually transforms a somewhat stagy villain into a new sort of full-sized hero. From Steerforth to Eugene Wrayburn is the road of self-discovery. Of all the would-be seducers in Dickens' novels, James Steerforth alone gets his prey; yet he is the only one, until

Wrayburn, whom Dickens seems to have wished to redeem. If we look at the facts of Steerforth's character, it may be difficult to see why. From the moment that he so revoltingly gets Mr. Mell dismissed at Creakle's school until his carefully planned seduction of Em'ly he *does* nothing to commend himself. Yet David (and surely Dickens) uses language that would save if it could—"But he slept—let me think of him so again—as I had often seen him sleep at school; and thus, in this silent hour I left him. Never more, oh God forgive you, Steerforth, to touch that passive hand in love and friendship. Never, never more!" . . . "Yes, Steerforth, long removed from the scenes of this poor history! My sorrow may bear involuntary witness against you at the Judgement Throne; but my angry thoughts or reproaches never will, I know." And at the last—"among the ruins of the home he had wronged, I saw him lying with his hand upon his arm, as I had often seen him lie at school." If Dickens could have redeemed Steerforth he surely would have done so. And, indeed, he did; for Eugene Wrayburn is as much a redemption of Steerforth as Pip is a scapegoat for the falsities in David. On the whole, as I suggest, redemption through Wrayburn is a somewhat arbitrary business; but before that redemption came about, the figure of Steerforth had suffered under many guises and, in the course of his translation to hero, had borne witness to many changes in Dickens' social and moral outlook, had even assisted in the birth of a heroine more adequate to Dickens' mature outlook than either Little Nell or Agnes, or indeed the strange hybrid figure of Little Dorrit.

To trace these changes we should perhaps go back before Steerforth to earlier seductions in the novels. At the start the seducer is a cynical rake or libertine—John Chester or Sir Mulberry Hawk. He stands full square for the aristocratic dandy whom the middle-class radical Dickens detests as the source of outdated arbitrary power. Yet we have only to look at Boz in his early pictures to see the beringed and ringleted dandy—or is it the "gent"? Dick Swiveller is kindly treated. In his adolescence surely it was among the would-be swells of Dick Swiveller's world that Dickens moved—the direct butt, no doubt, of any real dandy's contempt and laughter. The seducer, then, up to *Dombey*, is a crude class symbol.

Dombey and Son brings us farther forward. Carker has some genuine sensuality, of the cold, calculating, rather epicene imitation-Byron kind that the early nineteenth century must often have bred. True, he is vulgar, hypocritical, and apparently subservient—but then, unlike Steerforth, he has to scheme and work for his living. Like Steerforth, his Byronic professional seducing spills over into other sorts of pleasure-loving—a somewhat ornately comfortable villa. There are four things in which Steerforth differs from him, apart from age: Steerforth despises the world, he puts other values above work, he sometimes wishes that he was not wasting his life, he has the vestige of a power to love or at any rate to want to be loved. It is not very much luggage, yet it proves enough to make the long journey to Eugene Wrayburn. Carker fails in his seduction, but then in Edith Dombey he has a much more difficult job than little Em'ly presents to Steerforth. There were two roads open for the Dickensian seducer—glamour (it was presumably this that Steerforth used, though little Em'ly's last note to Peggotty shows small evidence that she has felt it) or boredom. Boredom and self-distaste, these were the marks of the woman who had already sold herself into loveless marriage—Edith, Louisa Bounderby, Honoria Dedlock, if she had not already been seduced before the novel began. Pride saves Edith Dombey; pride would have saved Lady Dedlock; pride and an instinct of self-preservation saved Louisa. Yet it is hardly a fair contest—Mr. Carker emits his faint ray of vulgar sensuality, James Harthouse his rather superior brand of Steerforth's worldly charm. But, if it only takes one to make a rape, it takes two to make a seduction; and there is nothing in Edith or Louisa to respond. They are looking for flight from a desperate situation and indeed they take it; but they are not looking for any species of sexual love. The female equivalent to the sort of professional minor Byronism that Steerforth and Harthouse and Gowan, no doubt, in his relations with Miss Wade, offer, is the minor, rather half-hearted coquetry that is touched on in Dolly Vardon, punished in Fanny Dorrit and Estella, and finally redeemed in Bella Wilfer. But Estella and Bella are more than coquettes, they are proud, frozen, unhappy women anxious to be free of desperate homes, they combine in fact the nearest approach that Dickens gets to a sensually alive woman with the proud cold beauties—Edith, Louisa, and Honoria. *Our Mutual Friend,* in fact, contains the developed hero and the most developed heroine in Dickens' fiction. The one has come a long journey from the seducer-villain; and the other, almost as long a journey from the coquette and the runaway wife. Even so they remain separate, each is reclaimed by a nullity, John Harmon and Lizzie Hexam. Yet in them Dickens had admitted to the saved a degree of sexual reality that argues well for the future.

We may leave Bella on one side; she has brought some frailty, some liveliness and some sexual warmth to Dickens' heroines; but she plays little part in the evolution of Dickens' social or moral outlook—it was not a woman's role to do so.

Eugene Wrayburn is a far more interesting case. His salvation is really immensely arbitrary. Even after he has left Lizzie for the last time be-

ore Headstone's murderous attack, he has not given up his ideas of seduc-
ion entirely—his father's voice tells him, "You wouldn't marry for
ome money and some station, because you were frightfully likely to become bored. Are you less frightfully likely to become bored marrying for
10 money and no station?" It is indeed his rival's blows that save him.
Yet we have seen that Steerforth had certain pleas to offer; Wrayburn
offers all the same pleas and by this time they have become more urgent
o Dickens. First, contempt for the world and for success—this, once a
1idden admiration, is now the center of Dickens' moral values. Private
ncome, public school, and university education, all these may be forgiven if they produce a despiser of bourgeois society. Dandy insolence,
once the mark of an arbitrary, outdated order, is now the badge of rejec-
cion of Podsnap. Other values above work and duty? This has been
amply confirmed by a rather separate but very successful hero, the sad,
Calvinist-destroyed Clennam. Then the vestige of regret for a wasted life
1as gone through many fires since Steerforth's day; it has been purified
by Richard Carstone and above all by Sydney Carton, whom Shrewsbury,
gentlemanly bohemianism, and the Bar could not entirely destroy. Above
all the need for love has also been through Carton's fire so that Lucie
can say to Darnay, "remember how strong we are in our happiness, and
1ow weak he is in his misery." Loneliness, failure, pride, bitter rejection
of all that made up Victorian progress and Victorian morality, a considered rejection of duty and hard work as moral ends—Dickens comes
through to acceptance of these in the person of Eugene Wrayburn. And
sensuality? Does he also redeem his own strong sensuality? This, I think,
s less certain. The thin, calculated sensuality that runs from the Byronic
Steerforth to the Yellow Book Wrayburn is not surely of the obsessive,
tortured kind that we suspect in Dickens. Does not this real sensuality
>eep through in more sinister places? In Pecksniff's scene with Mary
Graham, in Jonas's wooing of Mercy, in Uriah's glances at Agnes—there
s more real lust there than in all the wiles of Steerforth and Harthouse,
n all the brutalities of Gowan. And now the lust comes up again on the
wrong side, in slavery to the Victorian doctrines of hard work, of fact,
of ambition, and of self-betterment—all things that had played a large
part in Dickens' own life and which he had now rejected. The obsessive
ust of Bradley Headstone finds no redemption. Yet as he rolls on the
ground, after Charlie Hexam has left him, I believe that Dickens feels
as strong a pity for him as David had felt for Steerforth. Would Dickens
perhaps have left from here on another long pilgrimage deep into the
1oly places of his own soul? Can Jasper be the next strange step in that
1ew pilgrimage?

The Dickens World:
A View from Todgers's

by Dorothy Van Ghent

The course of things demonically possessed is to imitate the human while the course of human possession is to imitate the inhuman. Thi transposition of attributes, producing a world like that of ballet, is th principle of relationship between things and people in the novels o Dickens. The masks, the stances, and the shock-tempo are comic. Th style which they have for their perspective is the style of a world under going a gruesome spiritual transformation.

Things, like animal pets, have adopted the disposition and expressio of their masters. The "tight-clenched" old bureau of a miser has a "ba and secret forehead." But this argues a demonic life in things; and a it takes a demon to know a demon, they have maliciously felt out an imitated, in their relationships with each other and even with people the secret of the human arrangement. A four-poster bed in an inn is despotic monster that straddles over the whole room, "putting one o his arbitrary legs into the fireplace, and another into the doorway, an squeezing the wretched little washing-stand in quite a Divinely Right eous manner." The animation of inanimate objects suggests both th quaint gaiety of a forbidden life and an aggressiveness that has got out o control. Even a meek little muffin has to be "confined with the utmos precaution under a strong iron cover," and a hat, set on a mantelpiece demands constant attention and the greatest quickness of eye and han to catch it neatly as it tumbles off, but it is an ingenious demon an finally manages to fall into the slop-basin.

These continual broadsides of the pathetic fallacy might be considere as incidental embellishment if the description of people did not every where show a reciprocal metaphor. The animate is treated as if it wer

"The Dickens World: A View from Todgers's" by Dorothy Van Ghent. From *Th Sewanee Review*, LVIII (1950), 419-38. Copyright © 1950 by the University of th South. Reprinted by permission of the author and the editors of *The Sewanee Review*

a thing. It is as if the life absorbed by things had been drained out of people who have become incapable of their humanity. Grandfather Smallweed, in *Bleak House,* has to be beaten up periodically like a cushion in order to be restored to the shape of a man. The ignominy is horrifying, suggesting unspeakable deterioration. Those who have engaged, as Grandfather Smallweed has, in the manipulation of their fellows as if they were things, themselves develop thing-attributes, like Podsnap, the capitalist, who has hair-brushes on his head instead of hair; while those who suffer the aggressiveness which is the dynamics of this economy are similarly transformed, like the convict Magwitch, mechanized by oppression and fear, who has a clockwork apparatus in his throat that clicks as if it were going to strike, or poor little Twemlow, whose hosts put leaves in him like a dining-table, extending or depressing him according to the size of the party.

The progressive keys of the transformation may be illustrated by those people who have wooden parts, Silas Wegg and Sarah Gamp's famous husband offering the examples. The wooden leg of Mr. Gamp, "which in its constancy of walkin' into wine vaults, and never comin' out again 'till fetched by force, was quite as weak as flesh, if not weaker," has taken over the man. More ominous is the deliberate choice of a lower order of being, when the man takes over or becomes his member. (Lady Scadgers, in *Hard Times,* is "an immensely fat old woman, with an inordinate appetite for butcher's meat, and a mysterious leg which had now refused to get out of bed for fourteen years." The lady is "thinged" into her own leg, which is clearly the repository of all that butcher's meat.) In Silas Wegg, the humanity of the man with the wooden leg is so reduced to the quality of his appendage that he is expected to develop another leg of the same kind in about six months, if his development receive no untimely check. The inanimate member of the organism signifies spiritual necrosis, and Silas does in fact identify himself with his deceased member, which has been disposed of by the hospital porter to an articulator of bones. "Now, look here, what did you give for me?" he demands, and he bargains for his leg in a grotesque parody of the Resurrection of the Body. The man with the wooden leg, however harmless in appearance, is ominous of something out of nature; he is death-in-life. The comedy of this is comedy with immense stylistic tension.

Dickens told Forster that he was always losing sight of a man in his diversion by the mechanical play of some part of the man's face, which "would acquire a sudden ludicrous life of its own." His habit of seeing the parts of the body as separable and manipulable makes in his first writings for funny foolishness, as in the case of the tall lady, eating sand-

wiches, in *Pickwick,* who "forgot the arch—crash—knock—children look
around—mother's head off—sandwich in her hand—no mouth to put it
in." Where it is put to use most seriously and spectacularly, it is a technique of surgical division serving to characterize personality that has
given itself over to deceit, thus dividing itself unnaturally into a manip-
ulating and a manipulated part, a me-half and an it-half. General Scadder, the agent of the land-swindle in *Martin Chuzzlewit,* has one sight-
less eye that stands stock still: "With that side of his face he seemed to
listen to what the other side was doing. Thus each profile had a distinct
expression; and when the movable side was most in action, the rigid one
was in its coldest state of watchfulness." Pecksniff, warming his hands
before the fire "as benevolently as if they were somebody else's, not his,"
has divided himself from his imagination of himself, and the image is
one of mayhem and of a surgical graft. In Mr. Vholes, the lawyer in
Bleak House, deceit is not even a personal matter, as it is with Pecksniff.
Mr. Vholes is only a cog in the mechanics of Chancery, which has institutionalized the manipulation of living creatures as if they were not
human but things. The norms of this hell enable Mr. Vholes to do more
violent physical damage on himself than Pecksniff, a kind of damage of
which only the mediaeval and twentieth century imaginations have been
thought capable. He "takes off his close black gloves as if he were skin-
ning his hands, lifts off his tight hat as if he were scalping himself, and
sits down at his desk."

The more rugged criminals, among those who still move in respectable
society, are radically cloven into two people, and it is but a question of
point of view from the eccentric *appearance* of Mr. Flintwinch, in *Little
Dorrit,* whose neck is so twisted that he looks as if he had hanged himself at one time, to the schizophrenia of the murderer Jonas Chuzzlewit,
who, after his crime, is "not only fearful *for* himself but *of* himself," and
half expects when he returns home to find himself asleep in bed. The
ultimate development of this imagery of division is total transformation
of the me-half into the it-half, as in the spontaneous combustion of
Krook. Krook, not even a hanger-on of the colossal deceit of Chancery,
has established himself in a business which is a parody of Chancery; he
lives off the refuse paper of the court, and at the time of his decease has
just found a promising speculation in blackmail. Here personality has
so developed its thing-constitution that it has become a purely chemical
phenomenon, and the moment of Krook's death is the moment when
his chemicals (largely gin) have finally consummated their possession
of him. The nastiness of the image is proportional to the horror of the
idea. A defiling yellow liquor is the last of Krook, slowly dripping and
creeping down the bricks.

Krook's mortification is the savagely simple working out of the law of conversion of spirit into matter that operates in the Dickens world. In the case of Miss Havisham, in *Great Expectations,* the decayed wedding cake offers a supplementary image of the necrosis that is taking place in the human agent. Miss Havisham is guilty of aggression against life in using the two children, Pip and Estella, as inanimate instruments of revenge for her broken heart, and she has been changed retributively into a fungus. The cake on the banquet table acts by homeopathic magic, like a burning effigy or a doll stuck with pins: "When the ruin is complete," she says, pointing to the cake but referring to herself, she will be laid out on the same table and her relatives will be invited to "feast on" her corpse. But this is not the only conversion. The "little quickened hearts" of the mice behind the panels have been quickened by what was Miss Havisham, carried off crumb by crumb. The principle of reciprocal changes bears on the characteristic lack of complex inner life on the part of Dickens' people; it is inconceivable that the fungoid Miss Havisham or the spirituous Krook should have complex inner lives, in the moral sense. In the *art* of Dickens (distinguishing that moral dialectic that arises not solely from character but from total aesthetic occasion) there is a great deal of "inner life," transposed to other forms than that of character; partially transposed in this scene, for instance, to the symbolic activity of the speckled-legged spiders with blotchy bodies and to the gropings and pausings of the black beetles on Miss Havisham's hearth.

In Balzac, environment is literally natural; in Dickens, environment is literally *un*natural. Mme. Vauquer's pension or Old Grandet's house in Saumur, as physical constructions, partake eminently of the harshness and constriction of the forms of life which they help to render intelligible, but there is never any doubt as to their natural limitations; formally they correspond to the human nature for which they provide the scene, and they set physical and in time spiritual bonds to the human development within them; but in no sense do they actively intrude upon the human. Their symbolic value lies in their natural rigidity. They are that beyond which the soul cannot go. In Dickens, environment constantly exceeds its material limitations. Its mode of existence is altered by the human purposes and deeds it circumscribes, and its animation is antagonistic; it fearfully intrudes upon the soul.

The room occupied by Jonas Chuzzlewit at the time of the murder is charged with the tensions of a straining life—but not Jonas's life.

> The room in which he had shut himself up was on the ground-floor, at the back of the house. It was lighted by a dirty skylight, and had a door in the wall, opening into a narrow, covered passage or blind alley. . . .

It was a blotched, stained, mouldering room, like a vault; and there were water-pipes running through it, which, at unexpected times in the night, when other things were quiet, clicked and gurgled suddenly, as if they were choking.

It is not only that the water-pipes serve to interpret Jonas's fears—as if they had tattle-tale tongues—but they appear to have been released, by the act which dehumanizes Jonas, into a busy life of their own. What is shocking is not their relevance to the murder but their irrelevance to it. On a larger scale, the same transposition of attributes has taken place in Coketown, in *Hard Times*, whose fortifications are more alive than the race they shelter. The Coketown "hands" have been approximately reduced to those members for which they are named—or, Dickens says, they are "like the lower creatures of the seashore, only hands and stomachs"—while the two-way law has also had the effect of converting their material environment into passion, complicated, lunatic, and uncontrollable: Coketown is a labyrinth of "narrow courts upon courts and close streets upon streets, which had come into existence piecemeal, every piece in a violent hurry for some one man's purpose, and the whole an unnatural family, shouldering, and trampling, and pressing one another to death."

The description of Coketown is strongly felt because it represents an objective evil favored by industrialism; the image of a deformed, totem-like life in its chimneys and chimney-pots—"which, for want of air to make a draught, were built in an immense variety of stunted and crooked shapes, as though every house put out a sign of the kind of people who might be expected to be born in it"—has an hallucinatory vividness; but more hallucinatory is the relatively innocent prospect from the roof of Todgers's boarding-house, in *Martin Chuzzlewit*, a description which bears a curious resemblance to passages in M. Sartre's *La Nausée* and other writings, where non-human existences rage with an indiscriminate life of their own.

> The revolving chimney-pots on one great stack of buildings seemed to be turning gravely to each other every now and then, and whispering the result of their separate observation of what was going on below. Others, of a crook-backed shape, appeared to be maliciously holding themselves askew, that they might shut the prospect out and baffle Todgers's. The man who was mending a pen at an upper window over the way, became of paramount importance in the scene, and made a blank in it, ridiculously disproportionate in its extent, when he retired. The gambols of a piece of cloth upon the dyer's pole had far more interest for the moment than all the changing motion of the crowd. Yet

even while the looker-on felt angry with himself for this, and wondered how it was, the tumult swelled into a roar; the hosts of objects seemed to thicken and expand a hundredfold; and after gazing round him, quite scared, he turned into Todgers's again, much more rapidly than he came out; and ten to one he told M. Todgers afterwards that if he hadn't done so, he would certainly have come into the street by the shortest cut; that is to say, head-foremost.

Much of the description is turned upon the conservative "seemed to be" and "as if," and the pathetic fallacy provides a familiar bourgeois security, but the technique changes in the middle, betrayed by a discomfort which the "as if's" are no longer able to conceal. The prospect from Todgers's is one in which categorical determinations of the relative significance of objects—as of the chimney-pots, the blank upper window, or the dyer's cloth—have broken down, and the observer on Todgers's roof is seized with suicidal nausea at the momentary vision of a world in which significance has been replaced by naked and aggressive existence.

It has so often been said that Dickens' point of view is that of the undernourished child roving London streets at night, that one hesitates to say it again, although with no reference to biography. The point of view is hallucinated and often fearful, as the insecure and ill-fed child's might be. It is not childish. The grotesque transpositions are a coherent imagination of a reality that has lost coherence, comic because they form a pattern integrating the disintegrated and lying athwart the reality that has not got itself imagined. Everything has to be mentioned—like the "strange solitary pumps" found near Todgers's, "hiding themselves in blind alleys, and keeping company with fire ladders"—for, assuming that there is coherence in a world visibly disintegrated into things, one way to find it is to mention everything. Hence the indefatigable attention to detail. No thing must be lost, as it is doubtless essential to the mysterious organization of the system. The system itself is assumed to be a nervous one, and for this reason Dickens' language has its almost inexhaustible vitality and vivacity, inasmuch as its predications about persons or objects tend to be statements of metabolic conversion of one into the other.

II

The changes are still wrought out of the broad common intuition of the connections between moral and physical phenomena, often using the ancient image of the bacillus-like physical reality of the evil spirit. The moral atmosphere of the Merdle swindle, in *Little Dorrit*, is treated in terms of a malignant physical infection, that, disseminated in the air they breathe, lays hold on people in the soundest health. On the other hand, the physical plague that arises out of the slum district of Tom All Alone's, in *Bleak House*, and that creeps to the houses of the great, is itself a moral plague, the conditions for it having been created by moral acquiescence. Its ambiguity is enforced by the conversion of the slum-dwellers into vermin parasites—"a crowd of foul existence that crawls in and out of gaps in walls and boards; and coils itself to sleep, in maggot numbers, where the rain drips in; and comes and goes, fetching and carrying fever, and sowing . . . evil in its every footprint." The Transformation of spiritual into physical being is reversed by an imagery of inferno, which translates the physical fact as a spiritual one: "the crowd . . . hovers round the three visitors, like a dream of horrible faces, and fades away up alleys and into ruins, and behind walls; and with occasional cries and shrill whistles of warning, thenceforth flits about them until they leave the place." This is Hell, and however verifiable on earth, is "unnatural" in nature. It is representative of Dickens' method, which is a scrupulous rendering of nature gone wrong in all its parts.

Imperceptibly, by changes that are themselves psychologically valid, the atoms of the physical world have been impregnated with moral aptitude, so that it is not inconsistent that at the crisis of plot, a giant beam should loosen itself and fall on the head of the villain. Stephen Blackpool, returning home and thinking of the drunken wife whom he will find there in her filth and madness, has "an unwholesome sense of growing larger, of being placed in some new and diseased relation towards the objects among which he passed, of seeing the iris round every misty light turn red. . . ." Gaffer Hexam, coming from the river where he has been at his usual business of trolling for corpses, is shunned by the other river-men when they suspect him of improving his occupation by manufacture of the commodity on which he lives, and he says fiercely as he looks around, now over this shoulder, now over that, "Have we got a pest in the house? Is there summ'at deadly sticking to my clothes? What's let loose upon us? Who loosed it?" Pip, standing waiting for Estella in the neighborhood of Newgate, and beginning dimly to be aware of his implication in the guilt for which that establishment stands, has the same sensation of a deadly dust clinging to him and tries to beat it out of his clothes. Still not without psychological validity is the minute change from the subjective atmosphere of guilt, or the apprehension of evil, which *seems* to be reflected in the physical world, to its actualization in the behavior of physical things, as in those mysterious rustlings and tremblings which frighten Affery in *Little Dorrit,* "as if a step had shaken the floor, or even as if she had been touched by some awful hand," which are the real warnings of dissolution in the worm-eaten old house and of its final providential collapse on Blandois, when he is alone in it in the purity of his evil. Considered in this way, Dickens' use of physical coincidence in his plots is consistent with his imagination of a thoroughly nervous universe, whose ganglia spread through things and people alike, so that moral contagion, from its breeding center in the human, transforms also the non-human and gives it the aptitude of the diabolic.

Coincidence is the violent connection of the unconnected; but there is no discontinuity in the Dickens world, either between persons and things, or between the private and the public act. What connection can there be, Dickens asks, between proud Lady Dedlock and Jo the outlaw with the broom: "What connection can there have been between many people in the innumerable histories of this world, who, from opposite sides of great gulfs, have, nevertheless, been very curiously brought together!" What brings Lady Dedlock and Jo together, from opposite sides of great gulfs, is the bond between the public guilt for Jo and the private guilt of Lady Dedlock for her daughter, these two offering to each other—as usual in Dickens—the model of parental irresponsibility, and the models coalescing when the woman who has denied her child and the diseased boy to whom society has been an unnatural father are laid side by side in the same churchyard to be consumed by the same worms, physical nature asserting the organicity which moral nature had revoked. What brings the convict Magwitch across "great gulfs" to the boy Pip is again a profoundly implicit compact of guilt, as binding as the convict's leg-iron which is its recurrent symbol, and again the model is that of parental irresponsibility—although the terms shift subtly here, and it is sometimes Magwitch, the criminal foster-father, who is the abused child, and Pip, the corrupted child, who bears the social guilt for Magwitch. The multiplying likenesses in the street as Magwitch draws nearer, coming over the sea, the mysterious warnings of his approach on the night of his reappearance, are moral projections as real as the storm outside the windows and as the crouched form of the vicious Orlick on the dark stairs. The conception of what brings people together—the total change in the texture of experience that follows upon the private or the public act, the concreteness of its effect on the very atoms of external matter, as upon the heart, so that physical nature itself collaborates in the drama of reprisal—is deep and valid in this book. It is, however, the same conception of linked changes in the universe that, clumsily in *David Copperfield*, allows Steerforth's body to be washed up on the sands of Yarmouth just at David's feet. The sea itself has not remained neutral.

It is for this reason that the river is so effective a symbol in these novels, appearing in almost every story in closely observed, vivid, and obsessive detail. It is the common passage and the actual flowing element that unites individuals and classes, and it has a malignant potentiality that impregnates everything upon it—discolored copper, rotten wood, honeycombed stone, green dank deposit. The corpse is shunted there secretly at night; but the river has a terrible capacity to act, and it will turn suddenly upon the ghoul, reach up, crush him, suck him under, converting him into the commodity he has been engaged in producing; and at obscure intervals along the banks are those night-stations of the law, with nets and pumps, and with bookkeepers employed to docket the ordinary apparition—"a face, rising out of the dreaded water." Lizzie Hexam, waiting at the riverside for her father's return, feels in the tidal swell breaking at her feet, without her seeing how it had gathered, the rush of *her own thoughts*, dim before her like the great black river.

In *Great Expectations*, in a finely lucid atmosphere of fairy-tale, Dickens uses a kind of montage to represent an organization of reality crossing spatial and temporal determinations, superimposing them in a moral present; as in the scene in which Estella walks the casks in the old brewery. Estella's walking the casks is an enchanting ritual dance of childhood (like walking fence-rails or railroad-ties), but inexplicably present in the tableau is the suicidal figure of Miss Havisham hanging by the neck from a brewery beam. Accompanying each appearance of Estella—who is the star and jewel of Pip's great expectations, wearing jewels in her hair and on her breast ("I and the jewels," she says)—is a disturbing ghostly suggestion of the same kind, an unformed dread; the star shudders in the wind from over the marshes; Pip tries to strike the dust of Newgate from his clothes as he sees his face in a coach-window; her slender knitting fingers are suddenly horribly displaced by the marred wrists of a murderess. This duality of vision is paralleled by a psychological duplicity. In the sense that one implies the other, the glittering frosty girl and the decayed and false old woman, Miss Havisham, are not two characters but a single one, a continuum (representing the tainted wish, the unpurchased good); as the boy Pip and the criminal Magwitch form another continuum. This bears on the comonplace of criticism that Dickens was usually unable, as Edmund Wilson puts it, "to get the good and bad together in one character," a criticism which holds in a world of neutral and simple matter, with its qualitative and quantitative disjunctions, and where character alone feels the stress of spirit; but in Dickens' nervous world, one simplex is super-imposed upon or is continuous with another, and together they form the complex of good-in-evil or of evil-in-good. Pip carries Magwitch (his "father") within him, and the apparition of the criminal is the appari-tion of Pip's own guilt. Similarly Joe Gargery, saintly simpleton of the folk, and the journeyman Orlick, dark beast of the Teutonic marshes (who comes "from the ooze"), as the opposed extremes of spiritual possibility, form a spiritual continuum that frames and gives meaning to the others.

Two kinds of crime form Dickens' two chief themes, the crime against the child, and the calculated social crime. They are formally analogous, their form being the treatment of persons as things; but, on the usual principle of inherence that obtains here, they are also inherent in each other, whether the private will is to be considered as depraved by the operation of a public institution, or the institution as a bold concert of private depravities. The correspondence of the two is constantly sug-gested. In *Little Dorrit,* for example, where old Dorrit's exploitation of his daughter supplies the main substance of the story, the crime against the child is a private type of the public morality represented by the Merdle swindle and by the ineffably criminal business of the Circumlo-ution Office. (The name Merdle may be a play on both *merde* and murder. Having murdered public welfare on a grand scale, then mur-dered himself with a penknife, Mr. Merdle is discovered as "certain carrion at the bottom of a bath.") In the same book, Arthur Clennam lives under an oppressive conviction that his father has committed a crime; without knowing what it is, he feels that the expiation of it is part of his inheritance: "there was some one with an unsatisfied claim upon his justice." The suggestion is strong here that the public and the private guilt spring from each other, or from the same root: that the "father" is the social mechanism, informed by the corrupt individual will. In *Bleak House,* the public crime is the operation of Chancery, and clearly Chancery is the "father" of Richard Carstone, as the slum of Tom All Alone's is the "father" of the pariah Jo.

Generally, in the Dickens novels, the public and private crimes are infinitely serial (a fact which gives the later plots their elaborately epicyclic character), in a series that can never be really closed, but only cut off, for which reason the plot resolutions are as nominal as the

resolution of *Tartuffe* or *l'Avare;* for, seen thus serially, the crimes ar
actually bottomless. The bottomless permutation of the crimes of th
fathers and institutionalized crime is felt in the passage describing th
neighborhood of Arthur Clennam's grim home. Somewhere, hidden i
the corner of a desk-drawer, or behind the frame of a portrait, is th
secret of his own father's crime, and the whole neighborhood is tainte
by it.

> The dim streets by which he went, seemed all depositories of oppressive
> secrets. The deserted counting-houses, with their secrets of books and
> papers locked up in chests and safes; the banking-houses, with their
> secrets of strong rooms and wells, the keys of which were in a very few
> secret pockets and a very few secret breasts; the secrets of all the dis-
> persed grinders in the vast mill, among whom there were doubtless
> plunderers, forgers, and trust-betrayers of many sorts, whom the light
> of any day that dawned might reveal; he could have fancied that these
> things, in hiding, imparted a heaviness to the air.

Though the plot may discover the secret of the portrait-frame or of th
desk-drawer, that is, though it may particularize this or that crime, ther
is left over a pervasive anxiety about things in hiding, indefinitely an
obscurely webbed, as if the permutation of public and private crime
constantly created a new and autonomous mystery, like the secret tran
forming principle of the concentration camp. The prison-symbol i
Little Dorrit is a deliberate attempt to organize these perceptions; an
when old Dorrit, in his mad speech of welcome at the Roman recep
tion, says, "Welcome to the Marshalsea! The space is—ha—limited—
limited—the parade might be wider; but you will find it apparentl
grow larger after a time—a time, ladies and gentlemen . . ." the word
carry an equivocal sense which refers them beyond certain eviden
particular meanings (as that, among the elegant guests, there are cheat
and forgers; or that the economy of the great world demands a prison
like suppression of the human quality) to another that is less tangible
a mysterious impotence in the face of that inevitable adjustment to th
narrowness of the parade, a distracted hopelessness that will seize on th
specific reference (industrialism in Coketown, big business in the city
but that is not exhausted by the specific. Little Dorrit, it is said, "begai
with sorrowful unwillingness to acknowledge to herself, that . . . n
space in the life of man could overcome that quarter of a century behin
the prison bars." There is, one feels, a crime behind a crime, create
by or creating the other, and making of the earth a foul and pestilen
congregation of vapors, without revealing what it is.

It is somewhere behind, overlooking but not to be looked at, like th

Chief Butler, who undoubtedly is in the secret. One is seated at the table in the act of drinking, and one sees him through the wine-glass, the glazed fixedness of his cold and ghostly eye. One tries to recall having met him in prison, for his distant attention argues previous acquaintance, but his face is unfamiliar. His relationship with the Law is identified in the person of Jaggers, the criminal lawyer in *Great Expectations,* chief butler of Newgate, whose office is wholly pertinent to one's own case (for he is the Father's lieutenant) but also wholly ambiguous, and whose manner is "expressive of knowing something secret about every one of us that would effectually do for each individual if he chose to disclose it."

The prevailing anxiety, still exceeding its occasions, is felt in the "maze," the "labyrinth," and the "wilderness" of Dickens' streets. To find Todgers's

you groped your way for an hour through lanes and bye-ways, and courtyards, and passages; and you never once emerged upon anything that might be reasonably called a street. A kind of resigned distraction came over the stranger as he trod these devious mazes, and, giving himself up for lost, went in and out and round about and quietly turned back again when he came to a dead wall or was stopped by an iron railing, and felt that the means of escape might possibly present themselves in their own good time, but that to anticipate them was hopeless.

Todgers's is, in a sense, all of London, as London is the whole world; for it is impossible for the reader to dissociate these mazes of a squalid metropolitan district from the Coketown "labyrinth of narrow courts upon courts, and close streets upon streets"; or from the "wildernesses" of semi-fashionable Park Lane, with their be-crutched and scrofulous tenements "that looked like the last result of the great mansions' breeding in-and-in," where Arthur Clennam goes looking for Miss Wade; or from the maggoty honeycomb of Tom All Alone's; or, for that matter, from the corridors of the Circumlocution Office, which is a purely moral phenomenon. The anxiety is felt also in the immense number of claustral interiors—the chamber offered to the Misses Pecksniff at Todgers's, commanding "at a perspective of two feet, a brown wall with a black cistern on the top" ("Not the damp side," said Mrs. Todgers. "That is Mr. Jinkins's."); Jonas Chuzzlewit's "blotched, stained, mouldering room, like a vault"; Gaffer Hexam's hovel, "smeared with red-lead and damp, with a look of decomposition"; Grandfather Smallweed's "dark little parlour, certain feet below the level of the street"—interiors suggesting, in one detail or another of underground darkness and damp, the grave.

Dickens' plots seldom serve to canalize this submerged hysteria, to

resolve it with the resolution of the particular set of plotted circur
stances. The Todgers world requires an act of redemption. A symbol
act of this kind is again and again indicated, in the charity of the ur
cherished and sinned-against child for the inadequate or criminal fath
—what might be called the theme of the Prodigal Father, Dickens' usu
modification of the Prodigal Son theme. But the act should be suc
that it would redeem not only the individual fathers, but society
large; one might almost say—thinking of those grave-like rooms whe
this vast population burrows, and of the monstrous caricature of deat
which the living themselves offer—that it should be such as to redeer
the dead. *Great Expectations* is an exception in that, in this novel, th
redemptive act is adequate to and structural for both bodies of themat
material—the sins of the individual and the sins of society.

III

Pip first becomes aware of the "identity of things" as he is hel
suspended heels over head by the convict; that is, in a world literal
turned upside down. Thenceforth Pip's interior landscape is inverted b
his guilty knowledge of this man "who had been soaked in water, an
smothered in mud, and lamed by stones, and cut by flints, and stur
by nettles, and torn by briars," and it is as much as to say that the inve
sion of natural order begins with self-consciousness, that self-consciou
ness coincides with guilt. The "crime" that is always at the center o
the Dickens universe is thus identified in a new way—not primarily a
that of the father, nor as that of some public institution, but as that o
the child. It is for this reason that the child is able to redeem his worl
The guilt of the child is realized on several levels. Pip experience
the psychological form of guilt before he is capable of voluntary evi
he is treated by adults—Mrs. Joe, and Pumblechook, and Wopsle—a
if he were a felon, a young George Barnwell wanting only to murde
his nearest relative. This is the usual nightmare of the child in Dicken
a vision of imminent incarceration, fetters like sausages, lurid accusator
texts. He is treated, that is, as if he were a thing, manipulable by adul
for the extraction of certain sensations; by making him feel guilty an
diminished, they are able to feel virtuous and great. But the psycho
logical form of guilt acquires spiritual content when he formulates th
tainted wish (the wish to be as the most powerful adult) and begins t
treat others as things: at the literal level, Pip's guilt is that of snobber
toward Joe Gargery. Symbolically, however, it is that of murder: for h
steals the file with which the convict rids himself of his leg-iron, an

it is this leg-iron, picked up on the marshes, with which Orlick attacks Mrs. Joe; so that the child does inevitably overtake his destiny, which was, like George Barnwell, to murder his relative. But the "relative" whom the young George Barnwell, adopting the venerable criminality of society, is destined, in the widest scope of intention, to murder is not Mrs. Joe but his "father," Magwitch—to murder in the socially chronic fashion of the Dickens world, which consists in the dehumanization of the weak, or in moral acquiescence to such murder. These are the possibilities that are projected in the opening scene of the book, when the young child, left with a burden on his soul, watches the convict limping off under an angry red sky, toward the black marshes, the gibbet, and the savage lair of the sea, in a still rotating landscape.

In Dickens' modification of the folk-pattern of the fairy-wishing, Magwitch is Pip's "fairy god-father," and like all the fathers, he uses the child as a thing, in order to obtain through him sensations of grandeur. In relation to society, however, Magwitch is the child, and society the prodigal father; from the time he was first taken for stealing turnips, the convict's career has duplicated brutally and in public the pathos of the ordinary child. Again, in relation to Pip, Magwitch is still the child; for, having been dedicated from the first to criminality, Pip has carried his criminal father within him, and is projectively responsible for Magwitch's existence and for his brutalization; so that Pip is the father of his father. Thus the ambiguities of each term of the relationship between Pip and Magwitch are such that each is both child and father; and the act of love which is redemptive is reinforced fourfold, and the redemption is a fourfold redemption—that is to say, infinite, as it serves for all the meanings Dickens finds it possible to attach to the child-father relationship, and this is the only relationship that obtains among men.

As the child's original alienation is essentially mysterious—a guilty inheritance from the fathers which invades first awareness—the redemptive act is also a mysterious one. The mysterious nature of the act is first indicated, in the manner of a motif, when Mrs. Joe, in imbecile pantomime, tries to propitiate her attacker, the bestial Orlick. In Orlick is concretized all the undefined evil of the Dickens world, that has nourished itself underground and crept along walls, like the ancient stains on the house of Atreus; he is the lawlessness implied in the unnatural conversions of the human into the non-human, the retributive death that invades those who have grown lean in life and who have exercised the powers of death over others; he is the instinct of aggression and destruction, and Dickens does not try to "psychologize" him through plotted cause and effect. His modality is that character of the visitations of evil which Kierkegaard called "suddenness," and he emerges without warning "from the ooze" where he has been unconsciously cultivated. As Orlick is one form of spiritual excess, Joe Gargery is the opposed form, unqualified love. Given these terms of the spiritual framework, the redemptive act itself could scarcely be anything but grotesque, and it is by a grotesque gesture—one of the most profoundly intuitive things in Dickens—that Mrs. Joe is redeemed. What is implied by her humble bowing down to the beast is a recognition of the essentiality of evil, and of its dialectical relationship with love. The motif reappears in the moment of major illumination in the book. Pip "bows down," not to Joe Gargery, toward whom he has been privately and literally guilty, but to the wounded, hunted, shackled man, Magwitch. It is in this way that the manifold organic relationships among men are revealed, and that the Todgers world, with its baffling labyrinths, its animated chimneys, its illicit bacillary invasions, its hints and signals of a cancerous organization, is healed.

The Change of Heart
in Dickens' Novels

by Barbara Hardy

Moral conversion lies at the heart of many novels. And we might use William James's distinction between the sudden conversion, or *crisis,* of St. Paul, and the gradual conversion, or *lysis,* of Bunyan or Tolstoy, to distinguish between *Robinson Crusoe* and *Martin Chuzzlewit,* novels of abrupt change, and *Emma, Daniel Deronda,* and *The Ambassadors,* chronicles of gradual progress. Although Dickens must be classed with Defoe, in structure and psychology, as a novelist of *crisis,* the moral implications of his novels place him with Jane Austen, George Eliot, and Henry James. Robinson Crusoe, on the Island of Despair, is converted by storm, sickness, and vision, to a faith in his guiding Providence, and his material rewards are considerable. Both Providence and material success are tainted concepts for Dickens, George Eliot, and Meredith, and the typical conversion of the great Victorian novel is not a religious conversion but a turning from self-regard to love and social responsibility. A crude graph of Dickens' typical treatment of moral progress would also bring him close to George Eliot and James. In all three novelists (and in others) the hero is converted by seeing and understanding his defect and its origins. Insight and fairly explicit revaluation set him free for a fresh start. All three seem to be using their art to qualify a belief in determinism by a belief in freedom: environment, heredity, and chance combine to make conversion necessary, but individuals are given the insight and power to remake themselves. But the hero is not isolated as a typical heroic figure. He is controlled by social and moral variations which emphasize the power of environment and the difficulty of change: we observe Pecksniff and Jonas Chuzzlewit, as well as Martin; Bulstrode and Lydgate, as well as Dorothea; Chad and Way-

"The Change of Heart in Dickens' Novels" by Barbara Hardy. From *Victorian Studies*, V (1961-62), 49-67. Reprinted by permission of the author and the editors of *Victorian Studies*.

marsh and Jim Pocock, as well as Strether. But the fundamental concept of possible conversion, even in the muted forms of *Middlemarch,*
rests on an optimistic belief in will and intelligence. An important
feature in all these delineations of moral change is the hero's ability
to recognize and formulate his own limitations.

The variations are of course considerable, and this kind of rough
general summary looks inadequate when challenged by the rich variety
of actual cases. No formula can do justice to a form which includes
the comic education of Emma's sense and sensibility; the frustrated triumphs of Dorothea's painfully acquired faith and realism; and Strether's
slow and complex rejection, in a middle-aged *Bildungsroman,* of the
materialism and puritanism of Woollett and the pure aesthetic sense
of Paris. All these portrayals of change are complete and continuous
moral actions, accreted in a close imitation of persons, events, social
habits, and slow time. The theme of conversion is coextensive with the
whole form of the narrative, and the optimistic suggestion of moral
progress is part of a fine elaborate mesh of cause and effect. Dickens'
optimism may look cruder than George Eliot's because of the absence
of this fine mesh. His imitation of persons is conveyed in a stereotyped,
not a realistically complex, psychology, and his conversions often depend on a theatrical telescoping of time. Nor is the subject of moral
change his exclusive interest: at his weakest, in *Martin Chuzzlewit,* the
moral change is virtually insulated from the main flow of action, not
just because it is separated in place, but because Martin's early selfishness
and his later unselfishness are trivially substantiated and have little
influence on the action. Even at his best, with the progress of David
Copperfield or Pip, Dickens never endows a character with that imaginative sensibility and energy which gives weight and truth to the
progress of Gwendolen Harleth, Isabel Archer, or Harry Richmond.
Allowing for such major differences, it is still possible to recognize that
although Dickens' mode of presentation, for many reasons, depends on
fantasy rather than realism, his changing characters have something in
common with the changing characters of George Eliot and James.
Scrooge, Pip, and Bella Wilfer pass through some of the same stages of
vision and revision as Emma, Gwendolen, and Strether.

Sudden conversion has a long history, in the drama and the novel.
In Elizabethan and Jacobean drama (in Greene, Shakespeare, Jonson,
and Tourneur, for instance) it often comes as a convenient final reconciliation. Surprisingly, perhaps, it seldom has this kind of concluding
function in Dickens, though it sometimes has in Wilkie Collins. Dickens

never shows us a Moll Flanders. He does, it is true, convert Micawber from Micawberism, and he does unite Dombey and Florence, but neither conversion comes as a surprising flourish when the illusion is wearing thin and the need for plausible demonstration has disappeared. The change in both Micawber and Dombey is prepared. Micawber's administrative apotheosis follows his energetic triumph over Heep, and the possible implausibility of his actions is decorously covered by the transitional mystery of his changed behavior to Mrs. Micawber and David. Besides, there have been earlier triumphs of efficiency, like his masterly salvaging of David's disastrous dinner-party. Dombey is a more serious character and a more serious case of change, but Kathleen Tillotson has shown convincingly that this is not a case of abrupt change: Dombey's sensibility, silences, and his extravagant commitment to cruelty, as Dickens himself pointed out in reply to the charge of violent change, reveal his unspoken conflict.[1] There are occasional small conversions, like Tom Gradgrind's deathbed repentance, but they are not conspicuous. The kind of conversion I have in mind, however, does not usually conclude the novel; it is rather the moral change on which action hinges, or appears to hinge.

The change of heart may provide the chief interest of the story, as in *A Christmas Carol,* a large part of the interest, as in *Great Expectations* and *Our Mutual Friend,* or a relatively unsubstantial part, as in *Martin Chuzzlewit.* It may play an apparently small part, as in Tattycoram's conversion in *Little Dorrit,* but illuminate much more than its immediate area of action. It may be presented in terms of strict *Bildungsroman,* as part of the process of growing up, as in *David Copperfield,* or it may be the crisis of an ironically retarded education, as in *Hard Times.* All these examples of the change of heart have one thing in common: where George Eliot and James transcribe the moral process in slow motion and loving detail, allowing for its irregular pulse, its eddy, its wayward lapse and false start, Dickens shows it as quick, simple, and settled. The converted hero never looks back: not for Martin Chuzzlewit the lapses of Fred Vincy, not for David Copperfield Strether's discovery that the new value, like the old, may have to be revised. George Eliot and James show moral change as an accumulation of many actions and reactions, as a continuous process. Dickens' conversions are startlingly rapid in comparison, though not always as rapid as his own chosen convention makes them seem.

[1] *Novels of the Eighteen Forties* (London, 1958).

I

This chosen convention depends on the moral double or opposite. The hero is changed by seeing his situation or his moral defect enacted for him in external coincidence: by his twin, who forces a recognition of loathsome resemblance, or his opposite, who forces reluctant admiration and comparison. He sees his defect enlarged, isolated, unmistakably his own, but detached for inspection. And he acts on this recognition, and is irrevocably changed. The situation is crystallized and the double acts as devil's advocate, as in Stevenson's *Markheim* or Kipling's *Drama of Duncan Parrenness,* or as model and guide, like Poe's *William Wilson.* Many examples of doubles are discussed by Ralph Tymms,[2] but as his interest is confined to the double in the literal sense, he glances briefly at the Brothers Cheeryble, and at Darnay and Carton, and dismisses Dickens' use of the double as insignificant, typical of "the non-psychological approach of the time." This is hard on Dickens. His doubles are moral, seldom physical, but their role is often identical with the role of the double in Chamisso's "Erscheinung," which Professor Tymms notes as a good example of the *Seelenspiegel* or soul-mirror.[3] The double who has this converting role has little of the symbolic ambiguity of Conrad and Dostoevsky: he appears as part of the realistic action, as a substantial character, involved in personal, as well as moral, relations with the hero. Dickens' satirical habit of diffusing examples of specialized vices and virtues throughout the novel (from *Martin Chuzzlewit* onward) may deflect our interest from this role. The novels are full of twins and opposites, but in the crisis of conversion the mirror is offered to the character, in effective mime and therapy, as well as to the reader, in irony and generalization. The mime is simple, but its implications are many.

The example which will come to everyone's mind is the only example where an actual physical double is used to play a part in moral change. Lauriat Lane describes the twinship of Darnay and Carton, in *A Tale of Two Cities,* as a device which allows Dickens to bring about the perfect wish-fulfillment of sacrifice and happy ending. This is not

[2] *Doubles in Literary Psychology* (Cambridge, England, 1949).
[3] Lauriat Lane, in "Dickens and the Double" (*The Dickensian,* LV [1959], 47-55), goes to the other extreme, and far from confining himself to literal doubles, spends much of his time in exploring suggestions of the *alter ego* in the portraits of Jonas Chuzzlewit and John Jasper—in the latter case speculating freely. His interest lies in possible traces of a split-personality in Dickens' criminal psychology, and he is not concerned with the converting *Seelenspiegel.*

the whole story. It is significant that when Sydney Carton first sees Darnay, he performs a good act, using the striking resemblance to break down the witness who is identifying Darnay, and saving his double for the first time. When he draws the court's attention to the resemblance, it is strong, but a few minutes later the "momentary earnestness" disappears, giving away to his usual reckless and disreputable look, so that some of the onlookers "said to one another they would hardly have thought the two were so alike." When Carton takes his "counterpart" to dine, he rejects both resemblance and affinity, saying, "Don't let your sober face elate you, however; you don't know what it may come to." After they part, Carton looks at his face in the mirror, seeing himself, as Darnay has seen him, as a "Double of coarse deportment" and then making this explicit recognition: " 'Do you particularly like the man?' he muttered, at his own image; 'why should you particularly like a man who resembles you? There is nothing in you to like; you know that. Ah, confound you! What a change you have made in yourself! A good reason for taking to a man, that he shows you what you have fallen away from, and what you might have been!' " [4]

This doubling is an important part of the plot, bringing about the special irony when Darnay and Carton both fall in love with Lucie, and eventually enabling Carton to sacrifice himself for Darnay and redeem his wasted possibilities. (It takes a character in George Eliot, Mirah in *Daniel Deronda,* to comment on the emotional luxury of such an act.) But Carton is redeemed by the love of a good woman, not just by this image of what might have been. He tells Lucie that all his life "might have been," and she says, anticipating and inspiring his death, "I am sure that the best part of it might still be." It takes more (or less) than love to redeem Martin Chuzzlewit and Pip.

Love is relevant, however, to the discussion of Scrooge. Because this is the only example of an entirely fantastic treatment of conversion I should like to depart from chronology, and begin my illustration of this recurring convention with *A Christmas Carol.* Marley's ghost wrings his chained hands as he contemplates the moral plight of Scrooge, and laments: "Why did I walk through the crowds of fellow beings with my eyes turned down, and never raise them to that Blessed Star which led the Wise men to a poor abode!" (Stave I). Scrooge, like many another Victorian anti-hero, is the Utilitarian Wise Man, and he is forced to find the poor abode and forced to give. Before he can lift his eyes to the Star he has first to turn them on himself. Like all Dickens' Utilitarian

[4] Chap. iv. References are to the National Edition (London, 1907).

egoists, he needs to have his heart taken by storm, and the storm comes in the shape of nostalgia, pity, and fear. Humphry House calls it "crude magic of reformation" but this might be qualified.

Scrooge sees his own image in the most literal fashion, moving back in time and confronting himself at different stages in his process of deterioration. There is his old self, the child, loving and innocent opposite of the unloving old sophist. There is the transitional self, committed to loveless rationalism, but still holding some few warm contacts with the past. There is his mirror-image, the present self who echoes his own words and sentiments but in a context newly charged with feeling. The doubles, like the ghosts, are all potent in different ways, and indeed the ghosts are not only aspects of Christmas but in part at least aspects of Scrooge: his past, his present, and his suggestively anonymous future. The return to childhood restores him to the first springs of love in a way reminiscent of Wordsworth and George Eliot; the personal past is a tradition which can keep alive the feeling child, father of the rational man. It also gives a brief glimpse at the deprived and isolated child. Instead of a recognition of causality—though I think that is obliquely present for the reader—we have in Scrooge himself the equally effective stirring of love and pity. He sees his sister, rather as Silas Marner remembers his sister after he first sees Eppie, and the link is made with old affection and old sorrow. He "feels pity for his former self" and the pity brings with it the first movement of imaginative self-criticism. He identifies his old sorrow with sorrow outside himself: "There was a boy singing a Christmas Carol at my door last night. I should like to have given him something: that's all" (Stave II). This is of course the carol which gives the story its name, and also its theme: "God bless you, merry gentlemen, May nothing you dismay." Scrooge threatens the boy with his ruler, rejects the blessing, and Christmas brings him a strong but salutary dismay.

The Ghost of Christmas Past acts as devil's advocate, and his timing is admirable. Scrooge is identifying himself with his former self at Fezziwig's ball: "His heart and soul were in the scene, and with his former self. He corroborated everything, remembered everything, enjoyed everything, and underwent the strangest agitation" (Stave II). The Ghost pours cold water on the apprentices' gratitude: "A small matter . . . to make these silly folks so full of gratitude. . . . He has spent but a few pounds of your mortal money: three or four perhaps." So Scrooge is forced to defend the generous spirit, "heated by the remark, and speaking unconsciously like his former, not his latter, self: 'The happiness he gives, is quite as great as if it cost a fortune.' " Then he suddenly remembers his present self, and gently urged by his ghostly analyst, moves toward self-criticism. The process is continued by the second Ghost, in Stave III, who answers Scrooge's anxious question about Tiny Tim: "If he be like to die, he had better do it, and decrease the surplus population." When Scrooge is overcome "with penitence and grief" at his own words, the Ghost comes in quickly with the grave rebuke: "forbear that wicked cant until you have discovered What the surplus is, and Where it is." The Ghost employs the same mimicry when he shows the terrible children, Want and Ignorance. Scrooge's newborn horror, like his compassion, is answered by his own words: "Are there no prisons? . . . Are there no workhouses?" This technique of exact quotation comes decorously enough in the Christmas present, rubbing Scrooge's nose in his very recent refusal to give to the portly gentleman. The arguments for charity were also presented in personification ("Want is keenly felt, and Abundance rejoices") but they have to be acted out for the unimaginative man, forcing him to walk through the crowds and see them composed not of ciphers but of individuals. All the elements in this brief masque are appropriate. They show the hardened man the need and love in his own past; they show the old killjoy his dead capacity for joy. Having indicated causality and change the show ends with a *memento mori,* cold, solitary, and repulsive, in the new perspective of feeling. Effective argument is implied in the dramatic reclamation by love and fear, and we are left with the urgent question—is reclamation still possible?—which makes the modulation from nightmare to reality. The fantasy has a realistic suggestion of hypnotic therapy.

II

But the content is supernatural and the effects greatly foreshortened. The process of conversion is everywhere else in Dickens transferred to a rather more realistic mode. Martin Chuzzlewit's conversion, for example, is as traumatic as that of Scrooge. It comes with a violent and unreal change of environment, Pavlovian in kind and effect, after Martin's sickness and his disillusion with Eden. The mode of external moral enactment is very close to the masque of *A Christmas Carol,* though it is Mark Tapley, the double as opposite, who provides the mirror. Mark has been nursing Martin, then the roles are reversed, and it is "Martin's turn to work, and sit beside the bed and watch." Mark keeps on crying brightly, "I'm jolly, sir: I'm jolly!" and Martin's unimaginative egoism is jolted by the similarity and the difference in the two situations. The running title is "The Discovery of Self":

> Now, when Martin began to think of this, and to look at Mark as he lay there; never reproaching him by so much as an expression of regret . . . he began to think, how was it that this man who had had so few advantages, was so much better than he who had had so many? . . . he began to ask himself in what they differed.
>
> He was assisted in coming to a conclusion on this head by the frequent presence of Mark's friend, their fellow-passenger across the ocean: which suggested to him that in regard to having aided her, for example, they had differed very much. Somehow he coupled Tom Pinch with this train of reflection; and thinking that Tom would be very likely to have struck up the same sort of acquaintance under similar circumstances, began to think in what respects two people so extremely different were like each other, and were unlike him. At first sight there was nothing very distressing in these meditations, but they did undoubtedly distress him for all that. (chap. 33)

The reader has of course anticipated Martin's groping classification, but the obvious bracketing of Mark Tapley and Tom Pinch is an important moment of insight for a character so far placed firmly in the egoists' category. Dickens' organization of doubles and opposites seems a simple formal device for giving clarity to narrative and theme, but artifice and morality interact with each other just as they do in more subtle novelists where psychological realism and particularity blur the categories. Even here the form is in part the result of a way of looking at life, and the moment of conversion largely depends on the way in which the character catches up with the reader and becomes aware of the categories in which he is himself placed. In this moral crisis Martin's recognition precedes his movement from one category to another, and both recognition and change are made very self-conscious processes. But there follows immediately one of Dickens' quiet authorial comments. He takes a look at the origin of Martin's humor, as he has indeed done much earlier in the novel when Martin explains to Tom that he has been brought up by his "abominably selfish" grandfather, whose failings —family failings, he has heard—have fortunately not descended to him. Dickens here gives the detached explanation. Selfishness, he says, was the domestic vice propagated by Martin's grandfather, and Martin had acquired a defensive selfishness, reasoning, as a child, "My guardian takes so much thought for himself, that unless I do the like by *myself*, I shall be forgotten." This is a relatively cursory glance at causality,

but it is made. Dickens then comments truly that Martin had never
known his fault:

> If any one had taxed him with the vice, he would have indignantly re-
> pelled the accusation, and conceived himself unworthily aspersed. He
> never would have known it, but that being newly risen from a bed of
> dangerous sickness, to watch by such another couch, he felt how nearly
> Self had dropped into the grave, and what a poor dependent, miserable
> thing it was.
>
> It was natural for him to reflect—he had months to do it in—upon his
> own escape, and Mark's extremity. This led him to consider which of
> them could be better spared, and why? Then the curtain slowly rose a
> very little way; and Self, Self, Self, was shown below.

The discovery that his essential self is selfish (Dickens plays with the
double meaning) is tactfully described in this image of the slow curtain.
Dickens describes the process of change so briefly—making no attempt
to give any correlative for the passage of time—that even though he
says that the process took months, we are left with the implausible impression of violent change. Dickens is in fact *saying*, but not *showing*,
that this is no single leap of vision but a slow and complex process:
"It was long before he fixed the knowledge of himself so firmly in his
mind that he could thoroughly discern the truth; but in the hideous
solitude of that most hideous place, with Hope so far removed, Ambition quenched, and Death beside him rattling at the very door, reflection came, as in a plague-beleaguered town; and so he felt and knew
the failing of his life, and saw distinctly what an ugly spot it was."
Eden has been the reverse of hope and illusion and pride, but by
a further irony Martin's process reverses the Fall, for "So low had Eden
brought him down. So high had Eden raised him up." Here are the
elements of Scrooge's reclamation: insight is painfully born from a
detached and clear reflection, and there is a similar context of panic,
horror, and death. Even the masque is shadowed in the strong personifi-
cations of Hope, Ambition, Death, and the plague-beleaguered town,
which is both a metaphor and a real place.

III

Martin's conversion is much slower than Scrooge's immediate and
successful transformation, but although Dickens says it is slow, it is
shown in a way which gives no impression of the real pace. Dickens
is very often showing moral development in narrative *cul-de-sac*, not

equating the main action of the novel with the action of change. In
David Copperfield there is rather less of a gap between the flow of event
and the moral action. The nature of the moral change has been discussed by Gwendolen Needham, who points out that for David the moment of insight comes when he hears Annie Strong tell of "the first
impulse of an undisciplined heart" and "love founded on a rock." [5] Her
words strike home because they both duplicate and reverse his situation: she has felt the first impulse but not followed it. Insight does not
come all at once, and when David first hears Annie's words about disparity of mind and purpose, we are told, "I pondered on those words,
even while I was studiously attending to what followed, as if they had
some particular interest, or some strange application that I could not
divine" (chap. 45). Her comment on the undisciplined heart is spoken
"with an earnestness that thrilled." Then at the end of the chapter
David cannot attend to his aunt's words: "I was thinking of all that had
been said. My mind was still running on some of the expressions used.
'There can be no disparity in marriage like unsuitability of mind and
purpose.' 'My love was founded on a rock.' But we were at home; and
the trodden leaves were lying underfoot, and the autumn wind was
blowing." We reach something approaching explicitness in the pathetic
tone and associations—the "too late"—of the natural images, but David's
divination still lags a little behind the reader's. It is not until three
chapters later, after we have been shown yet another mirror in the story
of Betsy Trotwood's undisciplined heart, and after we have seen David
trying hard to correct Dora's "disparity," that we are told how full
recognition has pervaded his life with "the old unhappy feeling":

> "The first mistaken impulse of an undisciplined heart." Those words of
> Mrs. Strong's were constantly recurring to me, at this time; were almost
> always present to my mind. I awoke with them, often, in the night; I
> remember to have even read them, in dreams, inscribed upon the walls
> of houses. For I knew, now, that my own heart was undisciplined when
> it first loved Dora; and that if it had been disciplined, it could never
> have felt, when we were married, what it had felt in its secret experience.
> "There can be no disparity in marriage, like unsuitability of mind and
> purpose." These words I remembered too. I had endeavoured to adapt
> Dora to myself, and found it impracticable. It remained for me to adapt
> myself to Dora . . . This was the discipline to which I tried to bring
> my heart, when I began to think. (chap. 48)

The moment of insight is again spread out in time, though condensed

[5] "The Undisciplined Heart of David Copperfield," *Nineteenth Century Fiction*, IX
(1954), 81-107.

for the reader into one memorable scene. David does not leap into action, but accepts trial and error and bewilderment. Once more the character is made aware of the moral categories which shape the novel, and by the end we see that Annie Strong's situation, which first applied only in part to David's, is the complete parallel: for David, as for Annie and Peggotty, it is the heart's discipline which founds love on a rock. We might once more point to a discrepancy between the narrative action and the moral development: David's process is only briefly one of discipline, and then the artist's wish-fulfillment disposes of Dora and what remains is less a stern moral test than the slow discovery that Agnes is the rock on which he should found his love. He is blind ("blind! blind! blind!") to his dependence on her rather than to a weakness which life harshly corrects. But this is not the place to discuss all the implications of Dickens' morality: whatever the nature of the moral conversion, it is once more made, with brevity and insight, by this dramatic enactment outside the hero's consciousness.

Gradgrind, in *Hard Times*, is also converted by two images, his double and his opposite, made available by the usual pattern of moral stereotypes. The two are not combined, as they are for David, but split, as they are for Scrooge. Gradgrind's redeeming opposite is Sissy, the pupil who teaches her master that the truth of the heart can be stronger than the truth of the reason, and he can learn her lesson only when faced by the sterile fruits of his teaching in another pupil, his daughter. Then comes the moment of insight which is here partly retrospective, for he sees that "some change may have been slowly working about me in this house, by mere love and gratitude." But his double is as effective a master as the model, and more ironical. Full insight comes like Nemesis when he too is quoted out of his own mouth. His dishonest son says, "So many people are employed in conditions of trust; so many people, out of so many, will be dishonest. I have heard you talk, a hundred times, of its being a law. How can I help laws? You have comforted others with such things, father. Comfort yourself!" (Bk. III, chap. 7) The statistical unit confounds the statistician, and Tom is made even more detestable and ridiculous by the "disgraceful grotesqueness" of his comic minstrel disguise. The truth is driven home in the form of gross parody.

But there are three successful pupils who act as double. His son's parody is followed by a reenactment of the past. The question-and-answer of the first schoolroom scene is reversed when the perfect pupil of Utilitarianism gives the text-book answer: " 'Bitzer,' said Mr. Gradgrind, broken down, and miserably submissive to him, 'have you a heart?' 'The circulation, sir,' returned Bitzer, smiling at the oddity of

the question, 'couldn't be carried on without one' " (Bk. III, chap. 8).
The new Gradgrind goes on speaking of ordinary human values to
Bitzer, going innocently against the established grain of his own system,
arguing pathetically, "If this is solely a matter of self-interest with you"
and "You were many years at my school." In his need he sees not only
that his precepts are dust, but that they have hardened in the malice of
Bitzer's rational replies. His last instruction comes from the world of the
circus and its idle frivolity, making its point in comic lisp: "There ith a
love in the world, not Thelf-interetht after all." At the end Gradgrind
is far from his sophisticated pupils, and learns truth from dogs and
clowns.

There is a small and very characteristic example in *Little Dorrit*
which shows all the constituents of this kind of moral crisis. Miss Wade
first seduces Tattycoram by fanning her jealousy. She sees herself as she
watches Tattycoram's fit of fury and "ingratitude," and it is hard not
to feel that this is one of Dickens' smug diagnoses: "The observer stood
with her hand upon her own bosom, looking at the girl, as one afflicted
with a diseased part might curiously watch the dissection and exposition
of an analogous case" (Bk. I, chap. 2). And Tattycoram has just said
to her, "You seem to come like my own anger, my own malice . . ." Miss
Wade captures the analogous case, and tries to avenge herself by exacer-
bating Tattycoram's less unredeemable jealousy and resentment. It is
rather like a Morality abstraction influencing a more realistic mixed
character, and the result is a good example of the moral homeopathy I
have been illustrating, for the jealousy is purged not increased. Tattycoram explains:

> I was afraid of her, from the first time I ever saw her. I knew she had
> got a power over me, through understanding what was bad in me, so
> well. It was a madness in me, and she could raise it whenever she liked.
> I used to think, when I got into that state, that people were all against
> me because of my first beginning; and the kinder they were to me, the
> worse fault I found in them. I made it out that they triumphed above
> me, and that they wanted to make me envy them, when I know—when I
> even knew then, if I would—that they never thought of such a thing . . .
> I am not so bad as I was . . . I have had Miss Wade before me all this
> time, as if it were my own self grown ripe—turning everything the wrong
> way, and twisting all good into evil. I have had her before me all this
> time, finding no pleasure in anything but keeping me as miserable, sus-
> picious, and tormenting as herself . . . (Bk. II, chap. 33)

This is the purest example of conversion by double, and Tattycoram
gives obliquely the perfect comment on the distortions of Miss Wade's

autobiography. There is also of course the central figure of another waif, Little Dorrit, who comes in just after this speech. Tattycoram has been instructed by her own self grown ripe, a stronger devil who exorcises her own, and now Mr. Meagles tells her to regard her opposite, like Martin Chuzzlewit: "If she had constantly thought of herself, and settled with herself that everybody visited this place upon her . . . she would have led an irritable and probably a useless existence." Tattycoram's story, like Miss Wade's, is an antithetical variant of Dorrit's, another study in the novel's exploration of conditioning and freedom.

IV

Pip's progress in *Great Expectations* is probably the only instance of a moral action where the events precipitate change and growth as they do in George Eliot or Henry James. Pip is marked by a dominant flaw like Scrooge, but the flaw does not absorb the whole vitality of the character. He is a more realistic and analytical Martin Chuzzlewit and he is shown subjected to the influences of accident and environment, and hardening in his pride and ingratitude, though never without some measure of shame. The main converting event is his discovery of the source of his expectations, but this is a fairly complex business, involving the delicately handled shifting relationship with Magwitch. This is certainly not only a symbolic delineation of the criminal basis of wealth, though at times it carries that implication. Magwitch is also an important agent in the conversion of Pip. He first exacerbates and then exorcises pride and ingratitude.

Pip's view of this nemesis is still steeped in his twin failings: "But, sharpest and deepest pain of all—it was for the convict, guilty of I knew not what crimes, and liable to be taken out of those rooms where I sat thinking, and hanged at the Old Bailey door, that I had deserted Joe" (chap. 39). Here he is merely revaluing one particular instance of pride and ingratitude, and what he has to learn, like all unimaginative men, is a generalized and renewable morality. He has to revalue his defects, not an isolated example of them. Magwitch plays a role in this Morality rather like that of King Grizzlybeard in the fairy tale, who degrades pride and gives it a real cause and a fitting punishment. Pip, like a spoiled child, is really given something to cry about. Pip has winced at Joe's illiteracy and manners, and so he is forced into the gross parody and ordeal of stomaching Magwitch, who has paid for Pip's education and fastidiousness. Then Pip becomes involved in Magwitch's past and future, and Magwitch himself is given dignity and sympathy. Both he and Pip move out of aggressive pride into trust and love. Magwitch then provokes a further revaluation in Pip, based now on an appraisal of the convict's gratitude, and an acknowledgment of his own debt:

> When I took my place by Magwitch's side, I felt that that was my place henceforth while he lived.
>
> For now my repugnance to him had all melted away, and in the hunted wounded shackled creature who held my hand in his, I only saw a man who had meant to be my benefactor, and who had felt affectionately, gratefully, and generously, towards me with great constancy through a series of years. I only saw in him a much better man than I had been to Joe. (chap. 54)

Magwitch draws out and punishes Pip's pride and ingratitude,[6] then delineates Pip for himself and the reader in his role as moral opposite. Finally, he provides the final ordeal which proves Pip's conversion. Pip holds Magwitch's hand during the trial, and the spectators "pointed down at this criminal or at that, and most of all at him and me" (chap. 56).

Although Estella's relations with her benefactor largely parallel Pip's, her moral change takes place offstage, and it is Miss Havisham's conversion which corresponds to Pip's. She is like Miss Wade in strengthening her own ruling passion by encouraging it in someone else—a subtle form of self-justification and revenge. She of course propagates her lovelessness in her education of Estella, and like Gradgrind she is punished at the hands of the pupil who has learned only too well. Estella hears Pip's declaration of love unmoved, and explains, "It is in the nature formed within me." When Miss Havisham demands the one thing she has trained Estella not to give—"Would it be weakness to return my love?"—Estella can only ask:

> If you had taught her, from the dawn of her intelligence, with your utmost energy and might, that there was such a thing as daylight but that it was made to be her enemy and destroyer, and she must always turn against it, for it had blighted you and would else blight her;—if you had done this, and then, for a purpose, had wanted her to take naturally to the daylight and she could not do it, you would have been disappointed and angry? (chap. 38)

Miss Havisham is taught by her self-created double, but the encounter shows her that she is in fact teaching lovelessness while desperately

---

[6] Although I cannot entirely accept Dorothy Van Ghent's view of this relationship (*The English Novel: Form and Function* [New York, 1953]), this account is not irreconcilable with her interpretation.

needing love. She sees her error in this distorting mirror. Then, like Scrooge, she sees her old self in the image of Pip. He provides this image of love just after she has been rebuffed by the image of lovelessness, and she tells Pip, after his rejection by Estella, "Until you spoke to her the other day, and until I saw in you a looking-glass that showed me what I once felt myself, I did not know what I had done" (chap. 49). There is no action left for her, but she admits responsibility, and knows that she has shut Estella, like herself,' away from the influences that form "the natural heart," that "with this figure of myself always before her, a warning to back and point my lesson, I stole her heart away and put ice in its place." Estella comes to find that suffering is "stronger than all other teaching" but that is a process not demonstrated in the novel.

There remains Dickens' last portrayal of conversion. The central moral crisis in *Our Mutal Friend*, the conversion of Bella from mercenariness to love, shows Dickens' precise awareness of this kind of moral therapy. For Boffin and his wife deliberately act out the homeopathic cure, staging her mercenary values and repelling her into the right course. It is Dickens' great surprise, as he tells us in the Epilogue, the card hidden up his sleeve from which our attention has carefully been averted by the deliberately flaunted impersonation by Harmon. Harmon himself, again like King Grizzlybeard, personates the poor man, and he and the Boffins collaborate in Bella's conversion. At the climax Boffin is both double and alter ego, for he assumes the miser's mask, most unlike his true self, and presents with verve the exaggerated and logically active image of Bella's supposed values. This releases the true forces of benevolence with a powerful spring. After the deceptive appearance of the good man perverted by wealth we see the virtuous Golden Dustman, golden in the metaphorical sense after all. And Bella's rejection of his values comes with the joy at knowing that Boffin is untarnished too.

She is always shown as partly affecting her mercenariness. Her declaration to her father, who asks her when she felt it "coming on," has the tone of strained levity. When Boffin acts as devil's advocate his encouragement of her humor shows the gap between wholehearted mercenariness and her half-hearted version: " 'I hope, sir, you don't think me vain?' 'Not a bit, my dear,' said Mr. Boffin. 'But I think it's very creditable in you, at your age, to be so well up with the pace of the world, and to know what to go in for. You are right. Go in for money, my love. Money's the article . . .' " (Bk. III, chap. 5).

The Brer Rabbit technique is of course powerful:

Somehow, Bella was not so well pleased with this assurance . . . as she might have been. Somehow, when she put her arms round Mrs. Boffin's neck and said Good-Night, she derived a sense of unworthiness from the still anxious face of that good woman and her obvious wish to excuse her husband. "Why, what need to excuse him?" thought Bella, sitting down in her own room. "What he said was very sensible, I am sure, and very true, I am sure. It is only what I often say to myself. Don't I like it then? No, I don't like it, and, though he is my liberal benefactor, I disparage him for it." (Bk. III, chap. 5)

Next Boffin enacts his full-blown miserly humor, and though it is studded with slight *double-entendres* which Dickens plainly enjoyed enormously ("Believe me that in spite of all the change in him, he is the best of men") the masquerade has all the plausible gusto of the impersonations of Edgar and Vendice. Mrs. Boffin sheds real tears, for instance, though these are subsequently explained, but there are a number of details which perhaps explain why Gissing was convinced that Dickens had at one stage intended that Boffin should really turn miser. Bella is also in part acted on by genuine Good Angels, Lizzie Hexam and Harmon. Influenced from all sides she rejects Boffin after he explains to Harmon-Rokesmith, "We all three know that it's Money she makes a stand for—money, money, money—and that you and your affections and hearts are a Lie, sir!" (Bk. III, chap. 15). Then the deception thins gradually before the reader's eyes. Boffin snubs the Lammles and is shown on good terms with his wife.

When the final disclosure is made we are given two slightly different explanations. Boffin's version has the simple morality of a fairy-tale test: "If she was to stand up for you when you was slighted, if she was to show herself of a generous mind when you was oppressed, if she was to be truest to you when you was poorest and friendliest, and all this against her own seeming interest, how would that do?" (Bk. IV, chap. 13). This dovetails rather than conflicts with Bella's insight into the psychological machinery of her conversion:

> When you saw what a greedy little wretch you were the patron of, you determined to show her how much misused and misprized riches could do, and often had done, to spoil people; did you? Not caring what she thought of you (and Goodness knows *that* was of no consequence!) you showed her, in yourself, the most detestable sides of wealth, saying in your own mind, "This shallow creature would never work the truth out of her own weak soul, if she had a hundred years to do it in; but a glaring instance kept before her may open even her eyes and set her thinking." (Bk. IV, chap. 13)

She calls Boffin her "finger-post," just as Miss Havisham called Pip her looking-glass, and as Tattycoram saw in Miss Wade her own self grown ripe. This is the Dickensian version of the Whip and Bridle of Dante's Purgatory.

V

The moral stimulus of ideals and deterrents is not peculiar to Dickens' dramatization of change, but I know of no other novelist who uses this device with the consistency and emphasis which I have illustrated. In *Felix Holt*, for instance, to choose an example from a long novel, not a short fable like Poe's or Stevenson's, there are traces of this reliance on some concept of *similia similibus curantur*. Mrs. Transome's portrait with its "youthful brilliancy" contrasts with her present "joyless, embittered age" to haunt Esther with a warning hint of her own possible future, rather as Darnay's face haunts Carton as a reminder of his possible past. But this warning mirror is only one item in a complex pattern of disenchantment, desire, and moral influence both implicit and explicit. George Eliot, like Jane Austen, presents human relationships as the most potent influence in conversion, and in their novels the didactic voice (Mr. Knightley's or Daniel Deronda's) is stronger than any warning double. It might be argued that Dickens is summing up, in an especially condensed and theatrical way, these effects of human influence, but such argument obscures the suddenness of the vision—the "glaring instance" works, or is made to appear to work, by empathy rather than instruction. And the diabolical enactment is usually more instructive than the ideal. Dickens' convention puts great responsibility on this single influence, and it is presented with the vividness of hallucination: Tattycoram and Bella see themselves in their potential doubles, and the act of seeing works the miracle.

It is not enough to dismiss the convention as an unrealistic, theatrical shortcut. It is a device which has to be related to the whole narrative context. This context is not exclusively concerned with moral analysis, and even though Dickens at times testifies to the gradualness of his conversions, he seems to need the economy of concentrated incident. In context, this is appropriate, and it is related to other features of the novels. The characters are not imaginatively analytical, and it would be futile to expect them to cope with the gradual piecemeal assembling of experience which is the central activity—the education in general truth —in many novels by George Eliot and James.[7] As Bella says, she needs "the glaring instance."

[7] This kind of activity is usually missing in Dickens' portrayal of change. William James speaks of the sensation of detachment and passiveness which is a feature of

Condensation and theatrical vividness seem to be related to the passiveness of the converted characters. And this brings me to a brief comment on the gap between Dickens' moral action and his plot-action. In George Eliot and James the moral change determines the course of the action, though both novelists need to bring in the aids of accident and contrivance, and it is indeed an essential feature of George Eliot's action that chance or trivial action shall have great influence on destiny. But action is precipitated by the strengths and weaknesses of the characters, as when Maggie drifts away with Stephen, Dorothea marries Casaubon, or Daniel Deronda rescues Mirah. Martin Chuzzlewit, on the other hand, is a victim of Pecksniff rather than of his own egoism, Pip is trapped by Magwitch's gratitude, Bella's life is determined by a will and a benevolent intrigue. I do not want to exaggerate this passiveness: it is also true that Pip reacts to his great expectations as a proud and ungrateful boy, before they have worked on him strongly, and that Bella is susceptible to wealth's temptation. But the shape of the action is largely determined from outside. It has its origin in character, certainly: the plotting and mystery are not merely imposed by Dickens on his moral argument, but set going by Jonas Chuzzlewit, Dombey, Steerforth and Heep, Miss Havisham and Magwitch, Bradley Headstone, and John Jasper. It is, however, more often created by the villains than by the good or mixed characters. Even when it is created by a Magwitch, it is not Magwitch who is most changed by the action he precipitates. Gradgrind learns from the action he shapes, true, and he and Dombey are perhaps closest to the typical hero of George Eliot and James in being changed by feeling the weight of their own action. But the vital difference between George Eliot's conversions and most

---

many conversions: "Throughout the height of it [the converting experience] he undoubtedly seems to himself a passive spectator or undergoer of an astounding process performed upon him from above." Dickens' characters, unlike Defoe's and Dostoevsky's, do not have a feeling of submission to an outside force, but rather give an impression of passive detachment. The conversion transforms a passive spectator rather than an active protagonist. One might pursue this passiveness and find resemblances to victims of brainwashing, or subjects of hypnosis and religious and political conversion. Like hypnosis or some forms of psychotherapy, the Dickensian conversion involves an isolation of some aspect of personality for recognition. Like other forms of conversion, it may depend on change of environment, shock, fear, physiological lowering. And it works quickly. Dickens' own tendencies to hallucination and autosuggestion, and his susceptibility to cyclical change, may account for some of these features. Humphry House's essay, "The Macabre Dickens" (which uses Edmund Wilson's essay on "The Two Scrooges" and some comments by G. H. Lewes) includes suggestive remarks on the hallucinatory features of his treatment of villains which may apply also to the studies in conversion. But to argue in detail the psychological validity of these conversions might both exaggerate and obscure their literary interest.

of those in Dickens is that in George Eliot the character whose change is central to the action is changed in and by the action he initiates, in the process of recognizing moral causality and responsibility. Dickens' characters, further removed from this kind of tragic process, are changed less by seeing what they have done than by seeing what they are, and in the exaggerated form of "the glaring instance." Dickens' segregated and sensational converting vision is appropriate to, and perhaps to some extent produced by, his concept of action.

He is too interested in social satire, comic incident, and melodramatic intrigue and mystery, to give more space to moral action. This comment is not intended to ignore his simplified and sometimes cursory treatment of character, but even where the psychology is blunt—and it is not always—this is only a negative explanation of his treatment of moral change. It is as if he were committed to the imposed external action of some eighteenth century novels, like those of Fielding and Smollett, which he had read and admired. Wilkie Collins may have followed him, or added his influence, in this kind of plotting. But the interest of moral change in Collins is small, for his concept of character is much more arbitrary and plot-determined than Dickens'. Dickens' division into plotters and victims, and his frequent separation of moral change and adventure, bring him closer to Fielding and Smollett—in spite of the contemporary relevance of his *roman policier*—than to his fellow-Victorians. But he uses this split action and imposed plot for the expression of an essentially nineteenth century theme, that theme of the growth of love and social sense which may be more subtly explored by greater psychologists than Dickens, but which still shapes his moral categories. Even if his psychology is stereotyped, his categories melodramatically distinct, part of the force of his conversions lies in the implication that the mixed character, the redeemable Tattycoram or Bella, has an affinity with the riper and purer evil. It is this threat of affinity which makes the fingerpost an effective warning. The moral trap set by Harmon and Boffin for Bella is very like the trap set for Pecksniff by old Martin's impersonation: but Pecksniff is confirmed in his humor, not converted. Where Dickens appears to be using a fantastic machinery akin to the techniques of eighteenth century fiction, he can come close to the moral truth aimed at by his contemporaries. The enactment of conversion, the very hinge of the true novel of moral development, is more than an interesting and consistent technical device, for it seems to reveal some of the ways in which Dickens' imagination does and does not work.

The Poet
and the Critics of Probability

by George H. Ford

A reader's sense of probability depends in part upon literary convention and tradition, in part upon his own experience, and in part
upon his imagination. To satisfy the demand for probability, the novelist
faces more difficulties than the dramatist not only because the theatrical
three-sided box is an immediate admission of illusion, but because the
novel-reader is more likely to have been affected by realistic or naturalistic convention. In its extreme form, such a convention leads the reader
to expect not "a sense of fact" as Pater says, but fact itself. That Dickens
recognized his problem is evident in a letter written in 1859 which contains the best defense of his own methods:

> It does not seem to me to be enough to say of any description that it is
> the exact truth. The exact truth must be there; but the merit or art
> in the narrator, is the manner of stating the truth. As to which thing in
> literature, it always seems to me that there is a world to be done. And
> in these times, when the tendency is to be frightfully literal and catalogue-
> like—to make the thing, in short, a sort of sum in reduction that any
> miserable creature can do in that way—I have an idea (really founded
> on the love of what I profess), that the very holding of popular literature
> through a kind of popular dark age, may depend on such fanciful treat-
> ment.[1]

The recognition here of the inadequacy of naturalist cataloguing, a

[1] John Forster, The Life of Charles Dickens, ed. J. W. T. Ley, London and New
York, 1928, pp. 727-28.

"dreary, arithmetical dustyness that is powerfully depressing" as he said elsewhere,[2] and the recognition of the necessity for color, style, and manner, bring us to the core of Dickens' technique. It is a technique closer to that of poetic drama than of the more conventional novel. . . .

. . . An obvious example of its success is the characterization of Mrs. Gamp. Like the Wife of Bath, she is introduced by a brief description of her person, but thereafter, to enable her to take recognizable shape in the reader's mind, Dickens relies almost entirely upon her manner of speech.

> "Ah!" repeated Mrs. Gamp; for it was always a safe sentiment in cases of mourning. "Ah dear! When Gamp was summoned to his long home, and I see him a lying in Guy's Hospital with a penny-piece on each eye, and his wooden leg under his left arm, I thought I should have fainted away. But I bore up."

In this initial speech, and the subsequent discussion of Mrs. Harris and the bottle on the "chimley-piece," already caught are the distinctive and completely individual rhythms that characterize Sara Gamp, and the tone of genteel self-satisfaction that differentiates her from her partner Betsey Prig. In subsequent chapters we listen to these same distinctive rhythms during Sara's visits to Mr. Mould, and we witness the mighty clash scene in which Betsey, after a feast of pickled salmon, cucumbers, and several glasses of liquor, makes the epoch-making pronouncement that she does not believe in the existence of Mrs. Harris. As Sara adds afterwards: " 'Wot I have took from Betsey Prig this blessed night, no mortial creetur knows! . . . The words she spoke of Mrs. Harris, lambs could not forgive. No Betsey!' said Mrs. Gamp, in a violent burst of feeling, 'nor worms forget!' "

The illusion here is consistently sustained by distinctive dialogue and not by attestations that Sara is a representative example of conditions in the nursing profession before Florence Nightingale. Like most of Dickens' successful creations, Mrs. Gamp is a "triumph of style" rather than of analysis.[3] The real aim of the novel, says Gide's hero in *The Counterfeiters,* is "to represent reality on the one hand and on the other to stylize it into art." Those who make wholesale charges against improbability and exaggeration in Dickens' novels are usually readers who refuse to admit the desirability of stylization in fiction. Of them Dickens spoke in his Preface to *Chuzzlewit:*

---

[2] *The Letters of Charles Dickens,* ed. Walter Dexter (The Nonesuch Edition), London, 1937-1938, II, 352.
[3] Oliver Elton, *A Survey of English Literature 1830-1880,* London, 1948, II, 217.

What is exaggeration to one class of minds . . . is plain truth to another.
. . . I sometimes ask myself whether there may occasionally be a difference of this kind between some writers and some readers; whether it is
always the writer who colours highly, or whether it is now and then
the reader whose eye for colour is a little dull?

The most inimitable feature of Dickens, according to George Orwell,
is a fertility of invention, "which is invention not so much of characters
. . . and situations, as of turns of phrase and concrete details. The outstanding mark of Dickens' writings is the unnecessary detail." [4] Orwell
cites as examples Joe Gargery's speech about the robbers stuffing Mr.
Pumblechook's mouth "full of flowering annuals to perwent his crying
out," and Mr. Murdstone assigning mathematical problems to David
Copperfield: "If I go into a cheese-monger's shop, and buy five thousand
double-Gloucester cheeses at fourpence-halfpenny each, present payment. . . ." As Orwell adds, "Dickens' imagination overwhelms him.
The picturesque details are too good to be left out." [5]

In 1864, Dickens was reading some novels by other authors and was
irritated by the dialogue. "I have been trying [to read] other books;
but so infernally conversational, that I forget who the people are before
they have done talking, and don't in the least remember what they
talked about before when they begin talking again." [6] In view of Dickens'
own practice, his criticism is really leveled not at the quantity of conversation but at its lack of distinctiveness. For purposes of stylization he
was prepared to take the risk that his world of sharply marked manners
of speech might seem improbable to some sorts of novel readers. It has
often been pointed out that if Shakespeare's plays had been printed
without the names of the speakers, so distinct are the styles of each
one that there would usually be little difficulty in assigning the lines.
Dickens' aim is comparable.

A criticism that has been commonly made is that Dickens' characters
are all types rather than individuals. Henry James complained instead
that they are nearly all individuals and not types.[7] James seems to be
closer to the truth, but the whole question of particulars and universals
ought to be related to the context in which the characters are placed

---

[4] George Orwell, *Inside the Whale,* London, 1940, p. 69.—That *all* great novels "are
essentially lavish of particulars" is discussed by José Ortega Y Gasset in his *The
Dehumanization of Art and Notes on the Novel* (Princeton, 1948), pp. 97-103.

[5] See also R. C. Churchill's discussion of *Chuzzlewit:* "Throughout, it is the detail
which is so masterly. . . . It is always the *language* of Dickens that is so important;
his genius was essentially dramatic." *Scrutiny,* X (1942), 359.

[6] Forster, p. 744.

[7] James, *Partial Portraits,* London, 1888, p. 318.

rather than be settled offhand by rigid prescriptions. The uniqueness of Dickens' most successful creations is readily apparent in their speech. His really flat characters (his insipid heroes and heroines in many instances) have no distinctive style. They are mere types. They are more ordinary, more natural, and hence should supposedly be more probable. Instead they are mechanical and lifeless. Placed in a world of highly stylized, strongly-colored individuals, they are pale and insignificant, and, paradoxically, improbable.

The paradox is reinforced if we consider the dialogue employed by some of the novelists after Dickens. Typical of many is Galsworthy's, which is "natural," that is, it has the flatness of most ordinary speech. But in sacrificing stylized speech, Galsworthy attains a drabness which finally becomes incredible. After a diet of Dickens, how weary, flat, stale, and unprofitable seem the later volumes of *The Forsyte Saga*. Oscar Wilde once made a breezy remark about a man who wrote novels which were so like life that no one could possibly believe in their possibility.

A second aspect of Dickens' methods is his use of comic exuberance. He was aware that it, too, can lead to improbabilities: "Invention, thank God, seems the easiest thing in the world; and I seem to have such a preposterous sense of the ridiculous . . . as to be constantly requiring to restrain myself from launching into extravagances in the height of my enjoyment." [8] In *A Tale of Two Cities*, he made the experiment of subduing these comic extravagances by reducing dialogue and comic relief to the minimum. The results were disappointing, and he was happy to return to his more characteristic manner in *Great Expectations*, a novel which pivoted, as he said, upon a "grotesque tragi-comic conception." [9]

The tragi-comic mixture is more firmly ingrained in his novels than is sometimes recognized. The obvious place to look for it is in the structure of his books in which we find scenes of dramatic intensity followed by scenes of comedy, a method half-whimsically defended in an introductory chapter in *Oliver Twist*. This method was no doubt attributable to serial publication, but in Dickens it is a more deeply-rooted device which affects both structure and characterization. One suspects that he would have employed it even if his novels had been published as wholes. His letters indicate that he considered the juxtaposition of serious and comic necessary not only to the reality of the comic character but of the serious character as well. Lear without his fool is not Lear. Thus he

[8] *Letters*, I, 782.
[9] Forster, p. 734.

was disappointed in Wilkie Collins' novel *No Name,* in which the heroine was supposed to embody "steadiness and inflexibility of purpose." In Dickens' opinion, Collins failed to make the heroine probable because he told the story "severely and persistently" instead of employing comic contrast. "Contrast in that wise is most essential. She [the heroine] cannot possibly be brought out as he wants to bring her out, without it." [10]

The most interesting application of the mixture of genres can be found in the gallery of what may be called, in the general sense, his villains. The mixture here is employed not so much between the characters as within the characters. When Keats was developing his theory of negative capability, he spoke of the poetical character as having "no character." "It enjoys light and shade"; said Keats, "it lives in gusto, be it foul or fair. . . . It has as much delight in conceiving an Iago as an Imogen." [11] Dickens' method accords with Keats' theory. Bumble, Fagin, Squeers, Sampson and Sally Brass, Pecksniff, Uriah Heep, Creakle, Chadband, Podsnap, and other major and minor villains are conceived with gusto and delight. The gusto is apparent in the humor they provoke. They all represent vice or unpleasantness of different kinds, but they all share the characteristic of arousing not only dread but amusement. Stylization is achieved by the mixture of genres in the single character; the flat villain is thus made into something rounder and more complex. The grotesque humor of the scenes between Quilp and his wife may mean that Quilp is a less credible villain, but they make him into a more credible character. Concerning Major Bagstock in *Dombey,* Dickens told his illustrator that the Major was to be shown as "the incarnation of selfishness and small revenge" and hence gloating "in his apoplectico-mephistophelian observation of the scene." [12] Most of the Dickensian villains are similarly conceived; they combine a comic with a serious role. As a rule, it is only when he achieves this combination that his villains are animated and credible. The incredible villains, such as the purely melodramatic Carker and some of the other villains of his Dark Period novels, are played straight.

In the Preface to *Nicholas Nickleby,* Dickens raises the question constantly raised by his critics: how can an altogether evil character be probable?

[10] *Letters,* III, 284, and II, 852. On another occasion, he advised Collins: "I think the probabilities here and there require a little more respect than you are disposed to show them." *Letters,* II, 435-36.

[11] Letter to Richard Woodhouse, October 27, 1818.

[12] *Letters,* II, 17-18.

It is remarkable that what we call the world, which is so very credulous in what professes to be true, is most incredulous in what professes to be imaginary; and that, while, every day in real life, it will allow in one man no blemishes, and in another no virtues, it will seldom admit a very strongly-marked character, either good or bad, in a fictitious narrative, to be within the limits of probability.

Dickens' method is to make such "strongly-marked" black characters probable by greying them not with virtues but with humor. It is a form of complexity, different from George Eliot's for example, but still a form of complexity. For his white characters, whose goodness is "strongly-marked," he often uses no comparable method of greying. That is one of the reasons why the purely virtuous figures such as Little Nell, Agnes, and Little Dorrit, seem improbable. Their flatness is unrelieved. If we compare Nell in her determination never to desert her grandfather with another Dickens character who exclaims "I will never desert Mr. Micawber," the difference will be apparent. Humor is not a sign of illiteracy. It is an integral feature of Dickens' technique. When Dostoevsky was writing *The Idiot,* he noted that Don Quixote and Mr. Pickwick were rare examples of "positively good" characters who are probable. They are made probable because they are ridiculous, and the reader feels a sense of compassion "for the much ridiculed good man who does not know his own worth. . . . This rousing of compassion is the secret of humor." [13]

If we turn to the question of probability of plot and action, we find that Dickens' letters and prefaces provide less clues to his intentions, but there is an excellent substitute in some scattered remarks by Edwin Muir in his *Structure of the Novel.* The latter contains a stimulating analysis of the two kinds of traditional plots used by Dickens. The first is episodic; the characters move from place to place, but they do not develop. They are in this sense static.[14] The second kind is designed to show the development of character (such as Pip in *Great Expectations*), and clearly this second kind of plot raises different questions of probability. Instead of asking, as we do of the static character's actions, "Is he simply continuing to behave typically?" we ask instead, "Was his

---

[13] Quoted by Edward H. Carr, *Dostoevsky,* London, 1949, p. 205.

[14] Of Mrs. Gamp, R. H. Hutton remarked: "Indeed, just as the great mystery of physiology is said to be how a single living cell multiplied itself into a tissue composed of an indefinite number of similar cells, so the great intellectual mystery of Dickens's fertile genius was his power of reduplicating a single humorous conception of character into an elaborate structure of strictly analogous conceptions." *Brief Literary Criticisms* (1906), p. 50.

change of character motivated, and is his present behaviour explicable in view of what we have known of him?" Mr. Muir terms this second kind of structure *dramatic,* although there are inconvenient connotations when the term is applied to the novel.

The episodic plot is a device to set the characters "in new situations, to change their relations to one another, and in all of these to make them behave typically." As Muir adds, the task of the novelist who creates static characters is more like the choreographer's than the dramatist's.[15] In this sense, *Pickwick Papers* has the most satisfactory structure of all of Dickens' novels because it is most similar to the ballet. In his later novels, an attempt was made to devise more dramatic plots, to make the best of two traditions. *Dombey and Son,* for example, consists in part of a ballet sequence in which assorted groups of static characters are projected in successive scenes, throughout which they behave typically, and in part a foreground story of Florence and Walter, who are separated by some extraordinary and improbable accidents and coincidences. In the foreground, also, is Mr. Dombey himself, a serious study in the development of a proud man who, after a series of catastrophic events, is finally restored to humility. Dickens protested in a Preface that readers who failed to be convinced by Mr. Dombey's actions were lacking in knowledge of human nature. "Mr. Dombey undergoes no violent change either in this book, or in real life." But these foreground scenes, in which change occurs, are usually not so convincing as the more static background. One must except some of his last novels from this generalization. Old Dorrit, Pip, Bradley Headstone, show that Dickens was acquiring in his late years a new skill in the presentation of characters who change during the course of the novel. Usually, however, the static characters tend to crowd the developing characters off the stage. Novelists such as Austen and James, who have successfully used dramatic plot, have demonstrated that the scope of the novel form offers special resources for the exploration of motives of action so that character development seems probable. Dickens dismissed these special resources with the word "dissective." [16] He preferred to rely not on the resources of fictional drama but on stage drama, often of stage melo-

---

[15] Edwin Muir, *The Structure of the Novel,* London, 1946, p. 26.

[16] Concerning *The Woman in White* he wrote to Collins (January 7, 1860): "You know that I always contest your disposition to give an audience credit for nothing, which necessarily involves the forcing of points on their attention." "The three people who write the narratives . . . have a DISSECTIVE property in common, which is essentially not theirs but yours; . . . my own effort would be to strike more of what is got *that way* out of them by collision with one another, and by the working of the story."

drama. "Every writer of fiction," he said, "although he may not adopt the dramatic form, writes, in effect, for the stage." [17] In practice, this meant not merely a reduction of authorial comment and dissection, but a reliance upon stage motivation. Old Martin Chuzzlewit's strange behavior to his grandson, or Mr. Dombey assigning Edith to Carker for instructions in wifely obedience, or John Rokesmith's concealment of his identity—all such incidents might be passably probable in a fast-moving play, but in the slower pace of a novel they arouse incredulity.

As an example of the probability of action of the more static characters, Micawber's behavior in the exposure scene and later in Australia have seemed out of character to many readers. The stylized character does not lend himself to changes. As Muir says, in the novel of static character, "time is assumed, and the action is a static pattern, continuously redistributed and reshuffled in Space." Uncle Toby, Parson Adams, Mr. Collins, and Micawber "are beyond time and change" just as such a character as Pip is "completely enclosed" in time and change. Falstaff, as Muir continues, "remains quite unthreatened by the violent events in the two parts of Henry IV; the world in which Prince Henry and Hotspur fight and the king dies is not his world, but only a dream which passes over it." Falstaff and Micawber dwell in "a stationary spatial world in which time has reached an equilibrium." [18] Muir's explanation indicates why many readers have been disappointed by what finally happens to both Falstaff and Micawber; the illusion of permanence is threatened by the intrusion of time and change.

Let us leave the problem of endings, however, for too many discussions of probability are taken up with it exclusively, especially among certain readers (and movie-audiences) who have opinions about nothing else. The main impression Dickens' novels create depends less upon what *finally* happens to the characters than upon the characters themselves and the atmosphere in which they are surrounded. Dickens' lavish use of settings is one more indication of his predominant concern for spatial realities rather than for time realities. Perhaps it is inappropriate to apply the word *probability* in a discussion of Dickens' settings, but if we compare Todgers's boarding house with the Paris pension of Sophia Baines in *The Old Wives' Tale* or even with the Maison Vauquer in *Père Goriot,* the word is applicable. Todgers's is not like any other boarding house; it is not a type but an individual. It is stylized in the same way that the characters are stylized and is therefore equally offen-

[17] J. W. T. Ley, *The Dickens Circle,* New York, 1919, p. 87.
[18] Muir, pp. 63, 81-84.

sive to the strict realist. And because Todgers's is seen from the same imaginatively distorted angle as the characters, the description is entirely functional and satisfies Henry James' criterion of the organic relationship between the parts of a good novel. The setting of Todgers's and the character of Pecksniff mutually reinforce the credibility of each other. Dickens' awareness of his own method is apparent in some advice he gave to another novelist. It concerned a scene in which the characterization failed because of a lack of "the little subtle touches of description which, by making the country house and the general scene real, would give an air of reality to the people."

> The more you set yourself to the illustration of your heroine's passionate nature, the more indispensable this *attendant atmosphere of truth* becomes. It would . . . oblige the reader to believe in her. Whereas, for ever exploding like a great firework *without any background,* she glares and wheels and hisses, and goes out, and has lighted nothing.[19]

Descriptions of such background in Dickens are nearly always atmospheric rather than literal. He rejected one novel that had been submitted to him because the descriptions "make no more of the situation than the index might, or a descriptive playbill might." [20] His remark sounds like Willa Cather's essay, "The Novel Démeublé" which attacks the "popular superstition that 'realism' asserts itself in the cataloguing of a great number of material objects" or in explaining "mechanical processes." Our error, she says, consists in taking it for granted that "whoever can observe . . . can write a novel." Dickens' novels are certainly as crowded with furnishings as they are crowded with characters, but although he starts with observation, he rarely catalogues. His settings are integrated with what Cather would call "the emotional penumbra of the characters themselves." [21]

Dickens was his own best critic when he was replying in a letter to some charge of improbability in one of his novels:

> I work slowly and with great care, and never give way to my invention recklessly, but constantly restrain it; . . . [but] I think it is my infirmity to fancy or perceive relations in things which are not apparent generally. Also, I have such an inexpressible enjoyment of what I see in a droll light, that I dare say I pet it as if it were a spoilt child.[22]

The Circumlocution Office originated in its creator's observation of the

---

[19] *Letters,* II, 850 (italics mine).
[20] *Letters,* III, 462.
[21] Cather, *On Writing,* New York, 1949, pp. 35-37, 40.
[22] Forster, p. 721.

excessive reliance upon red tape of government officials during the Crimean War. But as his invention seized it for *Little Dorrit,* the Circumlocution Office was transformed into something rich and strange, something that the civil servants such as Fitzjames Stephen could only dismiss as fantastic, yet something which can have, for other readers, the same nightmare-like reality as Kafka's vision of an intricate bureaucracy under the Austro-Hungarian Empire.

Dickens' comments on the novel which have been quoted in this section show that he sometimes misunderstood the nature of his own writings, but in his preoccupation with the problem of probability he was usually trying to reestablish one old and well worn principle about how his novels should be read. Except when forced into a false position by reviewers, he urged that the reality of a novel, as of a play or narrative poem, depends upon imaginative imitation or stylization. His advice to his editorial assistant was the advice he tried to follow himself: "Keep Household Words Imaginative! is the solemn and continual Conductorial Injunction."

Dingley Dell
& the Fleet

by W. H. Auden

*To become mature is to recover that sense of seriousness
which one had as a child at play.*

F. W. Nietzsche

All characters who are products of the mythopoeic imagination are
instantaneously recognizable by the fact that their existence is not defined by their social and historical context; transfer them to another
society or another age and their characters and behavior will remain
unchanged. In consequence, once they have been created, they cease to
be their author's characters and become the reader's; he can continue
their story for himself.

Anna Karenina is not such a character for the reader cannot imagine
her apart from the particular milieu in which Tolstoy places her or the
particular history of her life which he records; Sherlock Holmes, on the
other hand, is: every reader, according to his fancy, can imagine adventures for him which Conan Doyle forgot, as it were, to tell us.

Tolstoy was a very great novelist, Conan Doyle a very minor one, yet
it is the minor not the major writer who possesses the mythopoeic gift.
The mythopoeic imagination is only accidentally related, it would seem,
to the talent for literary expression; in Cervantes' *Don Quixote* they are
found together, in Rider Haggard's *She* literary talent is largely absent.
Indeed, few of the writers whom we call great have created mythical
characters. In Shakespeare's plays we find five, Prospero, Ariel, Caliban,
Falstaff and Hamlet, and Hamlet is a myth for actors only; the proof
that, for actors, he is a myth is that all of them without exception, ir-
respective of age, build, or even sex, wish to play the part.

After Cervantes, as a writer who combines literary talent and a mytho-poeic imagination, comes Dickens and, of his many mythical creations, Mr. Pickwick is one of the most memorable. Though the appeal of mythical characters transcends all highbrow-lowbrow frontiers of taste, it is not unlimited; every such character is symbolic of some important and perpetual human concern, but a reader must have experienced this concern, even if he cannot define it to himself, before the character can appeal to him. Judging by my own experience, I would say that *Pickwick Papers* is emphatically *not* a book for children and the reflections which follow are the result of my asking myself: "Why is it that I now read with such delight a book which, when I was given it to read as a boy, I found so boring, although it apparently contains nothing which is too 'grown-up' for a twelve-year-old?" The conclusion I have come to is that the real theme of *Pickwick Papers*—I am not saying Dickens was consciously aware of it and, indeed, I am pretty certain he was not—is the Fall of Man. It is the story of a man who is innocent, that is to say, who has not eaten of the Tree of the Knowledge of Good and Evil and is, therefore, living in Eden. He then eats of the Tree, that is to say, he becomes conscious of the reality of Evil but, instead of falling from innocence into sin—this is what makes him a mythical character —he changes from an innocent child into an innocent adult who no longer lives in an imaginary Eden of his own but in the real and fallen world.

If my conclusion is correct, it explains why *Pickwick Papers* said nothing to me as a boy because, though no boy is innocent, he has no clear notion of innocence, nor does he know that to be no longer innocent, but to wish that one were, is part of the definition of an adult.

However he accounts for it, every adult knows that he lives in a world where, though some are more fortunate than others, no one can escape physical and mental suffering, a world where everybody experiences some degree of contradiction between what he desires to do and what his conscience tells him he ought to do or others will allow him to do. Everybody wishes that this world were not like that, that he could live in a world where desires would conflict neither with each other nor with duties nor with the laws of nature, and a great number of us enjoy imagining what such a world would be like.

Our dream pictures of the Happy Place where suffering and evil are unknown are of two kinds, the Edens and the New Jerusalems. Though it is possible for the same individual to imagine both, it is unlikely that his interest in both will be equal and I suspect that between the Arcadian whose favorite daydream is of Eden, and the Utopian whose favorite daydream is of New Jerusalem there is a characterological gulf as unbridgeable as that between Blake's Prolifics and Devourers.

In their relation to the actual fallen world, the difference between Eden and New Jerusalem is a temporal one. Eden is a past world in which the contradictions of the present world have not yet arisen; New Jerusalem is a future world in which they have at last been resolved. Eden is a place where its inhabitants may do whatever they like to do; the motto over its gate is, "Do what thou wilt is here the Law." New Jerusalem is a place where its inhabitants like to do whatever they ought to do, and its motto is, "In His will is our peace."

In neither place is the moral law felt as an imperative; in Eden because the notion of a universal law is unknown, in New Jerusalem because the law is no longer a law-for, commanding that we do this and abstain from doing that, but a law-of, like the laws of nature, which describes how, in fact, its inhabitants behave.

To be an inhabitant of Eden, it is absolutely required that one be happy and likable; to become an inhabitant of New Jerusalem it is absolutely required that one be happy and good. Eden cannot be entered; its inhabitants are born there. No unhappy or unlikable individual is ever born there and, should one of its inhabitants become unhappy or unlikable, he must leave. Nobody is born in New Jerusalem but, to enter it, one must, either through one's own acts or by Divine Grace, have become good. Nobody ever leaves New Jerusalem, but the evil or the unredeemed are forever excluded.

The psychological difference between the Arcadian dreamer and the Utopian dreamer is that the backward-looking Arcadian knows that his expulsion from Eden is an irrevocable fact and that his dream, therefore, is a wish-dream which cannot become real; in consequence, the actions which led to his expulsion are of no concern to his dream. The forward-looking Utopian, on the other hand, necessarily believes that his New Jerusalem is a dream which ought to be realized so that the actions by which it could be realized are a necessary element in his dream; it must include images, that is to say, not only of New Jerusalem itself but also images of the Day of Judgment.

Consequently, while neither Eden nor New Jerusalem are places where aggression can exist, the Utopian dream permits indulgence in aggressive fantasies in a way that the Arcadian dream does not. Even Hitler, I imagine, would have defined his New Jerusalem as a world where there are no Jews, not as a world where they are being gassed by the million day after day in ovens, but he was a Utopian, so the ovens had to come in.

How any individual envisages Eden is determined by his temperament, personal history and cultural milieu, but to all dream Edens the following axioms, I believe, apply.

(1) Eden is a world of pure being and absolute uniqueness. Change can occur but as an instantaneous transformation, not through a process of becoming. Everyone is incomparable.

(2) The self is satisfied whatever it demands; the ego is approved of whatever it chooses.

(3) There is no distinction between the objective and the subjective. What a person appears to others to be is identical with what he is to himself. His name and his clothes are as much *his* as his body, so that, if he changes them, he turns into someone else.

(4) Space is both safe and free. There are walled gardens but no dungeons, open roads in all directions but no wandering in the wilderness.

(5) Temporal novelty is without anxiety, temporal repetition without boredom.

(6) Whatever the social pattern, each member of society is satisfied according to his conception of his needs. If it is a hierarchical society, all masters are kind and generous, all servants faithful old retainers.

(7) Whatever people do, whether alone or in company, is some kind of play. The only motive for an action is the pleasure it gives the actor, and no deed has a goal or an effect beyond itself.

(8) Three kinds of erotic life are possible, though any particular dream of Eden need contain only one. The polymorphous-perverse promiscuous sexuality of childhood, courting couples whose relation is potential, not actual, and the chastity of natural celibates who are without desire.

(9) Though there can be no suffering or grief, there can be death. If a death occurs, it is not a cause for sorrow—the dead are not missed—but a social occasion for a lovely funeral.

(10) The Serpent, acquaintance with whom results in immediate expulsion —any serious need or desire.

The four great English experts on Eden are Dickens, Oscar Wilde, Ronald Firbank and P. G. Wodehouse.[1]

[A section is omitted in which Mr. Auden discusses the differences between a shame-culture and a guilt-culture—Ed.]

When the novel opens, Mr. Pickwick is middle-aged. In his farewell speech at the Adelphi, he says that nearly the whole of his previous life had been devoted to business and the pursuit of wealth, but we can no more imagine what he did during those years than we can

[1] N. B. To my surprise, the only creators of Edens during the last three centuries I can think of, have all been English.

imagine what Don Quixote did before he went mad or what Falstaff
was like as a young man. In our minds Mr. Pickwick is born in middle
age with independent means; his mental and physical powers are those
of a middle-aged man, his experience of the world that of a newborn
child. The society into which he is born is a commercial puritanical
society in which wealth is honored, poverty despised, and any detected
lapse from the strictest standards of propriety severely punished. In
such a society, Mr. Pickwick's circumstances and nature make him a
fortunate individual. He is comfortably off and, aside from a tendency
at times to overindulge in food and drink, without vices. Sex, for example, is no temptation to him. One cannot conceive of him either
imagining himself romantically in love with a girl of the lower orders,
like Don Quixote, or consorting with whores, like Falstaff. So far as
his experience goes, this world is an Eden without evil or suffering.

> His sitting-room was the first floor front, his bedroom the second floor
> front; and thus, whether he was sitting at his desk in his parlour or
> standing before the dressing-glass in his dormitory, he had an equal op-
> portunity of contemplating human nature in all the numerous phases it
> exhibits, in that not more populous than popular thoroughfare. His land-
> lady, Mrs. Bardell—the relict and sole executrix of a deceased custom-
> house officer—was a comely woman of bustling manners and agreeable ap-
> pearance, with a natural genius for cooking, improved by study and long
> practice, into an exquisite talent. There were no children, no servants, no
> fowls—cleanliness and quiet reigned throughout the house; and in it Mr.
> Pickwick's will was law.

His three young friends, Tupman, Snodgrass, and Winkle, are equally
innocent. Each has a ruling passion, Tupman for the fair sex, Snodgrass
for poetry, and Winkle for sport, but their talents are not very formid-
able. We are not given any specimen of Snodgrass's poems, but we may
presume that, at their best, they reach the poetic level of Mrs. Leo
Hunter's "Ode to an Expiring Frog."

> Say, have fiends in shape of boys
> With wild halloo and brutal noise
> Hunted thee from marshy joys
> With a dog,
> Expiring frog?

We are shown Winkle at a shoot and learn that the birds are in far
less danger than the bystanders. Tupman's age and girth are hardly
good qualifications for a Romeo or a Don Juan. Contact with the world
cures them of their illusions without embittering them, Eros teaches the

two young men that the favors of Apollo and Artemis are not what they desire—Snodgrass marries Emily and becomes a gentleman farmer, Winkle marries Arabella Allen and goes into his father's business—and Tupman comes to acquiesce cheerfully in the prospect of a celibate old age.

The results of Mr. Pickwick's scientific researches into the origin of the Hampstead Ponds and the nature of Tittlebats were no more reliable, we may guess, than his archaeology but, as the book progresses, we discover that, if his ability at enquiry is less than he imagines, his capacity to learn is as great. What he learns is not what he set out to learn but is forced upon him by fate and by his decision to go to prison, but his curiosity about life is just as eager at the end of the book as it was at the beginning; what he has been taught is the difference between trivial and important truths.

From time to time, Dickens interrupts his narrative to let Mr. Pickwick read or listen to a tale. Some, like the Bagman's story, the story of the goblins who stole a sexton, the anecdote of the tenant and the gloomy ghost, are tall tales about the supernatural, but a surprising number are melodramas about cases of extreme suffering and evil: a broken-down clown beats his devoted wife and dies of D.T.'s; the son of a wicked father breaks his mother's heart, is transported, returns after seventeen years and is only saved from parricide by his father dying before he can strike him; a madman raves sadistically; a man is sent to prison for debt by his father-in-law, his wife and child die, he comes out of prison and devotes the rest of his life to revenge, first refusing to save his enemy's son from drowning and then reducing him to absolute want.

Stories of this kind are not tall; they may be melodramatically written, but everybody knows that similar things happen in real life. Dickens' primary reason for introducing them was, no doubt, that of any writer of a serial—to introduce a novel entertainment for his readers at a point when he feels they would welcome an interruption in the main narrative—but, intentionally or unintentionally, they contribute to our understanding of Mr. Pickwick.

Mr. Pickwick is almost as fond of hearing horror tales and curious anecdotes as Don Quixote is of reading Courtly Romances, but the Englishman's illusion about the relationship of literature to life is the opposite of the Spaniard's.

To Don Quixote, literature and life are identical; he believes that, when his senses present him with facts which are incompatible with courtly romance, his senses must be deceiving him. To Mr. Pickwick, on the other hand, literature and life are separate universes; evil and suffering do not exist in the world he perceives with his senses, only in the world of entertaining fiction.

Don Quixote sets out to be a Knight Errant, to win glory and the hand of his beloved by overthrowing the wicked and unjust and rescuing the innocent and afflicted. When Mr. Pickwick and his friends set out for Rochester, they have no such noble ambitions; they are simply looking for the novel and unexpected. Their reason for going to Bath or to Ipswich is that of the tourist—they have never been there.

Don Quixote expects to suffer hardship, wounds, and weariness in the good cause, and is inclined to suspect the pleasant, particularly if feminine, as either an illusion or a temptation to make him false to his vocation. The Pickwick Club expects to have nothing but a good time, seeing pretty towns and countrysides, staying in well-stocked inns, and making pleasant new acquaintances like the Wardles. However, the first new acquaintance they make in their exploration of Eden is with the serpent, Jingle, of whose real nature they have not the slightest suspicion. When Jingle's elopement with Rachel Wardle opens his eyes, Mr. Pickwick turns into a part-time Knight Errant: he assumes that Jingle, the base adventurer, is a unique case and, whenever he comes across his tracks, he conceives it his duty not to rest until he has frustrated his fell designs, but his main purpose in travel is still to tour Eden. Rescuing unsuspecting females from adventurers has not become his vocation.

During his first pursuit of Jingle, Mr. Pickwick meets Sam Weller, decides to engage him as a personal servant, and in trying to inform Mrs. Bardell of his decision creates the misunderstanding which is to have such unfortunate consequences. Sam Weller is no innocent; he has known what it is like to be destitute and homeless, sleeping under the arches of Waterloo Bridge, and he does not expect this world to be just or its inhabitants noble. He accepts Mr. Pickwick's offer, not because he particularly likes him, but because the job promises to be a better one than that of the Boots at an inn.

> I wonder whether I'm meant to be a footman, or a groom, or a gamekeeper or a seedsman? I look like a sort of compo of every one of 'em. Never mind; there's change of air, plenty to see, and little to do; and all this suits my complaint uncommon.

But before the story ends, he is calling Mr. Pickwick an angel, and his devotion to his master has grown so great that he insists upon being sent to prison in order to look after him. For Sam Weller had, after all, his own kind of innocence: about the evil in the world he had learned as much as anybody, but his experience had never led him to suspect that a person so innocent of evil as Mr. Pickwick could inhabit it.

Mr. Pickwick has hardly engaged Sam Weller when the letter arrives from Dodson and Fogg, announcing that Mrs. Bardell is suing him for Breach of Promise, and his real education begins.

If, hitherto, he had ever thought about the Law at all, he had assumed that it was what the Law must always claim to be:

(1) Just. Those acts which the Law prohibits and punishes are always unjust; no just or innocent act is ever prohibited or punished.

(2) Efficient. There are no unjust acts or persons that the Law overlooks or allows to go unpunished.

(3) Infallible. Those whom the Law finds guilty are always guilty; no innocent person is ever found guilty.

He has got to learn that none of these claims is fulfilled, and why, in this world, they cannot be fulfilled.

Even were the Law formally perfect, its administration cannot be, because it has to be administered, not by angels or machines, but by human individuals who, like all human beings, vary in intelligence, temperament, and moral character: some are clever, some stupid, some kind, some cruel, some scrupulous, some unscrupulous.

Moreover, lawyers are in the morally anomalous position of owing their livelihood and social status to the criminal, the unjust and the ignorant; if all men knew the Law and kept it, there would be no work for lawyers. Doctors also owe their livelihood to an evil, sickness, but at least sickness is a natural evil—men do not desire ill health— but crimes and civil wrongs are acts of human choice, so that the contradiction between the purpose of Law and the personal interest of lawyers is more glaring. And then the complexity of the Law and the nature of the legal process make those who practice law peculiarly liable to a vice which one might call the vice of Imaginary Innocence.

No human being is innocent, but there is a class of innocent human actions called Games.

A game is a closed world of action which has no relation to any other actions of those who play it; the players have no motive for playing the game except the pleasure it gives them, and the outcome of the game has no consequences beyond itself. Strictly speaking, a game in which the players are paid to play, or in which they play for money stakes, ceases to be a game, for money exists outside the closed world of the game. In practice, one may say that a game played for stakes remains a game so long as the sums of money won or lost are felt by the players to be, not real, but token payments, that is to say, what they win or lose has no sensible effect upon their lives after the game is over.

The closed world of the game is one of mock passions, not real ones. Many games are, formally, mock battles, but if any one of the players should feel or display real hostility, he immediately ceases to be a player. Even in boxing and wrestling matches, in which the claim to be called games at all is doubtful, the ritual of shaking hands at the beginning and end asserts that they are not fights between real enemies.

Within the closed world of the game the only human beings are the players; the other inhabitants are things, balls, bats, chessman, cards, etc.

Like the real world, the game world is a world of laws which the players must obey because obedience to them is a necessary condition for entering it. In the game world there is only one crime, cheating, and the penalty for this is exclusion; once a man is known to be a cheat, no other player will play with him.

In a game the pleasure of playing, of exercising skill, takes precedence over the pleasure of winning. If this were not so, if victory were the real goal, a skillful player would prefer to have an unskillful one as his opponent, but only those to whom, like cardsharpers, a game is not a game but a livelihood, prefer this. In the game world the pleasure of victory is the pleasure of *just* winning. The game world, therefore, is an innocent world because the ethical judgment good-or-bad does not apply to it; a good game means a game at the conclusion of which all the players, whether winners or losers, can truthfully say that they have enjoyed themselves, a point which is made by the Little Man's speech after the cricket match between Dingley Dell and Muggleton.

> Sir, while we remember that Muggleton has given birth to a Dumkins and a Podder, let us never forget that Dingley Dell can boast of a Luffey and a Struggles. Every gentleman who hears me, is probably acquainted with the reply made by an individual who—to use an ordinary figure of speech—"hung out" in a tub, to the Emperor Alexander:—"If I were not Diogenes," said he, "I would be Alexander": I can well imagine these gentlemen to say. If I were not Dumkins, I would be Luffey; If I were not Podder, I would be Struggles.

The vice of Imaginary Innocence consists in regarding an action in the open world of reality as if it were an action in the closed world of the game.

If this world were the worst of all possible worlds, a world where everybody was obliged to do what he dislikes doing and prohibited from doing anything he enjoyed, this vice would be impossible. It is only possible because some people have the good fortune to enjoy doing something which society requires to be done; what, from the point of view of society, is their necessary labor, is, from their own, voluntary play. Men fall into this vice when, because of the pleasure which the exercise of their calling gives them, they forget that what is play for them may for others concern real needs and passions.

Before Mr. Pickwick has to suffer in person from this human failing, he has already witnessed a manifestation of it in the party politics of Eatonswill.

Party politics presupposes that it is possible for two people, equally rational and well-meaning, to hold different opinions about a policy and possible for a man to be convinced by argument that his opinion has been mistaken. It also presupposes that, however widely their political opinions may differ, all voters are agreed that the goal of politics is the establishment of a just and smoothly running society. But in Eatonswill the pleasure of party rivalry and debate has become an end in itself to both parties, a closed game world, and the real goal of politics has been forgotten.

> The Blues lost no opportunity of opposing the Buffs and the Buffs lost no opportunity of opposing the Blues . . . If the Buffs proposed to new skylight the market place, the Blues got up public meeting and denounced the proceeding; if the Blues proposed the erection of an additional pump in the High Street, the Buffs rose as one man and stood aghast at the enormity. There were Blue shops and Buff shops, Blue Inns and Buff Inns; there was a Blue aisle and a Buff aisle in the very church itself.

On such a parochial scale politics as a game is relatively harmless, though on a national scale it is vicious, but there can be no circumstances in which the practice of Law as a game is not vicious. People who are not lawyers never come into court for fun; they come, either because they have been arrested or because they believe they have been wronged and see no other way of redress. Winning or losing their case is never a mock victory or defeat but always a real one; if they lose, they go to prison or suffer social disgrace or are made to pay money.

Rightly or wrongly, it is believed in our culture that, in most criminal and civil trials, the best means of arriving at the ethical judgment guilty-or-not-guilty is through a kind of aesthetic verbal combat between a prosecuting and a defending counsel, to which the judge acts as a referee, and the verdict is given by a jury. To say that a lawyer is a good lawyer, therefore, is an aesthetic not an ethical description; a good lawyer is not one who causes justice to be done, but one who wins his cases, whether his client be innocent or guilty, in the right or in the wrong, and nothing will enhance his reputation for being a good lawyer so much as winning a case against apparently hopeless odds, a state of affairs which is more likely to arise if his client is really guilty than if he is really innocent. As men, Dodson and Fogg are scoundrels but, as lawyers, their decent colleague Mr. Perkins has to admit that they are very good.

> Mrs. Bardell, supported by Mrs. Chappins, was led in and placed in a drooping state at the other end of the seat on which Mr. Pickwick sat . . . Mrs. Saunders then appeared, leading in Master Bardell. At sight of her child, Mrs. Bardell started: suddenly recollecting herself, she kissed him in a frantic manner; then relapsing into a state of hysterical imbecility the good lady requested to be informed where she was. In reply to this, Mrs. Chappins and Mrs. Saunders turned their heads away and wept, while Messrs Dodson and Fogg intreated the plaintiff to compose herself . . . "Very good notion, that indeed," whispered Perkins to Mr. Pickwick. "Capital fellows those Dodson and Fogg; excellent ideas of effect, my dear sir, excellent."

Dodson and Fogg may be scoundrels but they are not wicked men; though they cause undeserved suffering in others, they have no malevolent intent—the suffering they cause gives them no pleasure. To them, their clients are the pieces with which they play the legal game, which they find as enjoyable as it is lucrative. So, too, when Sergeant Buzzfuzz expresses his detestation of Mr. Pickwick's character, or Mr. Sumpkins bullies the unfortunate witness Winkle, what their victims feel as real hostility is, in fact, the mock hostility of the player: had they been engaged for the Defense, their abuse would have been directed against Mrs. Bardell and Mrs. Chappins, and they will have completely forgotten about the whole case by the next morning. The Guild Hall which is a Purgatory to Mr. Pickwick is to them what Dingley Dell is to him, an Arcadia.

When he is found guilty, Mr. Pickwick takes a vow that he will never pay the damages. In so doing he takes his first step out of Eden

into the real world, for to take a vow is to commit one's future, and
Eden has no conception of the future for it exists in a timeless present.
In Eden, a man always does what he likes to do at the moment, but a
man who takes a vow commits himself to doing something in the future
which, when the time comes, he may dislike doing. The consequence
of Mr. Pickwick's vow is that he has to leave his Eden of clean linen
and polished silver for a Limbo of dirty crockery and rusty broken
toasting forks where, in the eyes of the Law, he is a guilty man, a
lawbreaker among other lawbreakers.

The particular class of lawbreakers among whom Mr. Pickwick finds
himself in the Fleet are debtors. In selecting this class of offender
rather than another for him to encounter, one of Dickens' reasons was,
of course, that he considered the English laws of his day concerning
debt to be monstrously unjust and sending his fictional hero there gave
him an opportunity for satirical exposure of a real social abuse. But
in a world where money is the universal medium of exchange, the
notion of debt has a deep symbolic resonance. Hence the clause in the
Lord's Prayer as it appears in the Authorized Version of St. Matthew—
"Forgive us our debts as we forgive our debtors"—and the parable of
the forgiving and unforgiving creditor.

To be in debt means to have taken more from someone than we
have given whether the *more* refers to material or to spiritual goods.
Since we are not autonomous beings who can create and sustain our
lives by ourselves, every human being is in debt to God, to Nature, to
parents and neighbors for his existence, and it is against this background of universal human debt that we view the special case of debt
and credit between one individual and another. We are born unequal;
even if all social inequalities were abolished, there would remain the
natural inequalities of talent and inherited tendencies, and circumstance outside our control will always affect both our need to receive
and our capacity to give. A rich man, in whatever sense he is rich, can
give more than a poor man; a baby and a sick person need more from
others than a healthy adult. Debt or credit cannot be measured in
quantitative terms; a relation between two persons is just if both take
no more than they need and give as much as they can, and unjust
if either takes more or gives less than this.

In prison, Mr. Pickwick meets three kinds of debtors. There are
those like Smangle who are rather thieves than debtors for they have
borrowed money with the conscious intention of not paying it back.
There are the childish who believe in magic; they intended to return
what they borrowed when their luck changed, but had no rational

reason to suppose that it would. And there are those like the cobbler
who have fallen into debt through circumstances which they could
neither foresee nor control.

> An old gentleman that I worked for, down in the country, and died
> well off, left five thousand pounds behind him, one of which he left to
> me, 'cause I'd married a humble relation of his. And being surrounded
> by a great number of nieces and nephews, as well always quarrelling and
> fighting among themselves for the property, he makes me his executor
> to divide the rest among 'em as the will provided, and I paid all the
> legacies. I'd hardly done it when one nevy brings an action to set the
> will aside. The case comes on, some months afterwards, afore a deaf old
> gentleman in a back room somewhere down by Paul's Churchyard . . .
> and arter four counsels had taken a day a piece to both him regularly,
> he takes a week or two to consider and then gives his judgment that the
> testator was not quite right in the head, and I must pay all the money
> back again, and all the costs. I appealed; the case comes on before three
> or four very sleepy gentlemen, who had heard it all before in the other
> court and they very dutifully confirmed the decision of the old gentle-
> man below. After that we went into Chancery, where we are still. My
> lawyers have had all my thousand pounds long ago; and what between
> the estate as they call it and the costs, I'm here for ten thousand, and
> shall stop here till I die, mending shoes.

Yet, in the eyes of the Law, all three classes are equally guilty. This
does not mean, however, that all debtors receive the same treatment.

> The three chums informed Mr. Pickwick in a breath that money was in
> the Fleet, just what money was out of it; that it would instantly procure
> him almost anything he desired; and that, supposing he had it, and had
> no objection to spend it, if he only signified his wish to have a room to
> himself, he might take possession of one, furnished and fitted to boot,
> in half an hour's time.

The lot of the penniless debtor, like the Chancery Prisoner, was, in
Dickens' time, atrocious, far worse than that of the convicted criminal,
for the convict was fed gratis by the State but the debtor was not, so
that, if penniless, he must subsist on the charity of his fellow prisoners
or die of starvation. On the other hand, for those with a little money
and no sense of shame, the Fleet Prison could seem a kind of Eden.

> There were many classes of people here, from the laboring man in his
> fustian jacket, to the broken down spendthrift in his shawl dressing-gown,
> most appropriately out at elbows; but there was the same air about them
> all—a listless jail-bird careless swagger, a vagabondish who's afraid sort
> of bearing which is indescribable in words . . . "It strikes me, Sam," said

Mr. Pickwick, "that imprisonment for debt is scarcely any punishment at all." "Think not, sir?," inquired Mr. Weller. "You see how these fellows drink and smoke and roar," replied Mr. Pickwick, "It's quite impossible that they can mind it much." "Ah, that's just the very thing sir," rejoined Sam, "*they* don't mind it; it's a regular holiday to them—all porter and skittles. It is t'other wuns as gets down over, with this sort of thing: them down-hearted fellers as can't swig away at the beer, nor play at skittles neither: them as would pay as they could, and get's low by being boxed up. I'll tell you wot it is, sir; them as is always a idlin' in public houses it don't damage at all, and them as is always a working wen they can, it damages too much."

His encounter with the world of the Fleet is the end of Mr. Pickwick's innocence. When he started out on his adventures, he believed the world to be inhabited only by the well-meaning, the honest, and the entertaining; presently he discovered that it also contains malevolent, dishonest and boring inhabitants, but it is only after entering the Fleet that he realizes it contains persons who suffer, and that the division between those who are suffering and those who are not is more significant than the division between the just and the unjust, the innocent and the guilty. He himself, for instance, has been unjustly convicted, but he is in prison by his own choice and, though he does not enjoy the Fleet as much as Dingley Dell, by the standards of comfort within the Fleet, he enjoys the advantages of a king, not because he is morally innocent while Jingle and Trotter are morally guilty, but because he happens to be the richest inmate while they are among the poorest. Then Mrs. Bardell, who through stupidity rather than malice is responsible for the injustice done to him, becomes a fellow prisoner. Mr. Pickwick is compelled to realize that he, too, is a debtor, because he has been more fortunate than most people, and that he must discharge his debt by forgiving his enemies and relieving their suffering. In order to do his duty, he has to do in fact what he had been falsely accused of doing, commit a breach of promise by breaking his vow and putting money into the pockets of Dodson and Fogg; for the sake of charity, he has to sacrifice his honor.

His loss of innocence through becoming conscious of the real world has the same consequences for Mr. Pickwick as a fictional character as recovering his sanity has for Don Quixote; in becoming ethically serious, both cease to be aesthetically comic, that is to say, interesting to the reader, and they must pass away, Don Quixote by dying, Mr. Pickwick by retiring from view.

Both novels are based upon the presupposition that there is a difference between the Law and Grace, the Righteous man and the Holy man: this can only be expressed indirectly by a comic contradiction in which the innocent hero comes into collision without appearing, in his own eyes, to suffer. The only way in which their authors can compel the reader to interpret this correctly—neither to ignore the sign nor to take it as a direct sign—is, in the end, to take off the comic mask and say: "The Game, the make-believe is over: players and spectators alike must now return to reality. What you have heard was but a tall story."

Oliver Twist:

"Things as They Really Are"

by John Bayley

Oliver Twist is a modern novel. It has the perennially modern pretension of rejecting the unreality of a previous mode, of setting out to show us "things as they really are." But its modernity is more radical and more unsettling than this pretension implies; it can still touch us— as few novels out of the past can—on a raw nerve; it can still upset and discountenance us. *Pickwick* is not modern. It is a brilliant and successful recreation of the English novel's atmospheres and personalities; but Dickens, like Kipling, had a bargain with his daemon not to repeat a success. It was not *Pickwick* that made Thackeray ruefully praise Dickens' perpetual modernity, or Chesterton announce that Dickens had remained modern while Thackeray had become a classic.

Oliver Twist lacks only one attribute of the modern novel—complete self-consciousness. No novelist has profited more richly than Dickens from not examining what went on in his own mind. His genius avoids itself like a sleepwalker avoiding an open window. Chesterton says what a good thing it is we are not shown Pecksniff's thoughts—they would be too horrible—but the point about Pecksniff is that he has no thoughts: he is as much of a sleepwalker as Dickens: he is the perfect hypocrite because he does not know what he is like. Dickens recoiled from what he called "dissective" art, and if he had been able and willing to analyze the relation between our inner and outer selves he could never have created the rhetoric that so marvelously ignores the distinction between them. Unlike us, he had no diagrammatic view of mind, no constricting terminology for the psyche. The being of Bumble, Pecksniff, Mrs. Gamp is not compartmented: their inner being *is* their outer self. When Mrs. Gamp says: "We never know what's hidden in each other's hearts; and if

"*Oliver Twist*: 'Things as They Really Are'" by John Bayley. From *Dickens and the Twentieth Century*, ed. John Gross and Gabriel Pearson (London: Routledge & Kegan Paul, Ltd., 1962; Toronto: University of Toronto Press, 1962). Copyright © 1962 by Routledge & Kegan Paul, Ltd. Reprinted by permission of the publishers.

83

we had glass windows there, we'd need to keep the shutters up, some of us, I do assure you"—she is saying something that will be true of John Jasper and Bradley Headstone, but the great early characters are in fact windowed and shutterless. Noah Claypole carousing with Charlotte over the oysters, a *mass* of bread and butter in his hand; Bumble announcing the cause of Oliver's rebellion to Mrs. Sowerberry—" 'It's not madness, Ma'am, it's meat,' said the beadle after a few moments of deep meditation"—their monstrosity luxuriates without depth or concealment. When Proust sets out to "overgo" the Dickensian monster with his Charlus and Françoise, the ebullience and energy are seen to proceed from a creative center which is meticulous, reflective, and the reverse of energetic: the peculiar Victorian harmony of created and creating energy is lost.

Their wholeness and harmony have a curious effect on the evil of Dickens' monsters: it sterilizes it in performance but increases it in idea. The energy of Fagin or Quilp seems neutral; there is not enough gap between calculation and action for it to proceed to convincingly evil works. By contrast, Iago and Verhovensky are monsters because they know what they are doing; their actions let us loathe them and recoil from them into freedom, but we cannot recoil from Dickens' villains: they are the more frightening and haunting because we cannot expel them for what they do; they have the unexpungable nature of our own nightmares and our own consciousness.

We cannot recoil—that is the point. For in spite of the apparent openness of its energy and indignation *Oliver Twist* is in fact the kind of novel in which we are continually oppressed by the disingenuousness of our own impulses and fantasies, the kind of novel in which the heroine, say, is immured in a brothel, and in which we, like her, both shrink from the fate and desire it. *Clarissa* is in the background. "Richardson," says Diderot in a famous passage, "first carried the lantern into the depths of that cavern . . . he breathes on the agreeable form at the entrance and the hideous Moor behind it is revealed." The lantern has been carried pretty often into the cave since then, and the hideous Moor has become a familiar enough figure: we are introduced in many a modern fiction to our hypothetical sado-masochistic interiors. But whereas a novel like *Death in Venice,* or *Les Caves du Vatican,* divides one aspect of the self from another with all the dramatic cunning and the nice impassivity of art—the author being perfectly aware what he is up to—Dickens presents the nightmare of what we are and what we want in its most elemental and undifferentiated form. All unknowing, he does not let us escape from the ignominy of our fascinations, because he does not try to escape from them himself.

Oliver Twist is not a satisfying novel—it does not liberate us. In achieving what might be called the honesty of the dream world it has to stay in prison. The sense of complete reality in fiction can perhaps only be achieved by the author's possessing, and persuading his reader to share, a sense of different worlds, different and indeed almost incompatible modes of feeling and being. The awareness of difference is the awareness of freedom, and it is, moreover, the knowledge of reality we normally experience in life. But in *Oliver Twist* there are no such contrasts, no such different worlds. Even the apparent contrast between Fagin's world and that of Rose Maylie and Mr. Brownlow is not a real one, and this is not because the happy Brownlow world is rendered sentimentally and unconvincingly by Dickens, but because the two do in fact coexist in consciousness: they are twin sides of the same coin of fantasy, not two real places that exist separately in life. And there is no true activity in the two worlds, only the guilty or desperately innocent daydreams of our double nature.

The superior power and terror of the unreal is continually harped on. Nancy tells Mr. Brownlow that she can think of nothing but coffins and had just seen one carried past her in the street.

> "There is nothing unusual in that. They have passed me often." *"Real ones,"* rejoined the girl. "This was not." (Chap. 46)

Where the reality of action is concerned, Fagin's world has the technical advantage over the Maylie one of *reporting*—as in the dialogue of the thieves' kitchen and the boys going out with Oliver to pick pockets—but it is significant that the long burglary sequence, when Sikes takes Oliver down to Chertsey to crack the Maylie house and the two worlds collide at last, is one of the most dreamlike in the novel. Dreamlike too is a later collision, the meeting of Nancy and Rose Maylie in the hotel bedroom: another novelist would make such a confrontation of worlds the most reality-enhancing note in his tale, but in *Oliver Twist* they only confirm the dream atmosphere. Even when he is firmly inside the Maylie world, Oliver can, so to speak, deprive another character of reality by compelling him to act out Oliver's fantasy of what life in such a world is like. Oliver goes out to gather flowers every morning, and when Henry Maylie returns home "he was seized with such a passion for flowers, and displayed such a taste in their arrangement, as left his young companion far behind."

As we shall see, Dickens frequently defends himself against the charge of using literary devices and conventions by pointing out their similarity to real life, and he seems to imply that he is using the dream atmosphere as a kind of convention in this spirit. He gives two accounts of the nature of waking dreams, the first at Fagin's, and the second when just after the flower episode Oliver sees Fagin and Monks at the window of the Maylie's parlour and their eyes meet. "There is a kind of sleep that steals upon us sometimes which, while it holds the body prisoner, does not free the mind from a sense of things about it, and enable it to ramble at its pleasure" (Chap. 34). So similar are the two accounts of this state that it seems likely Dickens repeated himself accidentally in the hurry of composition (for the second half of the novel was written under great pressure), but the effect is nonetheless potent for that. It is a dream from which Oliver awakes to find it true, even though no footprints of the pair can be found. It recalls the earlier waking dream, when he lay watching Fagin sorting his stolen goods, and we realize it is not physical distance that keeps him from Fagin's house, a house which had once belonged to respectable people like the Maylies, and in which the mirrors of the unused rooms where Fagin and Monks confer now only reflect the dusty floor and the slimy track of the snail.

That the two worlds are one in the mind appears even in Cruickshank's drawings, where Oliver often has a distinct look of Fagin. Henry James remarked that as a child the pictures of the good places and people frightened him more than the bad! It is often said, and with some justice, that Dickens muddles the message of his novel by making Oliver immune to an environment which is denounced as necessarily corrupting. But Oliver is not psychologically immune, nor is Dickens, nor are we. It is true that Dickens cheerfully adopts a vaguely Rousseauesque notion of the innocent warped and made evil by institutions—("what human nature may be made to be") and also seems to adopt with equal readiness the tory doctrine that birth and breeding will win through in the end. But however muddled as propaganda—indeed perhaps because they are muddled—these contradictions are entirely resolved in the imaginative certainty of the novel. Dickens might well proclaim, as he did to critics who found Nancy's love for Sikes implausible—that IT IS TRUE! His imagination makes nonsense, just as life does, of theories of how human beings will or will not behave in a given environment. Notwithstanding the claustrophobic nature of the book, and its heavy dream atmosphere, Dickens' triumph is to have made Oliver—and Charley Bates and Nancy too—free of all human possibility, free in spirit and impulse against all physical and factual likelihood. The world of the novel may be a prison but they are not finally enclosed in it. And he has made this ultimate freedom seem true.

Still, Fagin's wish to incriminate Oliver, and hence confine him for ever in the evil world, is an objective and social terror as well as a psychological one. There remains the plain and sickening fact that Fagin's school and all it stands for extinguishes the hope and chance of better things, though not necessarily the capacity for them: of his pupils, Oliver escapes by the needs of the plot, Charley Bates by the death of Sikes and Fagin, and Nancy not at all. Dickens himself had been at Fagin's school—the blacking factory—and the boy who chiefly befriended him there was actually called Fagin. No wonder Fagin the criminal is such an ambivalent figure when the real Fagin's kindness had, so to speak, threatened to inure Dickens to the hopeless routine of the wage-slave. So passionate was the young Dickens' desire for the station in life to which he felt entitled, and so terrifying his sense that it was being denied him, that he must have hated the real Fagin for the virtue which he could not bear to accept or recognize in that nightmare world, because it might help to subdue him into it. The real Fagin's kindness becomes the criminal Fagin's villainy.

Like Oliver reading the tales of crime in Fagin's den, Dickens "prayed heaven to spare him from such deeds." He came later, at the time of his readings from *Oliver Twist,* to have a clear and horrifying awareness of his split personality: he dreaded himself, and the possibility that he might be exiled by his own doing into the world of the murderer and the social outcast. The premise of *Oliver Twist* is the gnostic one of Melville's poem:

> Indolence is heaven's ally here
> And energy the child of hell . . .

Dickens feared the surrender to the demon of energy which his nature continually imposed on him. One of the many biographical glosses on the novel is the idyll which in the summer of 1849 he claimed to be enjoying with his family in the Isle of Wight, an idyll rudely interrupted when Dickens could stand it no longer and hurried them all away again from the picnics, the charades, and the flower gathering.

The power of *Oliver Twist* depends more than any other of Dickens' novels on his personality and background—that is why one has to insist on them so much. Everything in the novel means something else; it is shot through and through with involuntary symbolism, with that peculiar egocentric modernity which Edmund Wilson tells us to be fiction's discovery of its true self. Except possibly for Giles the butler, nobody and nothing exists merely in itself. Even the famous "household" passages, like Oliver asking for more, do not have the legendary authority of an epic moment but make a piercing appeal to something private and vulnerable in the memory of the reader. "Things as they really are" turn out to be things as the fantasy fears, and feared in childhood, that they may be. In *David Copperfield* childhood fantasy is also dominant, but in the objective setting of true existences, David's mother, Peggotty, Betsy Trotwood, and Barkis—there is the breadth and solidity of epic. In *Oliver Twist* the child is *right:* there is no suggestion that his vision of monsters is illusory or incomplete, and the social shock to us is that the child here is right to see things thus—the system is montrous because he finds it to be so. His vision is the lens to focus Dickens' *saeva indignatio.* The grotesque conversation between Noah, Bumble, and the gentleman in the white waistcoat, about what is to be done with Oliver, is true because it is just how Oliver would imagine it. But in *Copperfield* the child may be wrong; he only partially apprehends the existences around him, and Murdstone, for instance, is more arresting and intriguing than anyone in *Oliver Twist* because there is no assumption that David really knows what he is like.

Dickens' crusading purpose underwrites Oliver's view of things and creates a powerful satiric method at the cost of losing the actual child's involuntary existence. Indeed it is the loss of the mere condition of childishness, as an abused animal or bird loses its natural status, which is so heart-rending—Oliver is never allowed to *be* what he is, and when liberated he has to act the part, a fact unconsciously recognized by Cruickshank in drawings which have the look of a twenty-year old actor playing a schoolboy. Oliver has been cheated of childhood like his friend Dick, whose limbs are "like those of an old man." Acting, indeed, as Dickens implies in his facetious but revealing preamble to Chapter 17, is the clue to the mode by which we are to be moved by the persona and events of the story. We must put ourselves in their place and act as they are acting. We must be like the crazy old woman for whom her daughter's death was "as good as a play."

> It is the custom on the stage, in all good murderous melodramas, to present the tragic and comic scenes in . . . regular alternation. . . . We behold, with throbbing bosoms, the heroine in the grasp of a proud and ruthless baron: her virtue and her life alike in danger, drawing forth her dagger to preserve the one at the cost of the other; and just as our expectations are wrought up to the highest pitch, a whistle is heard, and we are straightway transported to the great hall of the castle: where a grey-headed seneschal sings a funny chorus.
>
> Such changes appear absurd: but they are not so unnatural as they would seem at first sight. The transitions in real life from well-spread boards to death-beds, and from mourning weeds to holiday garments, are not a whit less startling; only, there, we are busy actors, instead of passive lookers-on, which makes a vast difference. The actors in the mimic life of

the theatre, are blind to violent transitions and abrupt impulses of passion or feeling, which, presented before the eyes of mere spectators, are at once condemned as outrageous and preposterous.

It is a brilliant apologia for his whole creative method. He implies that it is *because* Oliver is an actor that the spectator should not withhold sympathy if the tale seems artificial and implausible, thus ingeniously confounding the stage actor with the actor in real life and claiming that in both cases the only true view is the participant's: we must ourselves participate in order to feel the truth of the thing, and not merely appraise it from outside.

In seeking to disarm criticism by drawing his readers into a hypnotic unity with the tale and the author, Dickens relies heavily on convention to increase both the shared hypnosis and the emotion of truth. As Forster tells us, he delighted in coincidence and in pointing out how common it was in life. And in *Oliver Twist* he positively takes refuge in melodramatic ceremonial: it would be a disaster if the taste of the age had allowed him to describe what must have been the continual and brutish sexual activity in Fagin's hole—(*Jonathan Wild,* and *The Beggar's Opera,* which Dickens protests is unrealistic, are much franker about this)—or to have rendered the actual oaths of Sikes instead of giving him grotesquely and perhaps deliberately exaggerated euphemisms like "Wolves tear your throats!" . . . Though he may not have been conscious of it, Dickens knew that such disguises and prevarications are indeed the truth of the fantasy. And he enhances their effect by putting them beside facts of a neutral and professional kind, like his catalogue of the districts—Exmouth Street, Hockley in the Hole, Little Saffron Hill, etc.—through which Oliver is led by the Artful Dodger, and through which Sikes wanders after the murder. The setting in which Noah eavesdrops on the meeting between Nancy and the Maylies is detailed with the offhand expertise of Kipling:

> These stairs are a part of the bridge; they consist of three flights. Just below the end of the second, going down, the stone wall on the left terminates in an ornamental pilaster facing towards the Thames. At this point the lower steps widen: so that a person turning that angle of the wall, is necessarily unseen by any others on the stairs who chance to be above him, if only a step. (Chap. 46)

The old device of the eavesdropper has never been more effectively localized. But reality depends on the convention. Dickens was the first to protest against the new French "realism," because he felt it might discredit his mystery. He has often been blamed for giving the happy

ending to *Great Expectations,* in deference to Bulwer Lytton, but he has
there a sure sense, as in *Oliver Twist,* not of what the *donnée* demanded,
but of upholding the kinds of agreement he had made with the reader.
The artistic rigor of a Flaubert alienates, and Dickens is faithful only
to what he and his audience can make of the thing together.

Yet in his last novels he is beginning to hold the reader off. It is extremely illuminating to compare *Oliver Twist* with *Edwin Drood,* because we are not required to participate in the exquisitely murderous
atmosphere of the last novel. We can stand back, and watch the familiar
two worlds—the world of goodness and innocence and the world of
murder and hallucination—conjured into a real and objective existence.
Canon Crisparkle and his mother, the Virginia creeper, and the home-
made wines and jellies, are solid and reassuring presences: they have
strength as well as gentleness. Rosa Budd and Helena Landless, "a beautiful barbaric captive brought from some wild tropical dominion," are as
meticulously alive as Jasper, raising his high voice in the shadowy choir
and hating the role he has made for himself. Dickens has adopted the
principle of depth; hypocrisy is real at last. Instead of the divided nature being flat and two-dimensional as a Rorschach ink-blot, spreading
over the whole of life, it now exists in and perceives an upper and lower
world. At the cost of transforming his social earnestness into an earnestness of craftsmanship Dickens keeps his imagination working at full pre-
sure, but in a new sphere of complication and plurality. His vision
proves to be as fecund as Shakespeare's, and to have the same power
of continued transformation. It was transforming itself afresh when he
died.

So far I have stressed the waking nightmare which is the imaginative
principle of *Oliver Twist,* and the way it dispels any true distinction between the world of darkness which Oliver is in, and the world of light
which he longs for. Nonetheless, the impressive power of the novel does
depend upon a most effective distinction, of quite another kind, and of
the force of which Dickens seems equally unaware. It is the distinction
between crime and murder.

We are apt to forget how early-Victorian society, the society of laissez-
faire, took for granted individual conditions of privacy and isolation. It
was a society where each unit, each family and household, led their secret
lives with an almost neurotic antipathy to external interference. It was
the age of the private gentleman who wanted nothing but to be left
alone. He could ignore politics, the Press, the beggar who happened to
be dying of hunger in the coach-house; he need feel no pressure of social

or national existence. Noah Claypole provides an ironic gloss when he says about Oliver: "let him alone! Why, everyone lets him pretty much alone!" And the poor had the same instincts as their betters. At the time of the Crimea, when a suggestion of conscription was raised, laborers and miners said they would take to the woods or go underground rather than be caught for it. There has probably never been a time when England was—in the sociological phrase—less integrated.

Dickens has a most disturbing feeling for this. Like most Victorians his sense of other things, other places and people, was founded on fear and distrust. The Boz of the Sketches seems to hate and fear almost everything, even though it fascinates him. For unlike other people he had no home to go to, no hole in which he could feel secure. Normal living and the life of crime are almost indistinguishable in *Oliver Twist*, for both are based on the burrow. Both Jacob's Island and the town where Oliver is born consist largely of derelict houses which are not owned or occupied in the normal way but taken possession of as burrows, or "kens," with an "aperture made into them wide enough for the passage of a human body." Fagin, who when out of doors is compared to a reptile "looking for a meal of some rich offal," has his den on Saffron Hill; when he first enters the district Oliver sees that from several of these holes "great ill-looking fellows were cautiously emerging, bound, to all appearance, on no very well-disposed or harmless errands." The stiltedness of the writing here somehow emphasizes the effect of evening beasts coming out on their normal business. Mr. Brownlow (whose name oddly suggests a fox) and Mr. Grimwig are holed up in Clerkenwell; Mrs. Corney has her snug corner in the workhouse; the Maylies live behind the walls of their Chertsey house as if it were in the Congo. The house to which Oliver is taken before the abortive "crack," and which he afterward identifies, is found then to have some quite different tenant, an evil creature who is hastily left to his own devices. A man on the run makes the round of the kens and finds them already full, as if they were shells tenanted by crabs.

All these people have the same outlook and the same philosophy of life, a philosophy which that private gentleman, Fagin, sums up as "looking after No. 1." As one would expect, Dickens can see nothing in the idea of "private vices, public virtues" except a degradingly mutual kind of blackmail. In presenting his characters as animals, purposeful, amoral, and solitary in their separate colonies, with no true gregariousness or power of cohesion, he draws a terrifying imaginative indictment of what private life may be like in an open society, in his age or in our own.

Murder transforms all this. Like a magic wand it changes the animals

back into men again: what we think of as "human nature" returns with
a rush. And it is an extraordinary and sinister irony that makes murder
the only imaginative vindication in the book of human stature and human meaningfulness. Though Dickens may not have bargained for the
effect it is the crowning stroke in the satirical violence of his novel. Just
as murder, in the Victorian literary mythology, was cleaner than sex, so
in Dickens' vision is it more human than crime and the inhumanity of
social institutions, for crime is the most characteristic aspect of the social
order. Bumble, Fagin, and the rest are evil beings because they are not
human beings; they are doing the best they can for themselves in their
business, and Sikes was similarly an animal in the business—"the mere
hound of a day" as Fagin says—until murder turns him into a kind of
man. Thereupon, too, society develops the cohesion and point that it had
lacked before—indeed this, like so much else in the book, is grotesquely
though effectively overdone. Nancy's murder assumes the proportions
of a national crisis, "Spies," we hear, "are hovering about in every direction." Significantly, until the murder no one seems to take notice of
Fagin—he is engrossed in his repellent business like any other citizen—
but after it he is nearly lynched. Crime is like animal or mechanical
society, cold, separated, and professional, but murder is like the warmth
and conviviality which Dickens always praises—a great uniter.

Undoubtedly Dickens is saying something here about society which
has lost none of its potency. With a shudder we realize what we are
still like. Of course, Dickens had a perfectly "healthy" interest in murder
and hanging, just as he took a normal English pleasure in illness, fu-
nerals, and ballads like "the blood-drinker's burial"; but murder in *Oliver
Twist* has a more metaphysical status, is less literary and less purely
morbid and professional, than any other in Dickens. His later murders,
beautifully done as they are, have by comparison a dilettante flavor. In
Our Mutual Friend and *Drood* other characters mime the murderous
atmosphere in proleptic touches that are almost Shakespearean. Lammle
wrenches the stopper off a siphon "as if he wanted to pour its blood
down his throat." At the end of term celebrations in the dormitory of
Miss Twinkleton's seminary, one of the young ladies "gives a sprightly
solo on the comb and curl-paper until suffocated in her own pillow by
two flowing-haired executioners." But murder in *Oliver Twist* is defi-
nitely not considered as one of the fine arts. It is not an aesthetic matter
sealed off in its artifice and our satisfaction, but a moral act which for
that reason penetrates not only the life of the novel but our own lives as
well.

Dostoevsky, a great admirer of *Oliver Twist,* also makes murder a kind of social revelation. Writers who learn from Dickens usually develop explicitly an effect which is implicit in their source, and Dostoevsky makes Raskolnikov a rebel who murders the old money-lender out of frustration, as a kind of thwarted substitute for idealist terrorism. We know from his diary that Dostoevsky was bothered by Raskolnikov's lack of an obvious motive—he realized that the significance with which the author endowed the crime was showing too clearly through the story. But Sikes' motive is brutally simple and straightforward. Nancy must be got rid of because she has betrayed the gang: the whole burrow principle of looking after No. 1 demands her instant elimination. Nonetheless, it is a duty, and duty is a human and not an animal concept.

> Without once turning his head to the right or left, or raising his eyes to the sky, or lowering them to the ground, but looking straight before him with savage resolution: his teeth so tightly compressed that the strained jaw seemed starting through his skin; the robber held on his headlong course, nor uttered a word, nor relaxed a muscle, until he reached his own door. (Chap. 47)

Like Macbeth, Sikes "bends up each corporal agent to this terrible feat." An animal kills naturally, like a cat killing a bird; and in Dickens' other murders the murderer's animality is increased by the deed. Jonas Chuzzlewit skulks like a beast out of the wood where his victim lies; Rogue Riderhood lives by furtive killing, and Dickens suggests his nature in two brilliant images—the fur cap, "like some small drowned animal," which he always wears, and the shapeless holes he leaves in the snow, "as if the very fashion of humanity had departed from his feet." Headstone's course is the exact opposite of Sikes': the lust to kill strips the veneer of decency and laboriously acquired culture from him, and turns him into the terrifying creature who grinds his fist against the church wall until the blood comes. Like Chuzzlewit he feels no remorse, only the murderer's *esprit de l'escalier*—he cannot stop thinking how much more ingeniously the deed might have been done. Reduced to the animal status of Riderhood, he loses even his own name, his last link with humanity, when at Riderhood's bidding he writes it on the school blackboard and then rubs it out.

But Sikes finds his name. It is on every tongue in the metropolis. Other murderers become conscienceless animals, but he acquires the form and conscience of a man, almost indeed of a spirit. "Blanched face, sunken eyes, hollow cheeks . . . it was the very ghost of Sikes." And as his killing of Nancy makes him a man, so her love for him transforms her into a woman. "Pity us," she says to Rose Maylie, "for setting our rotten hearts on a man. Pity us for having only one feeling of the woman left, and that turned into a new means of violence and suffering." The act she puts on when she enquires for Oliver at the police station, and helps to recapture him in the street, is a nightmare parody of social pretences and what they conceal, a sort of analogue to the pomposities of Bumble and the realities of the workhouse. Her revulsion when Oliver is brought back to Fagin's den is one of the most moving things in the book, but its denizens suppose she is still keeping up the part ("You're acting beautiful," says Fagin) and they eye her ensuing rage and despair with bestial incomprehension. "Burn my body," growls Sikes, "do you know what you are?" and Fagin tells her "It's your living."

> "Aye, it is!" returned the girl; not speaking, but pouring out the words in one continuous and vehement scream. "It is my living and the cold wet dirty streets are my home; and you're the wretch that drove me to them long ago, and that'll keep me there, day and night, night and day, till I die!" (Chap. 16)

Nancy's living is the living of England, a nightmare society in which drudgery is endless and stupefying, in which the natural affections are warped, and the dignity of man appears only in resolution and violence. It is a more disquieting picture than the carefully and methodically symbolized social panoramas of *Bleak House, Little Dorrit,* and *Our Mutual Friend.* It is as raw and extemporized as Nancy's outburst. *Oliver Twist* quite lacks the overbearing pretension of the later novels, a pretension which Edmund Wilson defers to rather too solemnly when he tells us that Dickens in *Our Mutual Friend* "had come to despair utterly of the prospering middle class." It is the same pretension which G. K. Chesterton notes apropos of Riah, the good Jewish money-lender introduced because of complaints from Jewish correspondents about Fagin: "It pleased Dickens to be mistaken for a public arbiter: it pleased him to be asked (in a double sense) to judge Israel."

Oliver is not in a position to despair of the middle class, or anything else, and the humility of this is communicated in some way to the author and moves us more than all his later stridency. Oliver is a true everyman: he does not, like David Copperfield or D. H. Lawrence, shriek at us incredulously—"They did this to *me!*" It is logical that he has no character, because he has no physical individuality—he is the child element in a nightmare which is otherwise peopled by animals, and precariously by men. Child, beast, and man indeed merge and change places phantasmagorically throughout the book. Oliver is sometimes adult, almost middle-aged, and sometimes like an animal himself, as when his eyes glisten at the sight of the scraps of meat in Mrs. Sowerberry's kitchen—one of the few really physical intimations of him we have. After the murder the lesser criminals are as lost and bewildered as children, and the hardened Kags begs for a candle, saying "Don't leave me in the dark." Sikes and Nancy, as hero and heroine, have their transformation from beast to man: only Fagin remains a reptile throughout and to the end, losing at last even his human powers of speech and intellect and crouching in the dock like something snared, his glittering eyes "looking on when an artist broke his pencil point and made another with his knife, as any idle spectator might have done." He has the animal victim's unnerving air of detachment from his own predicament, and the butchery of one kind of beast by another is the final horror of his execution. "Are you a man, Fagin?" asks the gaoler.

"I shan't be one long," he replied, looking up with a face containing no human expression but rage and terror. "Strike them all dead! What right have they to butcher me?"

It is a horribly penetrating appeal, when we think of society as *Oliver Twist* presents it. And in contrast to the almost heroic death of Sikes, Fagin will lose even his animal identity at the very end, and revert to a dreadful human simulacrum, "a dangling heap of clothes."

"To be thoroughly earnest is everything, and to be anything short of it is nothing." Dickens' credo about novel-writing is certainly true of *Oliver Twist*, but whereas in the later novels this seriousness extends to the technique which fashions symbols and symbolic atmospheres—the famous fogs, prison, dust, etc.—he does not insist on, or even seem aware of, the animal symbolism here: it hits the reader like a sleepwalker's blow, involuntarily administered. It seems a natural product of the imagination, like that of Shakespeare and Hardy; though Dickens' later symbolic technique is closer to Lawrence's, purposeful and claustrophobic, the meaning too unified to expand into an ordinary human range of possibility. Character remains imprisoned in the author's will and we are uneasily aware of the life that has been left out. The Dickens of *Hard Times*, whom Dr. Leavis admires, manipulates symbolic meaning in a manner that reaches its apotheosis with Clifford Chatterley sitting in his motor-chair. Nor do his "straight" characters always escape the same fate. It is with some complacency that he reports how his mother, his model for Mrs. Nickleby, protested that there could not be such a woman. One sympathizes with her, and one is inclined to think she was right. Her son was rather too confident that his imagination could give another being its real life, and that what Mrs. Nickleby (or

Mrs. Dickens) felt themselves to be was nothing in comparison with what Dickens saw them to be.

It is the more remarkable, therefore, that Sikes and Nancy have such a range. His intentions about them are overt enough. He says he is not going to abate one growl of Sikes or "one scrap of curl-paper in Nancy's dishevelled hair." This confidence of the realist is hardly very encouraging. The description of the Bow Street officers, based on a "Wanted" notice, "reveals them," says Dickens, "for what they are"; and we are not allowed to forget Cratchit's shawl-pattern waistcoat or the humorous overcoat sported by the Dodger. Sikes himself

> was a stoutly-built fellow of about five and thirty, in a black velveteen coat, very soiled drab breeches, lace-up half boots, and grey cotton stockings, which enclosed a bulky pair of legs, with large swelling calves—the kind of legs, which in such costume, always look in an unfinished and incomplete state without a set of fetters to garnish them. (Chap. 13)

The bit about fetters gives the game away, and shows that for all his protestations of realism Dickens is really drawing on Gay and Hogarth. But what brings Sikes and Nancy to life is the gap between what they look like and what they are like, between their appearance as Dickens insists we shall have it, and the speech and manner with which another convention requires him to endow them. They rise, as it were, between two stools; they achieve their real selves by being divided between two modes of artifice. Nancy looks like the slattern in curl-papers lifting the gin bottle and exclaiming "Never say die!" but inside there is the desperate being who confronts Fagin and bitterly describes herself to Rose Maylie. The Sikes in grey cotton stockings is the same man who goes to murder like Macbeth.

In asserting an apparent realism, Dickens actually achieves a striking balance—very rare in his characterization—between the outward and inward selves that make up a whole person. The nonsense talked by Bumble, Pecksniff, or Squeers, their total lack of the responsibilities of intercourse, mark Dickens' most contemptuous, though most inspired, refusal to recognize an inner self in such persons. But Sikes and Nancy have an eloquence, a brutal and urgent power of communication, that shows how seriously Dickens takes them, and how seriously they are compelled to take themselves. The dimension of these two is the triumph of the novel, and it closely corresponds to the main feat—surely unique in the history of the novel—which Dickens has achieved in combining the genre of Gothic nightmare with that of social denunciation, so that each enhances the other.

Martin Chuzzlewit:
The Self and the World

by Steven Marcus

The greatness of *Martin Chuzzlewit* begins in its prose. For the first time Dickens' narrative style becomes consciously mannered, although it never really abandons that affinity to the spoken language which gives his earlier prose its natural and perdurable vitality. The sentences of *Martin Chuzzlewit* are long and involved, their syntax strenuous, their punctuation often adventurous and peremptory. Moreover, the influence of Shakespeare on this novel is everywhere to be found. Just before Dickens boarded ship to Liverpool, Forster presented him with a pocket edition of Shakespeare; in America Dickens continually carried it with him in his greatcoat, and he wrote Forster that it provided him with "an unspeakable source of delight." [1] Virtually every chapter in *Martin Chuzzlewit* contains some allusion to Shakespeare, some play on a quotation or passage from him. But, beyond this, one feels that the extensive rereading of Shakespeare worked to release in Dickens his own most daring powers of invention. When Pecksniff is introduced, a veritable deluge of images pours forth as if to allay the urgency of Dickens' inspiration.

Perhaps there never was a more moral man than Mr. Pecksniff; especially in his conversation and correspondence. It was once said of him by a homely admirer, that he had a Fortunatus's purse of good sentiments in his inside. In this particular he was like the girl in the fairy tale, except that if they were not actual diamonds which fell from his lips, they were the very brightest paste, and shone prodigiously. He was a most exemplary

[1] *The Letters of Charles Dickens,* ed. Walter Dexter (The Nonesuch Edition), London, 1937-1938, I, 415.

man: fuller of virtuous precept than a copybook. Some people likened
him to a direction-post, which is always telling the way to a place, and
never goes there: but these were his enemies; the shadows cast by his
brightness; that was all. His very throat was moral. You saw a good deal
of it. You looked over a very low fence of white cravat . . . and there it
lay, a valley between two jutting heights of collar, serene and whiskerless
before you. It seemed to say, on the part of Mr. Pecksniff, "There is no
deception, ladies and gentlemen, all is peace, a holy calm pervades me."
(chap. 2)

Nor did Dickens hesitate to write what appears to be a three-page
digression on the wind, and five pages on coaching (chaps. 2, 36). At
the same time, Dickens' genius for compression, his ability to spring an
entire character from a single image, was never more animated. The
gathering of the Chuzzlewit family, for example, is struck off in a prose
of extraordinary concentration. There is Chevy Slyme, "whose great
abilities seemed one and all to point towards the sneaking quarter of
the moral compass." There is Anthony Chuzzlewit, "the face of the
old man so sharpened by the wariness and cunning of his life, that it
seemed to cut him a passage through the crowded room." There is the
impotently aggressive Mr. Spottletoe, "who was so bald and had such
big whiskers, that he seemed to have stopped his hair, by the sudden
application of some powerful remedy, in the very act of falling off his
head, and to have fastened it irrevocably on his face." There is the
anonymous young gentleman, known only as a grand-nephew of old
Martin, who was "very dark and very hairy, and apparently born for
no particular purpose but to save looking-glasses the trouble of reflecting
more than just the first idea and sketchy notion of a face, which had
never been carried out" (chap. 4).

In a prose of such suggestiveness, compact and sure of stroke, the
language itself seems an organ of perception, shaping the experience
almost as soon as it is received. In *Martin Chuzzlewit* this use of language is everywhere to be found. Furthermore, the transaction between
Dickens and his reader in respect of what is being experienced, or
"observed," is an epitome of the relation between author and audience
which characterizes the first major phase of the modern novel. Take for
example Dickens' introduction of Zephaniah Scadder, agent for the
Eden settlement in America.

He was a gaunt man in a huge straw hat, and a coat of green stuff.
The weather being hot, he had no cravat, and wore his shirt collar wide
open; so that every time he spoke something was seen to twitch and jerk
up in his throat, like the little hammers in a harpsichord when the notes

are struck. Perhaps it was the Truth feebly endeavouring to leap to his lips. If so, it never reached them.

Two grey eyes lurked deep within this agent's head, but one of them had no sight in it, and stood stock still. With that side of his face he seemed to listen to what the other side was doing. Thus each profile had a distinct expression; and when the movable side was most in action, the rigid one was in its coldest state of watchfulness. It was like turning the man inside out, to pass to that view of his feaures in his liveliest mood, and see how calculating and intent they were.

Each long black hair upon his head hung down as straight as any plummet line; but rumpled tufts were on the arches of his eyes, as if the crow whose foot was deeply printed in the corners had pecked and torn them in a savage recognition of his kindred nature as a bird of prey. (chap. 21)

The presence of the novelist—of his disciplined, magisterial sensibility, acting as a kind of deity, freely creating and controlling the experience he imposes on his readers—is as natural and appropriate here as is his absence in the later James and in Joyce, where the novelist has become a *deus absconditus,* asserting his godhead by his apparent indifference to his creation, by paring his nails or wrapping himself in the invisible cloak of "point-of-view."

Yet of all Dickens' novels, *Martin Chuzzlewit* is in one sense the most Joycean, for language itself is one of its subjects. The first chapter, a sardonic genealogy of the Chuzzlewit family, has as its point that the historic past is both misleading and incommunicable, but makes that point by demonstrating through a labyrinth of double-entendres, non sequiturs, and puns that language is itself essentially deceitful. It is especially deceitful in art, and in the way art is enlisted in the deception and manipulation of others: Tigg, that worshipper of Mind, who appeals "on Mind's behalf, when it has not the art to push its fortune in the world," speaks of the unregenerate Chevy Slyme as "the highest-minded, the most independent-spirited, most original, spiritual, classical, talented, the most thoroughly Shakespearean, if not Miltonic, and at the same time the most disgustingly-unappreciated dog I know" (chap. 7). Although Tigg knows that he will soon be " 'gone to that what's-his-name from which no thingumbob comes back,' " he faces this bleak prospect with composure. "Moralise as we will, the world goes on. As Hamlet says, Hercules may lay about him with his club in every possible direction, but he can't prevent the cats from making a most intolerable row on the roofs of the houses, or the dogs from being shot in the hot weather if they run about the streets unmuzzled" (chap. 4). Tigg's distortions of Shakespeare's language correspond exactly to the deceptiveness and ambiguity of his character. As do Pecksniff's. Drunkenly making love to Mrs. Todgers, Pecksniff says, "My feelings, Mrs. Todgers, will not consent to be entirely smothered, like the young children in the Tower. They are grown up, and the more I press the bolster on them, the more they look round the corner of it" (chap. 9), superimposing something of *Macbeth* onto something of *Richard III*. To these and many similar passages in *Martin Chuzzlewit* one can trace a direct line from Buck Mulligan and the library scene in *Ulysses*.

In *Martin Chuzzlewit*, as never before in Dickens, characters seem to create themselves simply by becoming involved in the complexities of language or by committing themselves to an appropriate rhetoric. The youngest gentleman at Todgers's, for instance,

> entertained some terrible notions of Destiny, among other matters, and talked much about people's "Missions": upon which he seemed to have some private information not generally attainable, as he knew it had been poor Merry's mission to crush him in the bud. He was very frail and tearful; for being aware that a shepherd's mission was to pipe to his flocks, and that a boatswain's mission was to pipe all hands, and that one man's mission was to be a paid piper, and another man's mission was to pay the piper, so he had got it into his head that his own peculiar mission was to pipe his eye. Which he did perpetually.
>
> He often informed Mrs. Todgers that the sun had set upon him; that the billows had rolled over him; that the Car of Juggernaut had crushed him; and also that the deadly Upas tree of Java had blighted him. His name was Moddle. (chap. 32)

That final sentence is a perfect stroke—everything we need to know about the inner meaning of that wild high style is thrust into the name of Moddle.

In respect of rhetoric, furthermore, Dickens' trip to America is of paramount interest; it would be no exaggeration to say that he took a six-months' voyage into the English language, and that he was one of the first writers to come up against what Dylan Thomas desperately described as the "barrier of a common language." [2] He immediately understood, as Tocqueville had a few years before him, that a new language was being born in America; that Americans were losing the habit of speaking conversationally and spoke in private situations as if they were addressing a public meeting; and that the language of journalism and party politics occupied a place in American life incomparably larger than its counterpart in England.[3] Although it is

---

[2] *Quite Early One Morning* (New York, 1954), p. 232; (London, 1954), p. 63.
[3] *Democracy in America* (New York, 1948), I, 250.

true that Dickens did not like what was happening in America, it is also true that he fell in love with America and its rhetoric in the same way that he did with his great wicked or foolish characters, like Quilp or Pecksniff or Flora Finching. Had he not, the chapters of Martin's transatlantic experiences would have fallen short of the brilliantly just satires that they are. The parody of the English language dramatized in the colloquy of Jefferson Brick and Colonel Diver in the offices of the New York Rowdy Journal (chap. 16) realized spontaneously and unsystematically what Joyce was to achieve systematically (but no less brilliantly) in the Aeolus episode of *Ulysses*.

Parody is one of the characteristic modes of representation in *Martin Chuzzlewit,* and every one of its major themes and characters is rendered in parodic equivalents. Joyce's parody of Dickens' sentimental style is justly celebrated, but no one to my knowledge has remarked the instances of Dickens in parody of himself—of which the following is a trenchant sample.

> Truly Mr. Pecksniff is blessed in his children. In one of them at any rate. The prudent Cherry—staff and scrip, and treasure of her doting father—there she sits, at a little table white as driven snow, before the kitchen fire, making up accounts! See the neat maiden, as with pen in hand, and calculating look addressed towards the ceiling, and bunch of keys within a little basket at her side, she checks the housekeeping expenditure! From flat-iron, dish-cover, and warming-pan; from pot and kettle, face of brass footman, and black-leaded stove; bright glances of approbation wink and glow upon her. The very onions dangling from the beam, mantle and shine like cherubs' cheeks. Something of the influence of those vegetables sinks into Mr. Pecksniff's nature. He weeps. (chap. 20)

This, one is forced to recall, is in the same book as Ruth Pinch and her beefsteak pudding, and it dramatizes one of the novel's continual preoccupations, the treachery of all appearance, of style itself.

But the supreme triumphs of language in the novel are to be found in the figures of Pecksniff and Mrs. Gamp. Their comedy naturally is rendered in their speech; but they are no mere rhetoricians—they are poets, geniuses of the language, enamoured of the sound of words. "Mr. Pecksniff was in the frequent habit of using any word that occurred to him as having a good sound, and rounding a sentence well, without much care for its meaning. And he did this so boldly, and in such an imposing manner, that he would sometimes stagger the wisest people with his eloquence, and make them gasp again" (chap. 2). The key to his character, Dickens adds, is his "strong trustfulness in sounds and forms," and out of this trustfulness springs the brilliant absurdity of his speech. The logic of comedy, says Bergson, is the logic of dreams; comic poetry is also that species of literary expression the logic of which most resembles the ritual of play, and the greatest comic poetry, whether we find it in the speech of Falstaff or of Pecksniff or Mrs. Gamp, realizes that special and necessary condition of freedom which it is also the function of play to perpetuate.[4] When Pecksniff remarks of a certain woman who has just been venomously denounced that he will not "go so far as to say that she deserves all the inflictions which have been so very forcibly and hilariously suggested" (chap. 4), or when Mrs. Gamp observes that "Rich folks may ride on camels, but it ain't so easy for 'em to see out of a needle's eye" (chap. 25), they are commanding the language with the god-like dominion of the comic poet, affirming their freedom from conditions, their mastery over circumstances, by twisting the tissue of syntax and usage and sense—in which we are confined to live as inescapably as in our tissue of flesh—to their own wills and interests, and to ours as well, else we would not be delighted. And here too we touch on another of the themes of *Martin Chuzzlewit*, a theme which asks, in the direct tradition of classical comedy: how is it possible in a world of conditions and circumstances to achieve a life of freedom?

Dickens soon became aware of how exceptional an accomplishment *Martin Chuzzlewit* was. As was becoming his custom, he had locked himself in his study during the period of extreme concentration which he referred to as "the agonies of plotting and contriving a new book," refused invitations, and set about his task like a general organizing a campaign. "In starting a work which is to last for twenty months there are so many little things to attend to, which require my personal super-intendence, that I am obliged to be constantly on the watch; and I may add, seriously, that unless I were to shut myself up, obstinately and sullenly in my own room for a great many days without writing a word, I don't think I ever should make a beginning." [5] Three months later, when the book was fully underway, he announced himself to be "in great health and spirits and powdering away at Chuzzlewit, with all manner of facetiousness rising up before me as I go on." [6] The letters of this period are intensely vivid, and Dickens himself is vibrant with energy.[7] Writing to his American friend Felton in apology for being remiss in correspondence, he described his state: "The truth is, that when I have done my morning's work, down goes my pen, and from that minute I feel it a positive impossibility to take it up again, until

[4] *Laughter* (New York, 1956), pp. 180-82; see also Huizinga, *Homo Ludens,* pp. 8-13.
[5] *Let.,* I, 487.
[6] *Let.,* I, 509.
[7] *Let.,* I, 534.

imaginary butchers and bakers wave me to my desk. I walk about brim-
ful of letters, facetious descriptions, touching morsels, and pathetic
friendships, but can't for the soul of me uncork myself." He then
casually remarks: "My average number of letters that *must* be written
every day is, at the least, a dozen" [8]—which, to uncork the image, is no
mean feat for a genie in a bottle. The pride and gratification Dickens
felt in his literary exertions were equaled only by the pleasure he found
in being himself, which he recognized as something of heroic proportions. He writes from Broadstairs: "In a bay-window in a one-pair sits,
from nine o'clock to one, a gentleman with rather long hair and no
neckcloth, who writes and grins as if he thought he were funny indeed.
His name is Boz. At one he disappears, and presently emerges from a
bathing-machine, and may be seen—a kind of salmon-coloured porpoise—splashing about in the ocean. After that he may be seen in another bay-window on the ground-floor, eating a strong lunch; after
that, walking a dozen miles or so, or lying on his back in the sand
reading a book. Nobody bothers him unless they know he is disposed to
be talked to; and I am told he is very comfortable indeed." [9] This comfort was not, however, to be uninterrupted.

As the novel progressed he became aware of the fact that he was
unreservedly serving his daemon and that this service was being rewarded. Discussing Pecksniff and Mrs. Gamp with Forster, he remarked:
"as to the way in which these characters have opened out, that is to me
one of the most surprising processes of the mind in this sort of invention. Given what one knows, what one does not know springs up; and
I am as absolutely certain of its being true, as I am of the law of gravi-
tation—if such a thing be possible, more so." [10] And nothing could
shake his conviction that *Martin Chuzzlewit* was his most accomplished
work. "You know, as well as I," he writes to Forster, "that I think
Chuzzlewit in a hundred points immeasurably the best of my stories.
That I feel my power now, more than I ever did. That I have a
greater confidence in myself than I ever had. That I *know*, if I have
health, I could sustain my place in the minds of thinking men, though
fifty writers started up to-morrow. But how many readers do *not*
think!" [11] For the well-known fact is that *Martin Chuzzlewit* was selling
far below expectations, and readers of every kind were being displeased
with it.

Although there has never been a bad day for speculating about the

[8] *Let.*, I, 535.
[9] *Let.*, I, 535.
[10] John Forster, *The Life of Charles Dickens*, ed. J. W. T. Ley, New York and London, 1928, p. 311.
[11] *Let.*, I, 545-46.

cause of this failure, certain considerations in connection with it are
relevant to an understanding of the novel.[12] To begin with, *Martin
Chuzzlewit* is not an easy book to read. It is the first of Dickens's novels
the prose of which, including some of the dialogue, makes an unremit-
ting demand on the reader's attention. In addition, the novel amounted
to something in the way of an assault upon Dickens' audience. It is,
among other things, about England and the national life: Dickens had
at first planned to print on its title-page the motto "Your homes the
scene, yourselves the actors, here," but was dissuaded by Forster.[13] It
is nonetheless evident that Pecksniff and the Chuzzlewits hit closer to
home than Bumble and Squeers. Indeed, *Martin Chuzzlewit* is the first
novel in which a separation between Dickens and his audience became
apparent; twenty-four years later, when the occasion for a new preface
arose, he took pains to address himself to this fact.[14] At the moment,
however, Dickens was chafed that "a great many people (particularly
those who might have sat for the character) consider even Mr. Pecksniff
a grotesque impossibility";[15] and the unsatisfactory reception of a work
"taking so much out of one as Chuzzlewit" prompted him to "leave the
scene" and go abroad once again. His sense of himself had dramatically
altered, and he refused, he said, to appear again "in my old shape." [16]
In July of 1844, Dickens left for Italy, where his new shape continued
to appear.

*   *   *

"What are the Great United States for," an American asks Martin,
"if not for the regeneration of man?" (chap. 21) One of the important
effects of Dickens' American experience was that it disburdened him of
this notion and left him convinced that whatever momentous changes
the self was undergoing in American society, it was not being regenerated, at least not in the direction of his expectations. In *Pickwick
Papers,* Dickens' first great comedy, the regeneration of man is a con-

---

[12] George H. Ford, *Dickens & His Readers,* Princeton, 1955, pp. 43-49, gives a useful
summary of *M.C.'s* reception and of the reasons that have been advanced for its
failure.

[13] Forster, p. 311.

[14] "What is exaggeration to one class of minds and perceptions," he wrote in that
Preface, "is plain truth to another. That which is commonly called a long-sight,
perceives in a prospect innumerable features and bearings non-existent to a short-
sighted person. I sometimes ask myself whether there may occasionally be a difference of this kind between some writers and some readers; whether it is *always* the
writer who colours highly, or whether it is now and then the reader whose eye for
colour is a little dull?"

[15] *Let.,* I, 555.

[16] *Let.,* I, 544, 546.

vincingly conceived and general possibility. In *Martin Chuzzlewit,* his second great comic novel, that possibility has all but receded: it brings, in Leslie Fiedler's apt phrase, an end to innocence.

Aside from the picture of America with respect to the theme of regeneration, special attention must be turned to Dickens's handling of the pastoral idea in *Martin Chuzzlewit.* This conception holds a place of peculiar significance in Dickens' development as a novelist. *Martin Chuzzlewit* opens on an autumn afternoon in "a little Wiltshire village, within an easy journey of the fair old town of Salisbury" (chap. 2). There follows an extended evocation of the traditional English agricultural scene, its rhythms and stability and security, which quickens, as night falls and the smith's fire burns brighter, into the briskness and finally into the gay "malicious fury" of the autumn wind, blowing through the village, whirling the fallen leaves, scattering the sawdust from the wheelwright's pit. The entire section is like an overture, ending with a masterfully controlled modulation out of the pastoral mode, as the first characters of the novel appear: the wind, taking advantage of "the sudden opening of Mr. Pecksniff's front-door," rushes into the passage, and "finding the back-door open, incontinently blew out the lighted candle held by Miss Pecksniff, and slammed the front door against Mr. Pecksniff who was at that moment entering, with such violence, that in the twinkling of an eye he lay on his back at the bottom of the steps" (chap. 2). It is here, with Pecksniff flat on his back, and the world spinning dizzily about him, that the novel properly begins. Picking himself up, Pecksniff is received solicitously by his daughters, whose behavior, Dickens remarks, "was perfectly charming, and worthy of the Pastoral age" (chap. 2). And later in the novel, when old Martin pays a sudden call on Pecksniff, that resourceful gentleman instantly mobilizes himself for action.

> Mr. Pecksniff, gently warbling a rustic stave, put on his garden hat, seized a spade, and opened the street door: calmly appearing on the threshold, as if he thought he had, from his vineyard, heard a modest rap, but was not quite certain. . . .
>
> "Mr. Chuzzlewit! Can I believe my eyes. . . . You find me in my garden-dress. You will excuse it, I know. It is an ancient pursuit, gardening. Primitive, my dear sir; or, if I am not mistaken, Adam was the first of our calling. *My* Eve, I grieve to say, is no more, sir; but": here he pointed to his spade, and shook his head, as if he were not cheerful without an effort: "but I do a little bit of Adam still." (chap. 24)

He does indeed, of the old Adam; and Pecksniff is a monumental parody of the ideal of pastoral innocence. For in *Martin Chuzzlewit* the pastoral vision is an illusion, an absurd identification of the self with nature, or a pretense of oneness with it. It is a relation to nature that is willed, wholly subjective, a mockery.

In *Martin Chuzzlewit,* the promise the pastoral idea once held for him has given way to a view of the Pastoral as a microcosm of the corruptions of society, disguising the disingenuousness of Pecksniffery, and tending to a denial of history and our condition in it. This denial is represented in Martin's chief experience in America, the journey to the settlement of Eden. At the geographical heart of the new continent, at the junction of the Ohio and Mississippi rivers, Martin is told, lies the new "terrestrial Paradise" (chap. 33).[17] In America, declares General Choke with unwitting irony, "man is in a more primeval state" (chap. 21), and Martin's journey to its interior, like Marlow's in *Heart of Darkness* (which owes something, I think, to this part of *Martin Chuzzlewit*), takes him into the primeval past.

> As they proceeded further on their track, and came more and more toward their journey's end, the monotonous desolation of the scene increased to that degree, that for any redeeming feature it presented to their eyes, they might have entered, in the body, on the grim domains of Giant Despair. A flat morass, bestrewn with fallen timber; a marsh on which the good growth of the earth seemed to have been wrecked and cast away, that from its decomposing ashes vile and ugly things might rise; where the very trees took the aspect of huge weeds, begotten of the slime from which they sprung, by the hot sun that burnt them up . . . this was the realm of Hope through which they moved.
>
> At last they stopped. At Eden too. The waters of the Deluge might have left it but a week before: so choked with slime and matted growth was the hideous swamp which bore that name. (chap. 23)

Whatever Eden might have been, this is what it has come to. Not only is there no regeneration in it, there is almost certain death. It is in fact an anti-Eden, just as in Dickens' mind America came to represent an anti-Paradise. Here, nature reveals itself as harshly primeval and cruelly uncivilized, and the pastoral vision reveals itself as a dangerous delusion. The people who settle at Eden "appeared to have wandered there with the idea that husbandry was the natural gift of all mankind," and though they try to cooperate "they worked as hopelessly and sadly as a gang of convicts in a penal settlement" (chap. 33). The fantasy of innocent nature has become a penal colony in a hostile jungle of swamp land. And later in the novel, back on English ground, when Dickens has Jonas murder Tigg in a pastoral setting and describes the murder

---

[17] For Dickens's account of the actual trip to "Eden" (Cairo, Illinois), see *American Notes,* chap. 12.

virtually in the pastoral style, the final reversal of the fantasy and its values is completed.

If, then, the self is to be neither established nor regenerated in natural innocence and primitive simplicity, we must turn back toward society, and somehow undertake to live in it. The novels of Dickens' middle period, from *Barnaby Rudge* through *David Copperfield,* have in common this impulse to reach some kind of reconciliation with society—although none of them succeeds in doing so. For all the ardency of their radicalism, and in contrast to the early novels, whose usual intention seems always to amount to a deliverance from society, each of these novels contains an attempt to achieve an accommodation within society. But it is no simple idea of society, either, which Dickens is turning to, and in *Martin Chuzzlewit* a great configuration of it unfolds in the chapter called "Town and Todgers's."

> You couldn't walk about in Todgers's neighbourhood, as you could in any other neighbourhood. You groped your way for an hour through lanes and bye-ways, and court-yards, and passages; and you never once emerged upon anything that might be reasonably called a street. A kind of resigned distraction came over the stranger as he trod those devious mazes, and giving himself up for lost, went in and out and round about and quietly turned back again when he came to a dead wall or was stopped by an iron railing. . . . Instances were known of people who, being asked to dine at Todgers's, had travelled round and round for a weary time, with its very chimney-pots in view; and finding it, at last, impossible of attainment, had gone home again with a gentle melancholy on their spirits, tranquil and uncomplaining. Nobody had ever found Todgers's on a verbal direction, though given within a minute's walk of it. . . . Todgers's was in a labyrinth, whereof the mystery was known but to a chosen few. . . . (chap. 9)

Embodying the essence of certain qualities of urban civilization, and of society itself, Todgers's is placed at the center of a labyrinth, one of Dickens' favorite symbols of the modern city. But here, unlike *Oliver Twist* in which the city as labyrinth was a mystery of darkness, anonymity, and peril, the labyrinth is benign, and being lost in it evokes the modern sadness of being adrift in life. The absurd and gratuitous mystification of Todgers's, the mystery of society itself, seems protective rather than sinister. When Dickens visited Philadelphia, he found the city handsome but "distractingly regular. After walking about it for an hour or two, I felt that I would have given the world for a crooked street." [18] And when he was taken beyond the outskirts of St. Louis to see a prairie he immediately perceived the bleakness, desolation, and

[18] *A.N.*, chap. 7.

terror of this characteristic American vista, and understood the endemic American affection, agoraphobia.[19] Todgers's is quite the reverse; it is, one keeps forgetting, a boardinghouse, a city within a city, a kind of encapsulated citadel of human society wherein is to be found the secret life of the metropolis:

> there were gloomy court-yards in these parts, into which few but belated wayfarers ever strayed, and where vast bags and packs of goods, upward or downward bound, were for ever dangling between heaven and earth from lofty cranes. . . . In the throats and maws of dark no-thoroughfares near Todgers's, individual wine-merchants and wholesale dealers in grocery-ware had perfect little towns of their own; and, deep among the foundations of these buildings, the ground was undermined and burrowed out into stables, where cart-horses, troubled by rats, might be heard on a quiet Sunday rattling their halters. . . . But the grand mystery of Todgers's was the cellarage, approachable only by a little back door and a rusty grating: which cellarage within the memory of man had had no connexion with the house, but had always been the freehold property of somebody else, and was reported to be full of wealth: though in what shape . . . was a matter of profound uncertainty and supreme indifference to Todgers's, and all its inmates. (chap. 9)

Congested, shabby, haphazard, impenetrable, irrational, and withal utterly humanized, the visible and palpable presence of a complex civilization and its history, eccentric, elaborate, thick, various, outlandish, absurd, Todgers's is a central item in Dickens' own list of Epsoms and Ascots. For its very chaos is human, inundated by the past, and reeking of mortality.

> There were churches also by dozens, with many a ghostly little church-yard, all overgrown with such straggling vegetation as springs up spontaneously from damp, and graves, and rubbish. . . . Here, paralysed old watchmen guarded the bodies of the dead at night, year after year, until at last they joined that solemn brotherhood; and, saving that they slept below the ground a sounder sleep than even they had ever known above it, and were shut up in another kind of box, their condition can hardly be said to have undergone any material change when they in turn were watched themselves. (chap. 9)

Even these stony old watchmen represent for Dickens at this moment something preferable to what he found in America. They do so by virtue of their relation to society, which is of course extreme, for they are as Dickens says "paralysed" by it and buried alive in it. Yet they

---

[19] *A.N.*, chap. 13.

are also at home in it, and so are the society of "commercial gentlemen" who board at Todgers's; for all their common circumstances, for all their limitations and absurdities, each of them is an individual identifiable by a particular "twist" of interest or character. There is "a gentleman of a sporting turn, who propounded questions on jockey subjects to the editors of Sunday papers, which were regarded by his friends as rather stiff things to answer . . . a gentleman of a theatrical turn, who had once entertained serious thoughts of 'coming out,' but had been kept in by the wickedness of human nature . . . a gentleman of a debating turn, who was strong at speechmaking . . . a gentleman of a literary turn, who wrote squibs upon the rest, and knew the weak side of everybody's character but his own." There are gentlemen of turns vocal, smoking and convivial; who have a turn for whist, billiards, and betting; for pleasure and for fashion—and all of them, Dickens reflects, "it may be presumed, had a turn for business" (chap. 9). They are foolish and inconsequent, shabby and pretentious. Limited by circumstances of birth and station, they have nevertheless undertaken to make the effort of a decent life, to cultivate their own and respect each other's oddities. If the purpose of civilization is to humanize man in society, then they are journeymen in that old and difficult enterprise. And there is no more important statement in the novel than that at Todgers's "every man comes out freely in his own character." The gentlemen at Todgers's represent the private life and self; each one is able to enact his own distinct conception of who he is—all of which stands in contrast to what Dickens saw occurring in America.

England is a great deal more than Todgers's, of course, as it is more than the characters and experiences that are on the side of virtue in *Martin Chuzzlewit*. It is also the colossal swindle of the Anglo-Bengalee, the smug and servile respectability of Pecksniff and everything else he stands for, the brutal materialism of Anthony and Jonas Chuzzlewit, the despotic authority of old Martin. In America, however, Dickens was able to see little to offset the Eden Land Corporation (counterpart of the Anglo-Bengalee), little to restrain the ruthless, aggrandising self, the unchecked and rapacious will. Although Dickens had always known that what he detested in society could not simply be severed as by the issuance of a moral fiat, in this novel he begins to grasp in a more fundamental way the interaction of those evils with the qualities which he regarded as indispensable to society, qualities that he approved and loved.

What Todgers's represents, in other words, could not alone suffice to sustain the self in modern society, or answer the needs for authority and independence. Dickens could not have read Keats's journal-letter of the spring of 1819, but a portion of it illuminates very clearly the inner drama of *Martin Chuzzlewit*. I refer to the famous passage in which Keats discusses "the most interesting question that can come before us": how far the ills and pains of human existence can be eliminated by the endeavors of civilization. Not very far, he argues, not beyond a certain point, and then he rounds upon this conclusion and examines the character of experience. "The common cognomen of this world among the misguided and superstitious is 'a vale of tears' from which we are to be redeemed by a certain arbitrary interposition of God and taken to Heaven—What a little circumscribed straightened notion! Call the world if you Please 'The vale of Soul-making.' Then you will find out the use of the world." And he then goes on to discuss how souls are made in the world, and asks how they are to "have an identity given them . . . peculiar to each one's individual existence? How, but by the medium of a world like this?" Do you not see, he says, "how necessary a World of Pains and troubles is to school an Intelligence and make it a Soul"? Our identities as men, he continues, must be formed through circumstances, which prove and fortify and alter our original undifferentiated natures—"and how is this Identity to be made . . . but in a world of Circumstances?" [20] This is the conception of experience, preeminently tragic as Keats states it, which in a curious, comic, and complicated way emerges in *Martin Chuzzlewit,* and which Dickens transforms, one might say, into the comedy of soul-making, of creating an identity in a world of circumstance.

Almost every character in the novel bears out this conception somehow. There is Tigg, who is able to "rise with circumstances" and attempts altogether to control them (chap. 27); there are those like Tom Pinch and Mary Graham, who have always to bear the heavy weight of circumstances, to "endure without the possibility of action" (chap. 33). The necessity of the world of delimiting circumstance is no less central to Dickens' satire of America, the new world which was supposed to have transcended circumstances somehow, at least the old humiliating ones of Europe, but which in fact had created new and perhaps equally humiliating ones. But the most conscious, articulate spokesmen for the world of circumstance are Mark Tapley and Mrs. Gamp.

Mark's overmastering impulse, his desire for adventure, is experienced as "a wish to come out strong under circumstances as would keep other men down" (chap. 13). For him this is not simply a way of proving himself, but virtually a scheme of salvation, for Mark wants to find

---

[20] *The Letters of John Keats,* ed. M. Forman (London, 1947), pp. 334-37.

"credit," that quintessentially protestant reward, in his undertaking. "Lookin' on the bright side of human life in short, one of my hopeful wisions is, that there's a deal of misery a-waitin' for me; in the midst of which I may come out tolerable strong, and be jolly under circumstances as reflects some credit," (chap. 48). It is Mark's "amazing power of self-sustainment" (chap. 33) that secures him his salvation, the wry comic nature of which he expresses in paradox: "Then all my hopeful wisions bein' crushed; and findin' that there ain't no credit for me nowhere; I abandons myself to despair, and says, 'Let me do that as has the least credit in it of all; marry a dear, sweet creetur, as is wery fond of me . . . lead a happy life, and struggle no more again' the blight which settles on my prospects' " (chap. 48).[21] Before he submits, however, he gives voice to a sentiment which is perhaps the soberest judgment on the uses of adversity, or circumstance, to be found in this novel. When Martin comes down with fever in the swamp of Eden and cries out in despair, "what have I done in all my life that has deserved this heavy fate," Mark, who is nursing him, replies encouragingly, *"that's* nothing. It's only a seasoning; and we must all be seasoned, one way or another. That's religion, that is, you know" (chap. 23). It is the religion of soul-making, this belief in being tempered and weathered in the world of circumstance.

The supreme embodiment of this conception of the world of conditioning circumstances, and at the same time of an almost supernatural accommodation to it, is Mrs. Gamp. At first we might conclude that she is simply one more instance of the comedy of absolute self which informs the central drama of the novel. She has, after all, invented a certain "Mrs. Harris," apparently for the purpose of attesting to her own goodness of heart and beneficence of conduct, constantly putting forth the evidence of this trusty witness to testify to the brightness of her inner light and thereby always diverting her acquaintances from making their own judgments on this score. But Mrs. Harris has been created by Mrs. Gamp "for the express purpose of holding visionary dialogues . . . on all manner of subjects," as much as for the purpose of "invariably winding up with a compliment to the excellence of her [Mrs. Gamp's] nature" (chap. 25), and thus is more than a hallucinatory phantom. She becomes as real to us as any other character, and without her we would have no proper image of Mrs. Gamp. Mrs. Gamp is that rare phenomenon, the character as creative artist, an imaginary person endowed with the same kind of vitality that imagined her, impelled to invent her own imaginary person in order to define and cele-

---

[21] Mark's counterpart and parody is of course young Moddle. See chaps. 46, 54.

brate herself and the world she lives in. She represents what might be called the schizophrenia of Election, just as Pecksniff sometimes represents the paranoia of it. The energy of her identity, moreover, is so impressive that the clothes she wears retain her shape even when she isn't in them—one can see her "very fetch and ghost . . . in at least a dozen of the second-hand clothes shops about Holborn." Like the novelist, she is prolific, always giving forth an abundance of observations, sentiments, feelings, experiences, quotations, maxims, gossip, etc., with an inventiveness that seems born out of a sheer excess of vitality. But unlike Pecksniff, Mrs. Gamp is not so much contriving reality as embellishing it. Nor, as we shall see, is she insisting on the virtue and authority of herself so much as on the existential authority of the world of circumstance—of birth, tribulation, and death—the very real world in which she lives and which with the aid of Mrs. Harris she is entirely at home in.

Mrs. Gamp is more than self. She is an incarnation of the world of circumstance and the human condition. When first introduced she is described as "a female functionary, a nurse, and watcher, and performer of nameless offices about the persons of the dead"; but in the higher walk of her art she is also a "monthly nurse, or, as her sign-board boldly had it, 'Midwife'" (chap. 19). She attends at the supreme ritual events of life and is herself a creature of ritual, of immemorial formulae and conventions for dealing with the life of adversity and pain. A gamey, squalid, fat old woman, "with a husky voice and a moist eye," a red nose and an insatiable thirst for gin, she represents in her very weaknesses and sordidness the principle of human endurance, and the conditions of comic triumph over the unendurableness of that endurance.

> Like most persons who have attained to great eminence in their profession, she took to hers very kindly; insomuch that, setting aside her natural predilections as a woman, she went to a lying-in or a laying-out with equal zest or relish.
>
> "Ah!" repeated Mrs. Gamp; for it was always a safe sentiment in cases of mourning. "Ah dear! When Gamp was summoned to his long home, and I see him a-lying in Guy's Hospital with a penny-piece on each eye, and his wooden leg under his left arm, I thought I should have fainted away. But I bore up."

And she goes on to say,

> "One's first ways is to find sich things a trial to the feelings, and so is one's lasting custom. If it wasn't for the nerve a little sip of liquor gives me (I never was able to do more than taste it), I never could go through with what I sometimes has to do. 'Mrs. Harris,' I says, at the very last case

as ever I acted in, which it was but a young person, 'Mrs. Harris,' I says, 'leave the bottle on the chimley-piece, and don't ask me to take none, but let me put my lips to it when I am so dispoged, and then I will do what I'm engaged to do, according to the best of my ability.'" (chap. 19)

Mrs. Gamp is a female Old Mortality, one of the guardians of human destiny in "this Piljian's Projiss of a mortal wale" (chap. 25). Her conversation is of birth and death and all the vicissitudes of life—of change, of "more changes too, to come, afore we've done with changes." Coarsened and chafed by the rough visitations of circumstance, there is little in the way of human pain, suffering, weakness and folly that is alien to her, that she cannot encompass in the ever-expanding circle of her imagination and "experienge."

"Although the blessing of a daughter was deniged me; which, if we had had one, Gamp would certainly have drunk its little shoes right off its feet, as with our precious boy he did, and arterwards send the child a errand to sell his wooden leg for any money it would fetch as matches in the rough, and bring it home in liquor: which was truly done beyond his years, for ev'ry individge penny that child lost at toss or buy for kidney ones; and come home arterwards quite bold, to break the news, and offering to drown himself if that would be a satisfaction to his parents." (chap. 25)

And when Ruth Pinch asks an innocent question, Mrs. Gamp launches into a declaration which might well be read as the metaphysics of the comedy of circumstance, of human mortality.

"Which shows," said Mrs. Gamp, casting up her eyes, "what a little way you've travelled into this wale of life, my dear young creetur! As a good friend of mine has frequent made remark to me, which her name, my love, is Harris, Mrs. Harris through the square and up the steps a-turnin' round by the tobacker shop, 'Oh, Sairey, Sairey, little do ye know wot lays afore us!' 'Mrs. Harris, ma'am,' I says, 'not much, it's true, but more than your suppoge. Our calcilations, ma'am,' I says 'respectin' wot the number of a family will be, comes most time within one, and oftener than you would suppoge, exact.' 'Sairey,' says Mrs. Harris, in a awful way, 'Tell me wot is my indiwidge number.' 'No, Mrs. Harris,' I says to her, 'ex-cuge me, if you please. My own,' I says, 'has fallen out of three-pair backs, and had damp doorsteps settled on their lungs, and one was turned up smilin' in a bedstead, unbeknown. Therefore, ma'am,' I says, 'seek not to proticipate, but take 'em as they come and as they go.' Mine," said Mrs. Gamp, "mine is all gone, my dear young chick. And as to husbands, there's a wooden leg gone likeways home to its account, which in its constancy of walkin' into wine vaults, and never comin' out again 'till fetched by force, was quite as weak as flesh, if not weaker." (chap. 40)

"As weak as flesh, if not weaker"—this is in the great tradition of comedy, and part of its greatness consists in its implicit recognition of a classic comic paradox: that it is the spirit, rather, which is weak, and the flesh, which it eternally tries to harness, that triumphs and comes out strong. It is in the bold confrontation of such contradictions that comedy performs its proper service, in the freedom, the release, the vindication we earn through recognizing the human condition, celebrating it, and at the same time enjoying momentary immunity from it under the sanction of art. In a way that reminds us of Molly Bloom, Mrs. Gamp is a kind of pagan, cockney goddess, beyond—like the Immortals—human suffering, but privileged to be a spectator and caretaker of it, to take delight in the occasions of it, and to observe and receive it from the Olympus of her immunity as only a goddess or a novelist could: as in the very nature of things. She is a squalid goddess of the earth, of the folk, of the flesh, and of the unreasoned primitive ritual life. She is a kind of brutalized goddess Hygeia,[22] and there is even something recognizably Homeric about her when she enunciates: "Bless the babe, and save the mother, is my mortar, sir; but I makes so free as to add to that, Don't try no impogician with the Nuss, for she will not abear it" (chap. 40). She is not the less reluctant to pronounce the terms of our a-bearing it in this vale of soul-making; and when Sweedlepipe, having just heard that Bailey is dead, cries out, "But what's a Life Assurance Office to a Life! And what a Life Young Bailey's was!" Mrs. Gamp "with philosophical coolness" replies. "He was born into a wale . . . and he lived in a wale; and he must take the consequences of sech a sitiwation" (chap. 49).

[22] The scene in which Mrs. Gamp and Betsy Prig take tea together and fall into a quarrel has something of the epic about it—they argue like goddesses in Homer, in long, set, superbly stylized speeches; like goddesses they are propitiated by ritual offerings of meat and drink, and stand watch, more or less ineffectively, over human fortunes; they are jealous of their status, protective of their place in a natural hierarchy, and quite clearly immortal. Like the Homeric goddesses, they are figures of comedy, though the mode and tone of the comedy are naturally different.

Dombey and Son

by Kathleen Tillotson

I

Dombey and Son stands out from among Dickens' novels as the earliest example of responsible and successful planning; it has unity not only of action, but of design and feeling. It is also the first in which a pervasive uneasiness about contemporary society takes the place of an intermittent concern with specific social wrongs. These are the main reasons why this novel rather than *Martin Chuzzlewit* or *David Copperfield* is here chosen to represent Dickens in the eighteen-forties; and these form the main headings—of unequal, but related importance—under which it will now be considered.

It is Dickens' seventh novel, and the fourth of those written in this decade. A gap unusually long for Dickens divides it from its predecessor; *Martin Chuzzlewit* was completed in July 1844, and the writing of *Dombey* was not begun until 27 June 1846.[1] The interval had been fully occupied in travel, theatricals, writing "Christmas books," founding and for a short time editing the *Daily News*; at the end of May came what Forster calls the "retreat to Switzerland," and it was at Geneva, Lausanne, and Paris that the first six numbers were written.[2] The writing was attended with many difficulties ("You can hardly imagine what infinite pains I take, or what extraordinary difficulty I find in getting on FAST"). He suffered from "the absence of streets and number of figures" —required not as material, but as stimulus—and from the new problem

"Dombey and Son" by Kathleen Tillotson. From "Part II, Four Novels" of *Novels of the Eighteen-Forties* (Oxford: Clarendon Press, 1954; paperback edition, 1961). Copyright © 1954 by the Clarendon Press. Reprinted by permission of the author and the publisher. Sections 5-7 are omitted.

[1] John Forster, *The Life of Charles Dickens*, Book v, Chap. 2; but it had been in his mind at least since the beginning of March (vi, 2) and probably earlier (v, 1).
[2] As a result of his absence from England the early stages of *Dombey* are fairly fully documented in letters to Forster; quotations from these are scattered through v, 2-7, vi, 1-2.

of beginning a novel and writing a "Christmas book" in the same months; but

> Invention, thank God, seems the easiest thing in the world; and I seem to have such a preposterous sense of the ridiculous after this long rest as to be constantly requiring to restrain myself from launching into extravagances in the height of my enjoyment.[3]

It was necessary for his illustrator to cooperate in avoiding "extravagances ("enormous care" is required with Dombey and Miss Tox, and "the Toodle Family should not be too much caricatured, because of Polly").[4] He wrote the christening scene with "the drag on," to avoid satire—"malice in christening points of faith." [5] There is evidence that he restrained himself especially in comic dialogue. When he had "overwritten" a number, it was the nonfunctional comic dialogue (between Miss Tox and Mrs. Chick) that was cut, as the original proofs show.

> I have avoided unnecessary dialogue so far, to avoid over-writing; and all I *have* written is point.[6]

This deliberate control of comic exaggeration and inventiveness marks one of the differences between *Dombey* and its predecessors; the comedy is in lower relief and is subordinated to the design of the whole.[7] The overflowing comic inventiveness is here kept within bounds; Dickens was setting himself new standards. His was the genius that "progresses and evolves and does not spin upon itself"; it would have been easy (and remunerative) for him to repeat the happy improvisation of his early novels—but this no longer contented him. With *Dombey* he began to write novels founded on a theme, embodied in a relation between characters. This more conscious technique (contrast "I thought of Mr. Pickwick") and the particular theme chosen, with its gravity, and its subtle and various relevance to his own time, give *Dombey and Son* a peculiar interest.

II

Despite the gap, there is a significant relation between *Dombey and Son* and its predecessor. In *Martin Chuzzlewit,* says Dickens,

---

[3] Forster, v, 5, letter of 30 August, written while at work on the second number.

[4] Forster, v, 3, letter of 18 July 1846; and *Letters,* ed. Walter Dexter (Nonsuch Edition), I, 768.

[5] Forster, vi, 2.

[6] Forster, vi, 2, letter of 6 December 1846, written while at work on the fourth number.

[7] On this, see Chesterton's Introduction to the Everyman edition of the novel, especially his remarks on Mrs. Skewton.

I have endeavoured to resist the temptation of the current Monthly Number, and to keep a steadier eye upon the general purpose and design. With this object in view I put a strong constraint upon myself.[8]

What was new was little more than the endeavor; the temptations were not always resisted nor the constraint effective. The origin of the book, we learn from Forster, lay in Pecksniff;

the notion of taking Pecksniff for a type of character was really the origin of the book; the design being to show, more or less by every person introduced, the number and variety of humours and vices that have their root in selfishness.[9]

This is a very general "purpose and design," leaving much room for improvisation and modification. There was no narrative plan, no dynamic view of the interaction of characters, such as we find in the long letter to Forster outlining the design of *Dombey*; evidence of foresight and design is found only after the writing, even the publication, is well under way. The plot of old Martin was drawn up when the third number was being written; Forster's comment on this bears upon *Dombey*:

the difficulties he encountered in departing from other portions of his scheme were such as to render him, in his subsequent stories, more bent on constructive care at the outset, and on adherence as far as might be to any design he had formed.

In *Dombey* he again had a "general purpose and design," which is explicitly compared to that of *Chuzzlewit*; it is "to do with Pride what its predecessor had done with Selfishness." [10] Rather, what he had *meant* its predecessor to do; he would learn from its stumbling endeavor and work out the design of *Dombey* more precisely. This novel, even without its numerous surrounding documents—number-plans, letters to Forster and Browne, corrected manuscript and proofs—is eloquent of his far greater success. To say this is not to belittle *Chuzzlewit*; but it is doubtful there whether a reader lacking preface or biography would recognize that Selfishness, or even Hypocrisy (it is never quite clear which Dickens means) was its theme. Circumstances worked against him; sales of early numbers were disappointing, and "America" was resorted to as an expedient to stimulate them. Although it is made relative to the theme (exposing Martin's selfishness, and magnificently illustrating the unconscious self-deception of another national character, which might be judged a kind of hypocrisy) it remains an expedient and an episode;

[8] Preface to first edition.
[9] Forster, iv, 1.
[10] Forster, vi, 2.

"a place Martin Chuzzlewit happens to go to." [11] And throughout this novel the details mask the "general purpose and design"; it is largely remembered and valued for single scenes and characters, either loosely attached to the theme or too expansively illustrative of it. Whereas *Dombey* has its firm center, of theme, character, and scene, Pecksniff and Martin divide the center, the one static, but giving out vitality, the other progressing, but uninteresting. There is no scenic center, and no coherent impression of period; no one would select *Chuzzlewit* as especially representative or reflective of the early eighteen-forties. We cannot mistake the earnestness of Dickens' moral and social concern to expose in Pecksniff a peculiarly English and contemporary vice,[12] as distinct from remediable and specific abuses. But for various reasons the exposure is not complete—far less so than in the smaller scale figures of Chadband and Podsnap. Dickens had not grasped the difficulty of having a hypocrite bearing the weight of a main character—he can hardly stand the strain if he is only to be exhibited, never analyzed. We need to know, at least to suspect, how he appears to himself; we are told that Pecksniff had solitary thoughts by the fireside, but never what they were.[13] Pecksniff exists mainly in the limelight of a series of superb scenes (and also as refracted in the contrasted natures of Tom and Martin); but under this continued exhibition, with its extravagantly comic dialogue, he becomes less not more repulsive. Dickens' comic inventiveness is still overflowing, neither subordinated to the general purpose nor fully contained by moral and social criticism. The resulting ambiguity is clearer still with Mrs. Gamp, who is almost extraneous to the plot. We are less aware of the horrors of her ministrations than of the private world she blissfully inhabits, "as light as any gash balloon," and which Dickens makes it seem a privilege to share. Contrast the continued yet unstrained harnessing of the comedy to the "general purpose and design" in *Dombey,* where the absurd is on the side of the angels. Toots and Susan Nipper and Captain Cuttle and Miss Tox, all, by their natures and their share in the action, supply continuous moral comment on the evil represented in Mr. Dombey; and they do so naturally and implicitly, without the copybook pointedness of Mark Tapley. So, from the other side, does Major Bagstock, whose function Dickens defined when he called him "a kind of comic Mephistophelean power" [14] (with Mr. Dombey as Faust?).

Not only the comedy, but all the characters and all the action are

[11] Chesterton, loc. cit.
[12] See Dickens' Preface, and Forster, iv, 2.
[13] Chap. 9 (which concludes Number III).
[14] Letter to Browne, 10 March 1847; *Letters,* II, 17.

subordinated to Mr. Dombey. This is the first novel of Dickens' to be dominated by a leading idea, embodied in a single character. He is the origin, center, and continuum of the novel, as no previous character of Dickens' had been. Before this is demonstrated in relation to the structural unity of the book it will be necessary to look into this idea and character, and the other character upon whom they chiefly act.

III

That the origin of the book lay in Mr. Dombey is not indeed clearly attested by direct external evidence, as it is with Pickwick and Pecksniff; but everything even outside the novel itself points that way. Forster's report that as first conceived "it was to do with Pride what its predecessor had done with Selfishness";[15] Dickens' anxiety for secrecy—"The very name getting out, would be ruinous";[16] the "outline of [his] immediate intentions" in the letter to Forster with the manuscript of Number I;[17] his "nervous dread of caricature in the face of his merchant-hero" [18]—all these agree in their emphasis. It is safe to assume that the originating idea took the form of a "merchant-hero," in whom business and family pride are twisted into a single hard knot; the continued interplay between the affairs of the firm and the family is emphasized by the early chapter titles[19] and "shadowed forth" in the semi-allegorical cover design; although in the working-out less is made of the firm than Dickens seems to have intended. The title is its epitome (there is no record of hesitation over this title as with most others); and is also deliberately misleading—serving to keep the secret of Paul's early death, and to point the irony of the book's true subject—which is, of course, Dombey and Daughter.[20] The relation between Mr. Dombey and Florence is the backbone of the whole book; structurally, the relation be-

[15] vi, 2; Forster is referring to what Dickens told him before he left England in May.

[16] v, 3; 18 July 1846.

[17] vi, 2; 25 July 1846.

[18] vi, 2; August 1846. To prevent caricature, Dickens asked for a sheet of sketches from which to select; this is reproduced by Forster.

[19] See chaps. 3, 13, 22.

[20] In the original edition, and in all editions up to 1858, the "turn" is emphasized by the closing words of No. V, chorically delivered by Miss Tox: "To think . . . Dombey and Son should be a Daughter after all!" (cf. letter to Forster, 25 July; vi, 2). When Dickens removed this sentence in 1859 (perhaps because it then seemed to him to mar the pathos of the conclusion) he forgot that it was echoed in chap. 59: "And so Dombey and Son, as I observed upon a certain sad occasion . . . is indeed a daughter, Polly, after all."

tween him and Paul, and that between Florence and Paul, are only means of exposing and developing it.

> From that time [Paul's death], I purpose changing his feelings of indifference and uneasiness towards his daughter into a positive hatred. . . . At the same time I shall change *her* feeling towards *him* for one of a greater desire to love him, and to be loved by him; engendered in her compassion for his loss, and her love for the dead boy whom, in his way, he loved so well too. So I mean to carry the story on, through all the branches and off-shoots and meanderings that come up; and through the decay and downfall of the house, and the bankruptcy of Dombey, and all the rest of it; when his only staff and treasure, and his unknown Good Genius always, will be this rejected daughter, who will come out better than any son at last, and whose love for him, when discovered and understood, will be his bitterest reproach.[21]

Through this changing relation works Mr. Dombey's pride, the master-motive of the novel, the mainspring of all its events. Much then depends upon the adequacy of these two characters, Mr. Dombey and Florence, to sustain this central interest, and especially upon Dickens' power—not hitherto manifested—to draw a character undergoing inner conflict.

This continued inner conflict was also a part of the original intention; the letter just quoted continues:

> For the struggle with himself, which goes on in all such obstinate natures, will have ended then; and the sense of his injustice, which you may be sure has never quitted him, will have at last a gentler office than that of only making him more harshly unjust.[22]

The last point alone shows Dickens' psychological insight; and it is repeated in the new Preface added by the author twelve years later—apparently in reply to criticism of the supposed "violent change" in the hero.[23]

> The two commonest mistakes in judgment . . . are the confounding of shyness with arrogance . . . and the not understanding that an obstinate nature exists in a perpetual struggle with itself.
>
> Mr. Dombey undergoes no violent change, either in this book, or in real life. A sense of his injustice is within him, all along. The more he represses it, the more unjust he necessarily is. Internal shame and external circumstances may bring the contest to a close in a week, or a

---

[21] Letter of 25 July 1846.

[22] Cf. chap. 59: "obstinate and sullen natures . . . struggle hard to be such. Ground long undermined, will often fall down in a moment."

[23] See Forster, vi, 2 (opening paragraph).

day; but, it has been a contest for years, and is only fought out after a long balance of victory.[24]

The moment in the novel when the contest is nearest to the surface is in chapter 35 where Mr. Dombey watches Florence, who believes him asleep.

> There are yielding moments in the lives of the sternest and harshest men, though such men often keep their secret well.

So begins the long paragraph in which his brief relenting is traced, and its hidden sources suggested. It ends with a dramatic turn; Edith enters, and, still unobserved, he witnesses her gentle and loving conversation with Florence—a double blow to his pride, and the stimulus to double revenge upon them.

"Such men often keep their secret well"; " 'Dombey,' said the Major . . . 'don't be thoughtful. . . . You are too great a man, Dombey, to be thoughtful.' " [25] The difficulty, especially to a writer more practised in exhibition than analysis, is to suggest the secret self-doubting of "stiff-necked sullen arrogance." Such suggestion is conveyed sometimes by the use of carefully timed silent pauses in the narrative, moments sharply presented to the sight and impressing the imagination: as when Mr. Dombey watches Florence carrying Paul up "the great, wide, vacant staircase" in the moonlight, and singing to him.[26] Or by a revealing but un-annotated gesture: as when Mrs. Chick, promoting the Brighton scheme, hesitantly submits that Florence must accompany Paul:

> "It's quite an infatuation with him. He's very young, you know, and has his fancies."
> Mr. Dombey turned his head away, and going slowly to the bookcase, and unlocking it, brought back a book to read.[27]

In Mr. Dombey Dickens achieves the remarkable feat of making us aware of the hidden depths of a character, while keeping them largely hidden; his method respects Mr. Dombey's own proud reserve. The only times his thoughts are unrolled at length before us it is through the

[24] The Preface was added in the edition of 1858, and revised for the collected "Charles Dickens" edition of 1867. I quote from the latter; in the passage quoted, the only differences are that 1858-62 read "no violent internal change . . . or in life"; "bring the contest to the surface"; and "is only fought out then." The Preface of 1848 is quite distinct—a brief farewell to readers, originally printed at the end of the concluding number.

[25] Chap. 20.

[26] Chap. 8. The moment is openly recalled at the end of chap. 18 and again at the end of chap. 36.

[27] Chap. 8.

phantasmagoria of the railway journey,[28] where Dickens can "analyse" as it were panoramically, with something of the picturesque freedoms of dream or allegory; and similarly again through the memories and visions called up when he roams through the silent house.[29] Mr. Dombey has "lonely thoughts, bred late at night in the sullen despondency and gloom of his retirement," [30] but the reader is seldom admitted to them; yet he is often reminded, both by oblique reference and momentary pictures of that silent brooding presence, the shadow behind the figure which Mr. Dombey presents to the world, "self-important, unbending, formal, austere." [31] What makes him interesting is the moral suspense: although Florence may serve partly as an externalized conscience, a troublesome and even hated reminder of the whole world of feeling that his pride has forsworn, she does so because something within him responds to her. Before Paul's birth, he had been merely indifferent; afterward this indifference turns to uneasiness and resentment,[32] which increase after Paul's death.[33] But in this resentment there is an unadmitted sense of guilt, and even the seeds of repentance. His love for his son, involved though it is in "a partial scheme of parental interest and ambition," is yet also the rift in the ice. We are aware of it even in the cruellest moment in which he repulses Florence's affection, and even aware of it as his justification for doing so: he watches her, silently and hopelessly ascending the stairs.

> The last time he had watched her, from the same place, winding up those stairs, she had had her brother in her arms. It did not move his heart towards her now, it steeled it: but he went into his room, and locked his door, and sat down in his chair, and cried for his lost boy.[34]

In his momentary relenting toward her (so abruptly terminated by a new jealousy)

> She became blended with the child he had loved, and he could hardly separate the two.[35]

Such evidence keeps before us the "contest [of] years, only fought out after a long balance of victory"; we can accept its bringing to a close, through "internal shame and external circumstances," in a single chap-

---

[28] Chap. 20.
[29] Chap. 59.
[30] Chap. 20.
[31] Chap. 27.
[32] Chap. 3.
[33] Chaps. 18, 20; and the reference to "hatred" in chap. 40.
[34] Chap. 18.
[35] Chap. 35.

ter of the closing number.[36] We may feel that for "internal shame" to reach the purpose of self-murder, and for "external circumstances" to bring Florence home in the nick of time, savors overmuch of the theater; we may feel that the year's lapse between the last two numbers[37] has cheated us, or spared us, too much of the slow undermining of Mr. Dombey's obstinate pride. But in the account of his days and nights of restless wandering through the desolate house, Dickens prevents us from feeling that the reconciliation is cheaply purchased. In a passage of no more than four pages he condenses Mr. Dombey's history and his present state. And he does it, as always, by a combination of picture and analysis. The deserted rooms, the staircase (that recurring symbol) with its remembered footsteps, carry us backward in time. In Mr. Dombey's thoughts, the whole of the original design of the novel is retraced. It is not a static view; the contest still continues. He has passed beyond Paul's death, the wreck of his marriage, his fallen fortunes:

> That which was his own work, that which he could so easily have wrought into a blessing, and had set himself so steadily for years to form into a curse: that was the sharp grief of his soul. . . .
>
> And yet—so proud he was in his ruin . . . that if he could have heard her voice in an adjoining room, he would not have gone to her. . . . He chiefly thought of what might have been, and what was not. What was, was all summed up in this: that she was lost, and he bowed down with sorrow and remorse.

Inevitably, the passage is introduced by a reiteration of the earlier prophecy: "Let him remember it in that room, years to come." [38] But the heavily emphasized pattern of sin, curse, retribution is not the "figure in the carpet" of *Dombey and Son*. Dickens' impulse toward the cruder simplifications should not obscure from us that his hero is a character of tragic stature. Not seldom, toward the close of the novel, we think of another unbending but vulnerable man of affairs, who wished to stand "as if a man were author of himself"; or of another proud father and banished daughter, Lear and Cordelia. And no more than there is the forgiveness a sentimental concession; the famous criticism that Mr. Dom-

---

[36] Chap. 59.

[37] I.e., before chap. 58, "After a lapse," "The year was out, and the great House was down." In the first part of this chapter (balancing chap. 59) is concentrated much of the effect on Mr. Dombey of the business failure, although he does not himself appear; and the better side of his pride is recognized by the unimpeachable Mr. Morfin: "He is a gentleman of high honour and integrity . . . resolved on payment to the last farthing of his means. . . . Ah, Miss Harriet, it would do us no harm to remember oftener than we do, that vices are sometimes only virtues carried to excess! His pride shows well in this."

[38] Chaps. 18, 59.

bey "becomes the best of fathers, and spoils a fine novel," [39] is wide of the mark. It might have been ill judged if he were fully shown as "the best of fathers"; but after this climax we see him only in the moral convalescence of physical illness, and in the afterglow of the epilogue.

IV

The contest for Mr. Dombey's soul requires no more of Florence than a perfect goodness and persistent affection; in the words of a chapter-heading, "The Study of a Loving Heart." But the balance of the novel requires her to be prominent, and she is not competely absent from the scene for more than a single number.[40] A character conceived in terms of pure feeling, passive, innocent to the point of being almost "incapable of her own distress," can hardly sustain this prominence. The dilemma, though it is doubtful if Dickens saw it as such, is clear. Conflict within her, introspection, or initiative, would mitigate the pathos of her situation; unmitigated, the pathos risks monotony, if not self-defeat. (It may even raise the more serious criticism that if her state of mind is not morbid, it is improbable;[41] and it is not within Dickens' range in *this* novel to regard it as morbid.)[42]

She has to be entirely lovable, in order to leave us in no doubt of the guilt of Mr. Dombey (and his own sense of it); for the same reason, she has to be, with that noticeable exception, universally loved. The love according to their lights of almost all the other characters carries conviction, and at times Florence gains some reflected vitality from Susan Nipper, Mr. Toots, and Captain Cuttle; even Mrs. Chick was on one occasion struck into silence and "lost . . . her presence of mind" at the sight of Florence grieving for Paul. But on the whole the effect is still of a space where Florence's character ought to be, with our attention drawn from the vacuum by the ring of admirers. Dickens' difficulties are not peculiar to him,[43] or to this novel; besides the timeless problem of

[39] Taine, *History of English Literature* (Paris, 1863-64; trans. H. Van Laun, 1871), Book V, ch. i, § 3. ii. Compare *Blackwood's* (October 1848), p. 469: "The entire change of character in Dombey is out of all nature."

[40] No. XVII (chaps. 52-54).

[41] So more than one reviewer thought; e.g. *Blackwood's*, October 1848: "nor does the extraordinary affection of the daughter spring from any known principle of humanity" (p. 469).

[42] Not that the emotional stresses of adolescent girlhood lay altogether outside Dickens' range; witness Tattycoram, also hungry for affection.

[43] Though perhaps accentuated for him by the pressure of his idealized memory of Mary Hogarth, who died at sixteen.

making perfect virtue, and especially the passive virtues, attractive, he has his age's problem of vitalizing a heroine in a period of limiting ideals for girlhood.[44] Yet let the Victorian novel itself dictate our standards, and we see what is lacking in Florence as a heroine attracting the reader; that endearing solidity, even of appearance, that touch of individualizing charm, which Trollope was able to give to all the fifty or so of his young heroines;[45] and which Dickens was to find for his less perfect ones—Dora, Pet, Bella, and Rosa.

This is not to say that Florence fails; only that one must approach her differently from Mr. Dombey, and see her as a character drawn wholly within the bounds of her situation; to an extent that she, and the pathos of that situation, are one and the same. Two approaches have at least the merit of being included in Dickens' own. First, by beginning with Florence as a child of six years old, he is able to sustain our pity and tenderness for her as a child, even after she grows to be seventeen. Because we have seen her "pressing her small hands hard together" [46] as she timidly enters her father's room, or ragged and lost in the City streets, or clinging crying to Polly's skirts; because we have seen her through Paul's eyes, and Walter Gay's, we continue to think of her, when she is thirteen, fifteen, seventeen, as a child still. Her fear of Carker is of the same coloring as her fear of Good Mrs. Brown; Walter is her "brother"; flying from her home, she is once again the lost child. Not with the Esthers and Agneses or the child-wives, but with the children of Dickens' novels—Nell, and Oliver—should Florence be classed. There is one qualification. Though her feeling for Edith may begin as childish—the "new mama"—it becomes more mature. When Florence, now sixteen, is drawn into the orbit of the unhappy domestic situation, Dickens does not leave her wholly innocent and bewildered. He attempts to suggest a transition from childhood;[47] which is indeed necessary if he is to lead up to her flight from home—the sole occasion on which she is to act as well as suffer. But in the Dombey-Carker-Edith situation she is chiefly a pawn in the game; and the idiom in which it is conducted makes her less and not more alive.

The other approach is by way of the mysterious simplicities of fairy-tale, never far away in Dickens' work. Walter Gay, before ever he has

[44] Heroines are a sadly featureless class of well-intentioned young women in these days" (*Blackwood's*, April 1855, pp. 464-65).

[45] "It is a wonder how finely he discriminates them" (Henry James, "Anthony Trollope," in *Partial Portraits*, 1888).

[46] Chap. 3.

[47] Chaps. 43, 47. "Florence's reflections," which open the former chapter, formulate the only doubt, the only complexity of feeling, which is ever attributed to her.

seen Florence, is compared by his romantic uncle to Dick Whittington, who married his master's daughter;[48] when he finds her as a lost child in the City streets, he feels like Cinderella's prince, and also

> not to say like Richard Whittington—that is a tame comparison—but like Saint George of England, with the dragon lying dead before him.[49]

The "great dreary house" where Florence lives alone is like a "magic dwelling-place in magic story, shut up in the heart of a thick wood," with the ironwork of the doorway instead of "two dragon sentries"; but she "bloomed there, like the king's fair daughter in the story." [50] When she has taken refuge with Captain Cuttle, they are compared to "a wandering princess and a good monster in a story-book." [51] With these as pointers,[52] we can discern other, unstated, analogues: the recurring witch-figure (Good Mrs. Brown, and Mrs. Pipchin, who has a black cat), the helpful animal (Diogenes attacking Carker), and the comic knight and squire of the anti-masque (Toots and the Game Chicken). The "adult" characters, Mr. Dombey, Edith, and Carker, are clear of this tincture of romance, but the children (and the fools) not wholly so. It affects us more than we are aware; and it relates *Dombey* to the world of the earlier novels—*Oliver Twist, Nicholas Nickleby,* and *The Old Curiosity Shop.* If we can see Florence as the princess under a spell, or the unrecognized child of royal birth from whom a strange light shines, or even as Spenser's Una, we may come nearer Dickens' own intention. The presence of different modes in a narrative is something we must accept in his novels, as in poetic drama.

[In the omitted sections, chapters 6 and 20 are used to illustrate "the integration of structure" of the novel—ED.]

VIII

These two chapters have also illustrated Dickens' use of the railway, both as topical coloring[53] and as symbol, underlining the contemporary intention of the novel and its offered social commentary. (He must be

---

[48] Chap. 4.
[49] Chap. 6.
[50] Chap. 23.
[51] Chap. 49.
[52] And others; Paul is compared to a changeling, Mrs. Pipchin's establishment to an ogress's castle.
[53] Cf. chap. 15 (disappearance of Staggs's Gardens) and chap. 55 (death of Carker). The railway references supply the chronological limits, and define them as about 1835 to 1845.

one of the earliest Victorian writers to seize the railways imaginatively.)
There are other recurrent symbols, and one, more obviously "poetic" in
itself and in intention, emphasizes rather the values of the "other world"
—not material progress or menace, but the mystery surrounding human
life.

Through the whole novel echoes the sea; from the close of the first
chapter, at the death of Mrs. Dombey with Florence in her arms—

> Thus, clinging fast to that slight spar within her arms, the mother
> drifted out upon the dark and unknown sea that rolls round all the
> world—

to the very end, when "autumn days are shining, and on the sea-beach"
Florence and Mr. Dombey walk together, with another Florence and
Paul. In all its recurrences the sea is charged with its inevitable associations of separation and reunion, death and eternal life. Seen in their
full context, the mysterious voice of the waves and the "invisible country
far away" of Paul's fancy are not a passing effect produced to intensify
pathos; they are part of a larger design. In the Brighton chapters at
least two further passages[54] prepare for the "waves" and the "river that
is always running on" of his dying hours; a much later chapter recalls
them, not too explicitly—the last illness, death, and burial of Mrs.
Skewton at Brighton.[55] The daydreams of Solomon Gills, the supposed
drowning of Walter Gay, the wedding voyage of Walter and Florence,
all reinforce this covering symbol. Even though its verbal patterns are too
pronounced for modern taste, they are at least based upon a perception
of something profoundly natural, not factitious.

> And see the Children sport upon the shore,
> And hear the mighty waters rolling evermore.

This was a calculated means of unity; the sea—beyond what the actual
incidents call for—is part of the semi-allegorical cover-design, and dominates the wholly allegorical frontispiece; the key phrases are often noted
ahead in the notes for coming chapters. But it is a unity that includes
much variety of tone. The shop of the Wooden Midshipman, that land-
locked harbor past which "the human tide is still rolling westward," is
picturesque embroidery; Master Bitherstone's schemes for reaching
Bengal are more absurd than pathetic; and in one of Paul's "old-fash-
ioned" colloquies his sickly fancy is boldly juxtaposed to comedy. Paul is
gazing out of his window at Dr. Blimber's:

[54] Chaps. 12, 13.
[55] Chap. 41.

"I say!" cried Toots, speaking the moment he entered the room, lest he should forget it; "what do you think about?"

"Oh! I think about a great many things," replied Paul.

"Do you, though?" said Toots, appearing to consider that fact in itself surprising.

"If you had to die," said Paul, looking up into his face—

Mr. Toots started, and seemed much disturbed.

"—Don't you think you would rather die on a moonlight night, when the sky was quite clear, and the wind blowing, as it did last night?"

Mr. Toots said, looking doubtfully at Paul, and shaking his head, that he didn't know about that.

"Not blowing, at least," said Paul, "but sounding in the air like the sea sounds in the shells. . . . I got up and looked out. There was a boat over there, in the full light of the moon; a boat with a sail."

The child looked at him so steadfastly, and spoke so earnestly, that Mr. Toots, feeling himself called upon to say something about this boat, said "Smugglers." But with an impartial remembrance of there being two sides to every question, he added "or Preventive."

"A boat with a sail," repeated Paul, "in the full light of the moon. The sail like an arm, all silver. It went away into the distance, and what do you think it seemed to do as it moved with the waves?"

"Pitch," said Mr. Toots.

"It seemed to beckon," said the child, "to beckon me to come!" [56]

The boldness is justified. Toots's literalness serves to "distance" Paul's fancies, suggesting a degree of detachment in the author (though insufficient for the modern reader. It also emphasizes the irrational bond between these two uncommunicative personalities, and this queer association starts Toots off on his eccentric but firm career through the narrative. He owes his very relation to the action to Paul's death, and is continuously faithful to its memory, but nevertheless "sinks into the Silent Tomb with a gleam of joy." Toots alone would justify Dickens' new technique in comedy; always subordinated to the main design, he yet gives ample elbow-room for Dickens' "preposterous sense of the ridiculous" . . . "And all I have written is point." Speech after speech of Toots could be selected for its ludicrous but unerring penetration to the heart of a situation; "children and fools speak the truth." His schooldays remain his touchstone for experience—"I never saw such a world. It's a great deal worse than Blimber's." He carries their innocence through the novel, as well as their scars.

The child's view of the world is also a source of unity in this novel; it is more important than in *Oliver Twist* and *The Old Curiosity Shop*, though the children there are hero and heroine, and do not grow up.

[56] Chap. 12.

But the children now affect the adults more deeply; the childhood love of Paul and Florence haunts Mr. Dombey, from the first chapter to the last. And their glance is more piercing. After *Dombey,* or even while writing it, Dickens was ready to write *David Copperfield.* The fourteenth chapter, "Paul . . . goes home for the holidays," is almost in the first person; the single point of view is held throughout, with the child's lucid confusion. And since, for all his mystified intimations of mortality, he is still a normal child enjoying a party and being the center of attention, it carries more conviction than the deathbed scene. The one has the mark of recovered experience on it; Dickens, after all, had never died. The essence of his childhood experience is of course already, in Oliver and Nell—the hapless, exploited child, tossed from place to place and from person to person. But in *Dombey* he began to use specific experience, and even to use it closely. Actual places and persons now appear, hardly disguised; Camden Town, and at least one of its denizens.

> I hope you will like Mrs. Pipchin's establishment. It is from the life, and I was there—I don't suppose I was eight years old; but I remember it all as well, and certainly understood it as well, as I do now. We should be devilish sharp in what we do to children.[57]

The child's-eye view, bewildered, yet implacable, is impressed upon the Brighton chapters, and especially on Mrs. Pipchin and her household. Perhaps some plausibility is here sacrificed; at least it needed a little manipulation to adjust this particular personal reminiscence to the much more prosperous Dombey family. The landlady takes a few steps up the social scale; her establishment is not in Camden Town, she has seen the better days which Susan Nipper pitied for having seen her, and no unpaid-for natural children[58] are mentioned among her boarders. The rest is evidently "from the life"; hence Dickens' bitter disappointment over the illustration.[59] Mrs. Roylance-Pipchin was the acknowledged breach in the wall that Dickens had built between himself and the darkest days of his childhood—a wall that is apt to crumble as middle age approaches, especially for a parent.[60] In the very letter

[57] Forster, vi, 2; cf. i, 2, where Mrs. Roylance is described as "a reduced old lady, long known to our family, in Little-College-street, Camden Town, who took children in to board, and had once done so at Brighton. . . ." Charles was lodged there while working at the blacking factory; later, on leaving the Marshalsea, the whole family went to live there for a time.

[58] i, 2.

[59] vi, 2; letter of November 1846.

[60] By 1846 Dickens had two daughters and four sons. Two of his sons were at a school where the master's daughter was "a thorough classical scholar and assisted him," which "suggested the Blimber notion" (Introduction by Charles Dickens, Jr., to edition of 1892).

which identifies Mrs. Pipchin, he first broaches the notion of writing the story of his childhood; he wrote it in 1848, and then wove it into *David Copperfield*. There were other events to awaken recollections; in 1846-47 Dickens' beloved elder sister Fanny had entered her last illness;[61] (the "Child's Dream of a Star," [62] avowedly written with her in mind, has its parallel in the relation of Paul and Florence). And he had as "a very young child" fancied the moonlight on the water as the pathway to heaven.[63]

Dombey and Son is also a plea for children; generally, for their right to be treated as individuals, instead of appendages and hindrances to parental ambition, and particularly, against the wrongs done to them in the name of education. It is a measure of this novel's largeness of scope that it is not often thought of as an exposure of misconceived schooling; but it is not less so than *Nicholas Nickleby* and penetrates into more protected places.[64] While forwarding the general design Dickens has shown, incidentally and half-humorously but unmistakably, what is wrong with Dr. Blimber's academy; what the plight of the cherished rich man's child [65] has in common with that of the foundling parish boy. Mr. Dombey's other educational mistake[66] is more briefly but more angrily[67] exposed: the committing of Robin Toodle to the mercies of the Charitable Grinders. And here he can venture to admit the twisting of a character by miseducation;[68] if not beyond repair,

[61] Forster, v, 7. She was the wife of Henry Burnett, and had two sons, one of whom, an invalid, is said to have been Paul's original. (The earliest evidence of this tradition seems to be in the recollections of a Manchester minister who had known them well: James Griffin, *Memories of the Past*, 1883, p. 209.)

[62] In the first number of *Household Words*, 30 March 1850. Forster links it with Fanny (vi, 4, last paragraph).

[63] *American Notes* (1842), chap. 16.

[64] This was recognized by several contemporary reviewers (e.g., *Westminster Review*, XLVII, April 1847) and by Edward Fitzgerald in a letter to Thackeray: "a very fine account of the overcramming educational system, worth whole volumes of essays on the subject. . . . The boy who talks Greek in his sleep seems to me as terrible as Macbeth" (Thackeray's *Letters*, ed. Gordon N. Ray, Cambridge, Mass., 1945-46, II, 226).

[65] He defines the limits of Mr. Dombey's obtuseness, however, by explicitly avoiding the public school; and has indicated his view of Sandhurst through Major Bagstock's grisly reminiscences (chap. 10).

[66] Another novelist might have made something of the complete neglect of Florence's education!

[67] Chap. 6 and chap. 20; and especially the last paragraph of chap. 38, given salience by being placed at the end of a number. Gissing calls Rob "one of the most important of Dickens's social studies" (*Charles Dickens*, 1898, p. 208).

[68] Dickens was growing interested in gradual moral deterioration. His first design was to show Walter Gay going wrong; counselled against it by Forster, he remembered it in Richard Carstone, and Pip.

since, restored to his parent and Miss Tox at the close, Rob is beginning
to reform.

But Dickens is not here concerned to attack specific abuses. He is not
so optimistic. Insofar as *Dombey and Son* is a "social" novel, its prevailing mood is one of deep disquiet about contemporary values, a suggestion that more is amiss with them than mere exposure and reform can
hope to touch. Dickens had formerly presented the wealthy man as a
benevolent fairy god-mother or Father Christmas, in Mr. Brownlow,
Abel Garland, or the Cheeryble brothers. There would be no place for
such characters here. *Dombey and Son* suggests the gloom of wealth
(more strongly even than Thackeray was to do) and its capacity to petrify
or poison human relations, in the family and in society. "Papa, what's
money? . . . It isn't cruel, is it?" Wealth is an evil, corrupting the heart;
prosperity a house built on sand. The moral of the "valuelessness in
themselves of the greatest earthly possessions" commended by one
critic[69] and patent to all readers, is inwoven with the main design. The
potential cruelty, the emptiness, the cold isolation of a Mammonist
society is repeatedly emphasized: but rarely in a didactic way. Dickens
is not writing a tract for the times, even at the distance of allegory.
There is no overt social reference in his draft of his general design, in
his working notes, or his Preface; but in a letter written when he was
halfway through he said:

> There is a great deal to do—one or two things among the rest that
> society will not be the worse, I hope, for thinking about a little.[70]

As we have seen, these "one or two things" become a natural part of
the narrative; still more effectively, they become part of the picture.
House and firm together dominate the story, and the house, scenically
central,[71] is also an emblem of the social theme.

The social intentions of the novel are pointed by the title, and the
status of the hero. He is Palmerston's "princely merchant in his counting
house"; a character "which could only be produced in a country whose
commerce embraces the globe, whose merchants are potentates." [72]

---

[69] *English Review* (December 1848), p. 271; and cf. *Christian Remembrancer* (December 1847), p. 347.

[70] Letter to Dr. Hodgson, 4 June 1847; *Letters*, II, 28.

[71] Although there is much variety (Brighton, Leamington, Dijon outside London;
Leadenhall St., Princess's Place, Brig Place, Brook St., Staggs's Gardens, and the
Carker suburb within London), over a third of the chapters are set or partly set in
the Dombey house, and these are among the "high-lights" of the novel, such as
chaps. 3, 18, 23, 28, 36, 40, 43, 47-48, 51, 59.

[72] Taine, *History of English Literature* (Paris, 1863-64), trans. H. Van Laun, 1871,
ed. 2; Book V, ch. i, § 3. ii.

Such a merchant-prince no longer, of course, lived in the City, nor
even, like Mr. Osborne and Mr. Sedley, near its borders in Russell
Square. He has followed the tide of fashion to "the shady side of a tall,
dark, dreadfully genteel street in the region between Portland-place
and Bryanstone-square" . . .[73] "a house of dismal state." We come to
know all its appurtenances: the lustres, chandeliers, and marble floors,
its statuary, its bookcase which "repudiated all familiarities," "glazed
and locked." The changing state of the house marks the movement of
the narrative; we see its dreary magnificence abandoned to neglect in
the months of Florence's solitude,[74] then garishly revived in preparation
for the second marriage,[75] stripped by the auctioneers—"the house is a
ruin, and the rats fly from it," and lastly

> frowning like a dark mute on the street; baulking any nearer inquiries
> with the staring announcement that the lease of this desirable Family
> Mansion was to be disposed of.[76]

> The dreadful spectacle of that sad House of Pride.[77]

Compared with this distinctness and load of significance, the firm of
"Dombey and Son," "wholesale, retail, and for exportation" is dimly
treated;[78] it is the off-stage source of wealth, rather than the hub of
activity, and its export trade is distinguished only by the dispatch of
Walter Gay. It lives rather through the characters it involves. Firm and
household are used skillfully to define the social pyramid, from the
loftiest to the lowest, from Mr. Carker the Manager down to Mr. Perch
the messenger, while the servants are "carried through"—Dickens' own
phrase—from beginning to end.[79] Every family event has its reverbera-
tions in the humming chorus of the servants' hall—"misfortune in the
family without feasting in these lower regions couldn't be"; below Susan,
and Polly, and (later) Mrs. Pipchin, is ranged the household hierarchy,
from the lugubrious Towlinson to the young kitchenmaid in black
stockings whose single recorded contribution marks the completeness
of the collapse—"Supposing the wages shouldn't be paid!" [80] More faintly

[73] And therefore well within the purview of Devonshire Terrace (opposite York
Gate), which was Dickens' home when in London from 1839 to 1850.

[74] Chap. 23.

[75] Chap. 28.

[76] Chap. 59.

[77] *The Faerie Queene,* I, v, 53.

[78] The "exposition" in chap. 4 (through Walter Gay) and the description in chap.
13 stand almost alone; in the office scenes the details are never either sharply visual
or symbolic.

[79] Note in plan of No. X; cf. chap. 31. But this had begun much earlier; see the
openings of chaps. 3 and 18.

[80] Chap. 59.

indicated, the clerk's chorus is set in apposition to the servants' chorus
in the closing act.[81] Other houses, and one other business, contribute
their variations on the theme; one, the town house of Cousin Feenix,
confirms the dreariness and heartlessness of wealth with its "black hatch-
ments of pictures," its "dark-brown dining-room, which no confectioner
can brighten up, let him garnish the exhausted negroes with as many
flowers and love-knots as he will";[82] others (the Toodles', the Wooden
Midshipman) mark a contrast, with their cosy contrivances of ingenious
frugality. Of these, the Wooden Midshipman is used with a twofold
purpose of contrast: it is shown not only as a humble source of loyalty
and affection, but as an outmoded retail concern representing a super-
seded past. No customers come to it—as Sol Gills laments, in almost
too pointed exposition, "Competition, competition—new invention,
new invention . . . the world's gone past me." (So much for the England
of thirty years before—"when that uniform was worn . . . fortunes
were to be made.") [83] This pocket of the past, in "the immediate vicinity"
of the offices of Dombey and Son, serves to emphasize the modernity and
prosperity of the firm. (At the close, when the firm has fallen, "Mr.
Gills's old investments are coming out wonderfully" and he was after all
not "behind the time" but "a little before it";[84] a consummation perhaps wisely left vague.) One other recurrent "place" deepens the contemporary picture. Four phases of the narrative are punctuated by scenes
in the same church: Paul's christening, his funeral, Edith's wedding, and
Florence's visit to Paul's grave before her own wedding.[85] In three of
these the physical atmosphere is defined, in terms of chill and dust and
wheeziness, with choric commentary from the two dried-up professional
ministrants, Mr. Sownds and Mrs. Miff. Dickens spares nothing in his
suggestion of a soulless society; he seems to point at house, firm, and
church as three hollow shells of the established order.

Across the social picture are ruled the ruthless lines of the new order,
symbolized in the railway. It links high and low, devastates Camden
Town, uproots Staggs's Gardens, provides employment for Mr. Toodle,
bears Mr. Dombey from grim past to grimmer future, and finally
obliterates Carker. Its appearance on each of the four carefully spaced
and placed occasions[86] is emphasized by a volcanic upsurge in the
style, by description much overflowing its narrative function. In these

[81] Chaps. 51, 58, 59.
[82] Chap. 31.
[83] Chap. 4.
[84] Chap. 62.
[85] Chaps. 5, 18 (very briefly touched), 31, and 57.
[86] Chaps. 6, 15, 20, 55.

descriptions may be discerned the fascination of the new as well as the horror of the strange; but the tone is mainly that of dread. Twice the railway is used to highlight the darker thoughts of hero and villain, thoughts of fear and hate and death.[87] The train is seen only as destructive, ruthless, an "impetuous monster," a "fiery devil." There is no suggestion of hope, of social progress. This coloring of gloom and horror may derive from the overriding mood of the novel; it may be a picturesque reflection of contemporary doubts; but more probably, from the evidence of the later novels, it represents a persistent shade in Dickens' own social view, which contains at least as much pessimism as optimism, and always more of the visionary than of the reformer.

The social criticism in *Dombey and Son* cannot be abstracted from the novel, and even such disengaging as is attempted here perhaps distorts it. It is pervasive, unformulated; not documentary in origin or usefulness; no purposeful journeys or reading of newspaper reports lie behind it, and it is not a convenient source for social historians. Partly for this reason, that it is inseparable, it assists instead of disturbing the firm unity of the design. It is part of the "Idea of the world" which protects Dickens from being "prevailed over by the world's multitudinousness." [88]

[87] Chaps. 20 and 55.
[88] *Letters of Matthew Arnold to Arthur Hugh Clough*, ed. H. F. Lowry (1932), p. 97; letter of 1848.

Chance and Design
in *Bleak House*

by W. J. Harvey

Two approaches to *Bleak House* have been adequately explored. These offer a view of the novel as a social document and as a work of dense, intricate, and powerful symbolism. I wish rather to consider the larger structural properties of the book. This may throw light on the transmutation of social concern into art and may even help us to test the validity of symbolic interpretation. *Bleak House* is so complicated that I shall examine only two aspects of its elaborate architecture. These are Dickens' use of double narration and his use of coincidence.

First, however, I should make explicit the general critical thesis from which this interest stems. Dickens has often been likened to a Jacobean dramatist both for his vivid, exuberant, "poetic" use of language and for his methods of characterization. There is a third point of likeness. Critics frequently discuss Jacobean plays in terms of "episodic intensification." By this they mean the impulse to exploit to the full possibilities of any particular scene, situation, or action without too much regard for the relevance of such local intensities to the total work of art. Clearly much of Dickens' fiction is of the same order. To admit this is to risk the displeasure of much modern criticism of fiction which, largely deriving from James, lays great stress on the organic unity of the novel and demands that no part shall be allowed autonomy if this threatens the integrity of the whole.

We can defend in four ways the novel of episodic intensification from such criticism. First, we may admit that in some cases the work may fail as a whole while succeeding in some part. The result may be a dead or crippled work which yet intermittently achieves the vigor of a masterpiece. We may admire what we can and regret the waste of so

"Chance and Design in *Bleak House*" by W. J. Harvey. From *Dickens and the Twentieth Century*, ed. John Gross and Gabriel Pearson (London: Routledge & Kegan Paul, Ltd., 1962; Toronto: University of Toronto Press, 1962). Copyright © 1962 by Routledge & Kegan Paul, Ltd. Reprinted by permission of the publishers.

much else. This, I think, is true of *Barnaby Rudge*. Second, we may deny the fiat of organic unity and maintain that in *some* cases a novel achieves no more than episodic intensification and yet possesses so much vitality that we are content simply to accept its greatness. In James's terms there must be room in the house of fiction for such "loose, baggy monsters." With much less certainty I would place *Pickwick Papers* in this category. Third, we may accept the idea of organic unity and yet maintain that by its standards Dickens' novels are entirely successful. Sometimes he achieves an economy, firmness, and clean-cut clarity of control that can only be called classical. This is surely true of *Great Expectations*. Finally, we may accept the idea of organic unity but argue that the criteria by which we judge its presence or absence have been too narrowly conceived and that there exist conventions and methods of organization which are non-Jamesian but still appropriate and effective. (James, unlike some more recent critics, admitted as much.) *Bleak House* is here a relevant example. Indeed, I would say that one of the reasons for its greatness is the extreme tension set up between the centrifugal vigor of its parts and the centripetal demands of the whole. It is a tension between the impulse to intensify each local detail or particular episode and the impulse to subordinate, arrange, and discipline. The final impression is one of immense and potentially anarchic energy being brought—but only just—under control. The fact that the equipoise between part and whole is so precariously maintained is in itself a tribute to the energy here being harnessed.

How well does an examination of the novel's structure support this general view? *Bleak House* is for Dickens a unique and elaborate experiment in narration and plot composition. It is divided into two intermingled and roughly concurrent stories; Esther Summerson's first-person narrative and an omniscient narrative told consistently in the historic present. The latter takes up thirty-four chapters; Esther has one less. Her story, however, occupies a good deal more than half the novel. The reader who checks the distribution of these two narratives against the original part issues will hardly discern any significant pattern or correlation. Most parts contain a mixture of the two stories; one part is narrated entirely by Esther and five parts entirely by the omniscient author. Such a check does, however, support the view that Dickens did not, as is sometimes supposed, use serial publication in the interest of crude suspense. A sensational novelist, for example, might well have ended a part issue with chapter 31; Dickens subdues the drama by adding another chapter to the number. The obvious exception to this only proves the rule; in the final double number the suspense of Bucket's search for Lady Dedlock is heightened by cutting back to the omniscient narrative and the stricken Sir Leicester. In general, however, Dickens' control of the double narrative is far richer and subtler than this. Through this technique, as I shall try to show, he controls the immense, turbulent, and potentially confusing material of his novel. Indeed, the narrative method seems to me to be part of the very substance of *Bleak House,* expressive of what, in the widest and deepest sense, the novel is about.

Let us first examine the structural functions of Esther Summerson and her narrative. Esther has generally been dismissed as insipid, one of Dickens' flat, non-comic good characters, innocent of imaginative life, more of a moral signpost than a person. Even if we accept this general judgment, we may still find good reasons why Dickens had necessarily to sacrifice vitality or complexity here in order to elaborate or intensify other parts of his novel. If Dickens, far from failing to create a lively Esther, is deliberately suppressing his natural exuberance in order to create a flat Esther, then we may properly consider one of Esther's functions to be that of a brake, controlling the runaway tendency of Dickens' imagination—controlling, in other words, the impulse to episodic intensification.

Can we possibly accept this view? The contrasting styles of the two narratives, while they offer the reader relief and variety, also seem to me evidence of Dickens' control in making Esther what she is, even at the risk of insipidity and dullness. The omniscient style has all the liveliness, fantastication, and poetic density of texture that we typically associate with Dickens. Esther's narrative is plain, matter-of-fact, conscientiously plodding. Only very rarely does her style slip and allow us to glimpse Dickens guiding her pen—as when, for instance, she observes "Mr. Kenge, standing with his back to the fire, and casting his eyes over the dusty hearthrug as if it were Mrs. Jellyby's biography" (chap. 4) or when, as Turveydrop bows to her, she could "almost believe I saw creases come into the white of his eyes" (chap. 14). Here one may glimpse Dickens chafing at his self-imposed discipline. Such moments apart, any stylistic vivacity or idiosyncrasy in Esther's prose comes from the oddities and foibles of other characters. Dickens imagines them; Esther merely reports them. Even when, at moments of emotional stress, her prose strays into the purple patch one still feels that this is the rhetoric of an amateur, not to be compared, for instance, with the controlled crescendo of Jo's death. Similarly, whenever the straightforward flow of Esther's narrative falters—as in her over-casual mention of Allan Woodcourt at the end of chapter 14—we prefer to see this as appropriate to her character rather than to spot Dickens signaling a new relationship to us behind her back. That, of course, is precisely what he is doing, but the disguise of style persuades us to focus on Esther and not on her creator. (There is, I think, a corresponding and quite remarkable impersonality about the omniscient narrative. The general impression is of a vast, collective choric voice brilliantly mimicking the varied life it describes, yet able to generalize and comment without lapsing into the idiom of one man, of Dickens himself. Obviously the style exploits and manipulates our sympathies; yet surprisingly rarely do we feel that Dickens is directly button-holing us.)

As I have said, the two narratives are *roughly* concurrent. Deliberately so; Dickens juggles the two chronologies by keeping the details sufficiently vague. Only rarely do we feel any awkwardness in this temporal matching together and any obvious discontinuity generally has a specific narrative or dramatic point. Esther's tale, taken in isolation, plods forward in the simplest kind of sequence. Yet, being autobiographical, it is retrospective and was written, so we are told at the very end, seven years after the main events. This simplicity is rarely disturbed; only occasionally does Esther sound the note of "If I had known then what I know now"; only occasionally does she throw an anticipatory light forward into the shadowy future of her tale as, for example, she does at the end of chapter 37. The reason is that, despite the retrospective nature of her story, Esther must *seem* to be living in a dramatic present, ignorant of the plot's ramifications. Dickens is *really* omniscient in the other narrative; god-like he surveys time as though it were an eternal present and Esther must seem to belong to that present. It is a convention most readers readily accept.

In what ways does Esther's tale throw light on its teller? During his later period Dickens showed considerable interest in the possibilities of the first-person narrative. In some cases—*David Copperfield, Great Expectations*—the adult narrator judges, implicitly or explicitly, his growth toward maturity. Esther is clearly not in this category; she swiftly advances from child to woman and scarcely changes at all. We feel that she was "born old"—a feeling reflected in the nicknames given her, though in fact she is little older than Ada Clare. On the other hand, she cannot be classed with Miss Wade, of *Little Dorrit,* whose story is taken by some critics as an early exercise in that kind of point-of-view technique which dramatizes a limited or crippled consciousness so that what is conveyed to the reader differs radically from the intention of the narrator. Clearly, we are meant to take Esther on trust. If what she tells us is wrong or limited this signifies no moral blind spot in her, no flaw in her sensibility, but only her necessary innocence of the full ramifications of the plot. Dickens' treatment of Esther is devoid of irony. We have only to imagine what narrative would have resulted if the teller had been Skimpole—or even Richard Carstone—to see that Esther's responses, attitudes, and actions are never qualified or criticized. She is, in short, thoroughly idealized.

One result of the idealizing process is the static nature of Esther's character, the essentials of which we quickly come to know. These never change; her story merely exhibits them in a variety of situations in which she is generally the patient rather than the agent. That is, Esther *does* very little in the sense of initiating a chain of actions by a deliberate choice. Things are done to her or because of her rather than by her. Devastating things happen to Esther from the moment of her birth, but she generally emerges with her usual placidity and acceptance of duty. Indeed, at times Dickens takes care to subdue the effect on the reader of these crises through which Esther as patient must pass. The chapter which deals, for example, with the recognition scene between Esther and her mother closes in fact with Esther's reunion with Ada. The curious thing is the feelings aroused by the Esther-Ada relationship seem more intense—and intensely rendered—than those aroused by the Esther-Lady Dedlock encounter.

Esther then is static, consistent, passive. She is also good. The difficulties of combining these qualities to produce a compelling character are so immense that we should wonder not that Dickens fails, but that his failure is so slight. Still, he does fail. The exigencies of the narrative force him to reveal Esther's goodness in a coy and repellent manner; she is, for instance, continually imputing to others qualities which the author transparently wishes us to transfer to her. Esther's goodness is acceptable when she is least conscious of its effects radiating out to impinge on others. Similarly, her narrative is most acceptable when she is pushed from the center of the stage by the typical inhabitants of the Dickens world. Happily this is usually so. In other words, Dickens has to reconcile in Esther the demands of a narrator and a main character and he chooses to subdue Esther as a character in the interests of her narrative function. We do not, so to speak, look *at* Esther; we look *through* her at the teeming Dickensian world. This viewpoint is no Jamesian dramatization of a particular consciousness; Esther is as lucid and neutral as a clear window. We look through at a human landscape but we are not, as with James, constantly aware that the window is limited by its frame or that it has a scratch here and an opaque spot there. The penalty Dickens pays for this is the insipidity of Esther's character. But then, *Bleak House* is a thickly populated novel; each character claims his own share of attention and all are connected by a complicated series of interlocking actions. There is no single center, no Jamesian *disponible*; rather we have a complex field of force, of inter-acting stresses and strains. Given this complication it would be too much to ask of the reader that he concentrate on the perceiver as well as the perceived. Were Esther to be complicated the novel would have to be correspondingly simplified and the Dickens world depopulated. Who would wish it so? If the real subject-matter of a novel is a subtly dramatized consciousness then the objects of that consciousness will tend to the sparse refinements of the closet drama. Dickens is the opposite of this; he is to Shakespeare as James is to Racine.

While this, I hope, explains the necessary limitations of Esther's character, it only pushes the real problem one stage farther back. Why was it necessary to have a narrator of this kind at all? Any adequate an-swer must also take into account the omniscient narrative as well. The two narratives are the systole and diastole of the novel and between them they produce the distinctive effect of *Bleak House*; something that I can only call, in a crudely impressionistic manner, the effect of *pulsa-tion,* of constant expansion and contraction, radiation and convergence.

The famous first chapter of *Bleak House* has had more than its fair share of critical attention; at the risk of tedium, therefore, I wish to isolate two striking features of Dickens' method. The omniscient eye which surveys the scene is like the lens of a film camera in its mobility. It may encompass a large panoramic view or, within a sentence, it may swoop down to a close scrutiny of some character or local detail. Closely related to this mobility is the constant expansion and contraction from the omniscient eye to Esther's single viewpoint. Closely related again is the constant expansion and contraction of the total narrative; now con-centrating at great length on some episode, now hustling the plot along with a rapid parade of characters. Dickens' narrative skill is nowhere more evident than in his control of tempo.

All this I mean by *pulsation*. But chapter 1 displays yet another re-lated effect. The scene contracts to the Court of Chancery at the heart of the fog but suddenly this process is reversed; Chancery monstrously expands to encompass the whole country:

> This is the Court of Chancery; which has its decaying houses and its blighted lands in every shire; which has its worn-out lunatic in every madhouse, and its dead in every churchyard. . . .

The heart of Chancery in this respect is Tom-All-Alone's, the breed-ing-ground of disease (again the radiation of infection). The two are appropriately linked for Chancery *is* a disease and is constantly described in these terms.

This theme is, of course, abundantly worked out in the novel—in Miss Flite, in Gridley, and above all, in Richard Carstone. The idea of corruption radiating out from a rotten center (Chancery *and* Tom-All-Alone's) is reflected, in geographical terms, in the constant to-and-fro movement between London, Bleak House, and Chesney Wold. But this idea is counterpointed, in plot terms, by the sense one has of convergence, especially the sense of something closing-in on Lady Dedlock. Geography and plot coalesce in the final constriction of the chase and the discovery of Lady Dedlock dead near her lover's tomb.

This pulsation, this interaction of radiation and convergence, is also temporal. The case of Jarndyce and Jarndyce does not merely fan out in the present to enmesh innocent and remote people; it also has a terrible history:

> Innumerable children have been born into the cause; innumerable young people have married into it; innumerable old people have died out of it. Scores of persons have deliriously found themselves made parties in Jarndyce and Jarndyce, without knowing how or why; whole families have inherited legendary hatreds with the suit.

Diverse pressures from the past converge to mold the present; Jarndyce and Jarndyce bears down on Richard Carstone; the past catches up with Esther and finally with her mother. This temporal convergence is reflected in the structure of the novel as a whole and locally, in its parts. Thus the first chapter given to Esther (chap. 3) quickly brings us from her childhood back to the dramatic present already described in the omniscient first chapter. Sometimes the dramatic present is illuminated by a shaft driven back into the past; thus both Boythorn and Miss Barbary are in some sense enlarged by the revelation of their abortive love long ago. Or again, the dramatic present will be left unexplained until time has passed and many pages have been turned; thus, on a small scale, the mystery of Jo's disappearance from Bleak House or, on a large scale, Bucket's uncovering of Tulkinghorn's murderess.

Granted the extremely complicated tangle of effects I have labeled *pulsation,* the desirability of a simple, lucid, straightforward narrative such as Esther's should be obvious. It offers us stability, a point of rest in a flickering and bewildering world, the promise of some guidance through the labyrinth. The usual novel may be compared to a pebble thrown into a pool; we watch the ripples spread. But in *Bleak House* Dickens has thrown in a whole handful of pebbles and what we have to discern is the immensely complicated tracery of half-a-dozen circles expanding, meeting, interacting. Esther—to change the metaphor—has the stability of a gyroscope; by her we chart our way.

She is, of course, much more than this. She is, as well, a moral touchstone; her judgments are rarely emphatic but we accept them. She can see Richard more clearly than Ada; through her Skimpole is revealed in his true colors and the Growlery becomes a sign of Jarndyce's obtuseness. She is also the known constant by which we judge all the other variables of character. Through her we can see the horrifyingly vivid notation of decay and infection that signals the slow process of Richard's destruction. (Among other things, the intertwining of the two narratives enables Dickens drastically to foreshorten and mold the *apparent* time sequence here.) Again, by her consistency Esther contributes to the wonderfully skillful characterization of Sir Leicester and Guppy, who change by fits and starts throughout the novel. Because these characters demand very different reactions from us at different times we impute complexity and development to them. In fact they are not so much complex as discontinuous. Dickens' art lies in masking this discontinuity and Esther in large part provides a convincing façade; because she is a simple unity we are conjured into believing that the heterogeneity of Guppy or Sir Leicester is a unified complexity.

Finally—and perhaps most important—by intertwining the two narratives Dickens compels us to a double vision of the teeming, fantastic world of *Bleak House*. We—and Esther—are within; we—and the omniscient author—are outside. This double perspective forces us as readers to make connections which because *we* make them have more validity than if Dickens had made them for us. The most crucial instance is Esther's ignorance of so much that surrounds her. What she sees she sees clearly; but she cannot see more than a fraction of the whole. In this she is not alone; one of the triumphs of the novel is the delicacy with which Dickens handles the knowledge, suspicions, guesses, and mistakes of the various characters. Some of them are limited to one or other of the narrative streams; Esther is never seen by the omniscient eye nor does Tulkinghorn ever appear personally in Esther's narrative. This corresponds to their limited knowledge; Tulkinghorn, for all his plotting, never knows of Esther's relation to Lady Dedlock while there is no substantial evidence that Esther knows anything of her father until after her mother's death.

Granted this, the opportunities for dramatic irony are clearly enormous and it is to Dickens' credit as an artist that with great tact he refuses many of the chances for irony offered by the interlocking narratives. How close—all unknowing—is Esther to meeting her father during her first visit to Krook's? Yet we scarcely perceive this, even on a re-reading of the novel. A lesser artist would have wrung dry the irony of such an incident but Dickens is sound in his refusal to do so. For the novel, as it stands, is so taut, so potentially explosive that to expatiate on, or to underline, its implications would make it quite intolerable. Of course the irony is there but it is kept latent and, so to speak, sub-critical; it does not explode in the reader's conscious attention. In nothing is Dickens' virtuosity more astonishing than in his control of that aspect of the novel which, together with the double narrative, determines its structure and the quality of its irony. I mean his use of coincidence.

I cannot think of another novel in which coincidence plays so essential a part as it does in *Bleak House*; Hardy's tragedies of circumstance are simple and crude by comparison. As an example we may briefly recall chapter 24. Richard has decided to join the army and is taking sword-lessons; his teacher turns out to be George Rouncewell, who is thus brought into contact with Esther and Jarndyce. Thus the various narrative strands converging on George (the reader particularly remembers Smallweed and his interest in Captain Hawdon) begin to tangle with the already tangled strands of Esther's past and future. (This is gently hinted by George's bewilderment at the familiarity of Esther's face; the reader has already encountered something like this when Guppy connected Esther with Lady Dedlock's portrait.) One coincidental connection, acknowledged as such by Esther, is almost immediately made—George's knowledge of Gridley. Esther then goes to the Court of Chancery; coincidentally Guppy is there with Mrs. Chadband, who turns out to be the Mrs. Rachael of Esther's childhood. George appears with a message from Gridley to Miss Flite; providentially Esther is there to introduce them. They go to George's shooting gallery and by chance Bucket turns up at this moment to arrest Gridley on a warrant from Tulkinghorn (one of the few times he is ever mentioned in Esther's narrative); thus Bucket meets Esther for the first time—an important detail since when much later Bucket finds Esther's handkerchief in Lady Dedlock's room he has to ask George where Esther lives in London in order that she may help him search for her mother. In the space of ten pages, then, several chance encounters—most of some consequence for the future of the novel—casually occur.

So casually, indeed, are these quite typical coincidences insinuated into the novel that I doubt whether any relaxed, non-analytical reader would recognize more than one of them (probably Mrs. Rachael-Mrs. Chadband) as coincidental. Certainly one does not feel that the characters are thereby made puppets or that the elaborate plot creaks with obvious contrivance; one accepts coincidence as a natural part of the *Bleak House* world. There are exceptions; Sir Leicester's visit to Jarndyce in chapter 43 perhaps reveals Dickens in the act of contriving and faking. But by and large, coincidence is to the microcosm of the novel what the law of gravity is to the macrocosm of the real world. We accept both as natural laws and are largely unconscious of their operation.

Only very detailed analysis could properly show how Dickens attains this end. But we may note four main factors combining to merge the various coincidences into the very fabric of the story. The first of these is the interlocking twin narratives we have already examined. Many of the coincidences Esther takes for granted because she is ignorant of something of which the omniscient narrative informs us. But because she takes them for granted and because we trust her, therefore we tend to take them for granted too.

Second, Dickens *does* combine coincidence with a good deal of naturalistic, rational explanation. Clearly in a complex novel dealing so centrally with the consequences, anticipated or unforeseen, of human actions some such explanation will be needed. Dickens had failed badly when faced with this problem early in his career. In *Oliver Twist*, after the mystery of a powerfully imagined Fagin we are offered in an undigested lump the tangled motivations of a feebly imagined Monks. In *Bleak House,* by contrast, such explanations are carefully broken-up, placed, and distributed. Frequently they occur long after the event to be explained has taken place; thus we rarely bother to check their validity. We are never offered too much explanation at one time; thus the Esther-Lady Dedlock relationship is cleared up relatively early. (By this stroke Dickens achieves many ends. He avoids cluttering up the end of the novel with too many climaxes and he misdirects the reader who thinks that the essential mystery is now cleared up and is thus unprepared for the subsequent mystery of Tulkinghorn's death. A similar tactic is central to *Our Mutual Friend* where the reader, having solved the problem of the hero's identity, is liable to take Boffin's pretence at its face value.)

Moreover, what seems coincidental is often the result of plotting and *Bleak House* is full of conspirators. The interesting thing to notice is how often their plots go astray, how often what man proposes is thwarted by the bias of chance, of unforeseen circumstances, of the merely random. No one, not even Bucket, is infallible. Partly because of this, because plotters, plots, and coincidences often cancel each other out, we accept Dickens' scheme of things. Coincidence is not the malign symptom of some metaphysical destiny inexorably hunting down a selected victim; we do not rebel because we feel Fate is unfair; chance reigns with fine impartiality over all.

Finally and paradoxically, it is because coincidence is so extensive in the novel that it becomes so natural. It seems true because it is congruent with the rest of the book. But more important, in the last analysis it expresses a truth about the real world. It expresses our sense that real life blends the casual and the causal, that things are connected and contingent, patterned and random, that we are both free and determined. This sense of life's contradictions is a common sense and we take commonsensically that which, if examined closely, would turn into wonder and mystery, into a world of speculation, dense with *ifs* and *perhapses* and *might-have-beens*. We walk in the real world as Esther walks, through a labyrinth of the conditional; we are surrounded, as she is, by other lives and other narratives; what seems to us a straight path is nothing but a series of crossroads.

So much is true and trite. Yet Dickens refreshed this cliché, expressed it with such imaginative force that it seems an original and profound intuition about the nature of things. At the heart of his work—beneath his immediate topical or satiric concerns—lie a number of such intuitions, darkly entangled with a number of private obsessions. Together they express something like Dickens' vision of the universal human predicament or, to be more modest and less portentous, the predicament of man in modern industrial society. Such, for instance, is his sense of the fragmented individual. One remembers here the sharp division between public and private, the official and the person; one recalls Bucket the person and Bucket the detective, Vholes the lawyer and Vholes as parent and child. The logical conclusion of this is the happy dichotomy of Wemmick in *Great Expectations*. In a different vein, one remembers Sir Leicester, decent enough but hopelessly locked within the prison of his class and caste; one remembers Lady Dedlock masking her guilt and suffering by a frozen disdain. As with the individual so with the fragmented society; what can the Boodles know of Jo or Jenny when Snagsby, who lives not far away, can be appalled by the unfamiliar hell of Tom-All-Alone's? Against isolation and alienation Dickens poses connection—whether of love, charity, and responsibility or the sinister negations of these, embodied in the infections of Chancery and the slums.

Yet even such basic intuitions as these depend upon that sense of the world I have tried to describe. The most explicit expression of this sense occurs in Forster's frequently quoted report of Dickens:

On the coincidences, resemblances, and surprises of life Dickens liked especially to dwell, and few things moved his fancy so pleasantly. The world, he would say, was so much smaller than we thought it; we were all so connected by fate without knowing it and people supposed to be far apart were so constantly elbowing each other; and tomorrow bore so close a resemblance to nothing half so much as yesterday.

This theme is heavily stressed in the opening chapters of *Little Dorrit*; in *Bleak House* it is given only brief and oblique expression by several of the characters. But it is implicit in the whole structure of the novel. Through the double narrative Dickens refracts, reflects, varies, distorts, reiterates his major themes, and the disturbing resonance thus set up is expressive of his deepest sense of what life is like.

"Trust in nothing but Providence and your own efforts. Never separate the two," Jarndyce tells Richard Carstone and unconsciously sums up this deepest sense of the intricate meshing of chance and choice in the affairs of men. Dickens recognized, of course, that chance is often cruel and that there is a world where Jo and Jenny have no choice but to suffer and die. For them he could see no easy remedy; no trust was to be placed in the Boodles of his world. For the rest of us, all we can do —as Esther would say—is to perform our duty; freedom lies in the recognition of *that* necessity. This, then, is what I take to be the essential substance of *Bleak House* and the form of the novel is expressive of its substance. Here, at the deepest level, the twin narratives and the widespread use of coincidence unite; out of a world of mingled chance and choice Dickens had created the design necessary to a great work of art.

Little Dorrit

by Lionel Trilling

Little Dorrit is one of the three great novels of Dickens' great last period, but of the three it is perhaps the least established with modern readers. When it first appeared—in monthly parts from December 1855 to June 1857—its success was even more decisive than that of *Bleak House,* but the suffrage of later audiences has gone the other way, and of all Dickens' later works it is *Bleak House* that has come to be the best known. As for *Our Mutual Friend,* after having for some time met with adverse critical opinion among the enlightened—one recalls that the youthful Henry James attacked it for standing in the way of art and truth—it has of recent years been regarded with ever-growing admiration. But *Little Dorrit* seems to have retired to the background and shadow of our consciousness of Dickens.

This does not make an occasion for concern or indignation. With a body of works as large and as enduring as that of Dickens, taste and opinion will never be done. They will shift and veer as they have shifted and veered with the canon of Shakespeare, and each generation will have its special favorites and make its surprised discoveries. *Little Dorrit,* one of the most profound of Dickens' novels and one of the most significant works of the nineteenth century, will not fail to be thought of as speaking with a peculiar and passionate intimacy to our own time.

Little Dorrit is about society, which certainly does not distinguish it from the rest of Dickens' novels unless we go on to say, as we must, that it is *more* about society than any other of the novels, that it is about society in its very essence. This essential quality of the book has become apparent as many of the particular social conditions to which it refers have passed into history. Some of these conditions were already of the past when Dickens wrote, for although imprisonment for debt was indeed not wholly given up until 1869, yet imprisonment for small

debts had been done away with in 1844, the prison of the Marshalsea
had been abolished in 1842, and the Court of the Marshalsea in 1849.
Bernard Shaw said of *Little Dorrit* that it converted him to socialism; it
is not likely that any contemporary English reader would feel it appropriate to respond to its social message in the same way. The dead hand
of outworn tradition no longer supports special privilege in England.
For good or bad, in scarcely any country in the world can the whole
art of government be said to be How Not To Do It. Mrs. General
cannot impose the genteel discipline of Prunes and Prisms, and no
prestige whatever attaches to "the truly refined mind" of her definition
—"one that will seem to be ignorant of the existence of anything that
is not perfectly proper, placid, and pleasant." At no point, perhaps, do
the particular abuses and absurdities upon which Dickens directed his
terrible cold anger represent the problems of social life as we now
conceive them.

Yet this makes *Little Dorrit* not less but more relevant to our sense
of things. As the particulars seem less immediate to our case, the general
force of the novel becomes greater, and *Little Dorrit* is seen to be about
a problem which does not yield easily to time. It is about society in
relation to the individual human will. This is certainly a matter general
enough—general to the point of tautology, were it not for the bitterness
with which the tautology is articulated, were it not for the specificity
and the subtlety and the boldness with which the human will is anat-
omized.

The subject of *Little Dorrit* is borne in upon us by the symbol, or
emblem, of the book, which is the prison. The story opens in a prison
in Marseilles. It goes on to the Marshalsea, which in effect it never
leaves. The second of the two parts of the novel begins in what we are
urged to think of as a sort of prison, the monastery of the Great St.
Bernard. The Circumlocution Office is the prison of the creative mind
of England. Mr. Merdle is shown habitually holding himself by the
wrist, taking himself into custody, and in a score of ways the theme of
incarceration is carried out, persons and classes being imprisoned by their
notions of their predestined fate or their religious duty, or by their
occupations, their life schemes, their ideas of themselves, their very habits
of language.

Symbolic or emblematic devices are used by Dickens to one degree
or another in several of the novels of his late period, but nowhere to
such good effects as in *Little Dorrit*. The fog of *Bleak House*, the dust
heap and the river of *Our Mutual Friend* are very striking, but they
scarcely equal in force the prison image which dominates *Little Dorrit*.

This is because the prison is an actuality before it is ever a symbol;[1] its connection with the will is real, it is the practical instrument for the negation of man's will which the will of society has contrived. As such, the prison haunted the mind of the nineteenth century, which may be said to have had its birth at the fall of the Bastille. The genius of the age, conceiving itself as creative will, naturally thought of the prisons from which it must be freed, and the trumpet call of the "Leonore" overture sounds through the century, the signal for the opening of the gates, for a general deliverance, although it grows fainter as men come to think of the prison not as a political instrument merely but as the ineluctable condition of life in society. "Most men in a brazen prison live"—the line in which Matthew Arnold echoes Wordsworth's "shades of the prison-house begin to close / Upon the growing boy," might have served as the epigraph of *Little Dorrit*. In the mind of Dickens himself the idea of the prison was obsessive, not merely because of his own boyhood experience of prison life through his father's three months in the Marshalsea (although this must be given great weight in our understanding of his intense preoccupation with the theme), but because of his own consciousness of the force and scope of his will.

If we speak of the place which the image of the prison occupied in the mind of the nineteenth century, we ought to recollect a certain German picture of the time, inconsiderable in itself but made significant by its use in a famous work of the early twentieth century. It represents a man lying in a medieval dungeon; he is asleep, his head pillowed on straw, and we know that he dreams of freedom because the bars on his window are shown being sawed by gnomes. This picture serves as the frontispiece of Freud's *Introductory Lectures on Psychoanalysis*—Freud uses it to make plain one of the more elementary ideas of his psychology, the idea of the fulfillment in dream or fantasy of impulses of the will that cannot be fulfilled in actuality. His choice of this particular picture is not fortuitous; other graphic representations of wish-fulfillment exist which might have served equally well his immediate didactic

---

[1] Since writing this, I have had to revise my idea of the actuality of the symbols of *Our Mutual Friend*. Professor Johnson's biography of Dickens has taught me much about the nature of dust heaps, including their monetary value, which was very large, quite large enough to represent a considerable fortune: I had never quite believed that Dickens was telling the literal truth about this. From Professor Dodds' *The Age of Paradox* I have learned to what an extent the Thames was visibly the sewer of London, of how pressing was the problem of the sewage in the city as Dickens knew it, of how present to the mind was the sensible and even the tangible evidence that the problem was not being solved. The moral *disgust* of the book is thus seen to be quite adequately comprehended by the symbols which are used to represent it.

purpose, but Freud's general conception of the mind does indeed make
the prison image peculiarly appropriate. And Freud is in point here
because in a passage of *Little Dorrit* Dickens anticipates one of Freud's
ideas, and not one of the simplest but nothing less bold and inclusive
than the essential theory of the neurosis.

The brief passage to which I make reference occurs in the course of
Arthur Clennam's pursuit of the obsessive notion that his family is in
some way guilty, that its fortune, although now greatly diminished, has
been built on injury done to someone. And he conjectures that the
injured person is William Dorrit, who has been confined for debt in
the Marshalsea for twenty years. Clennam is not wholly wrong in his
supposition—there is indeed guilt in the family, incurred by Arthur's
mother, and it consists in part of an injury done to a member of the
Dorrit family. But he is not wholly right, for Mr. Dorrit has not been
imprisoned through the wish or agency of Mrs. Clennam. The reasoning
by which Arthur reaches his partly mistaken conclusion is of the
greatest interest. It is based upon the fact that his mother, although
mentally very vigorous, has lived as an invalid for many years. She has
been imprisoned in a single room of her house, confined to her chair,
which she leaves only for her bed. And her son conjectures that her
imprisoning illness is the price she pays for the guilty gratification of
keeping William Dorrit in *his* prison—that is, in order to have the right
to injure another, she must unconsciously injure herself in an equivalent
way: "A swift thought shot into [Arthur Clennam's] mind. In that long
imprisonment here [i.e., Mr. Dorrit's] and in her long confinement to
her room, did his mother find a balance to be struck? I admit that I was
accessory to that man's captivity. I have suffered it in kind. He has decayed in his prison; I in mine. I have paid the penalty."

I have dwelt on this detail because it suggests, even more than the
naked fact of the prison itself, the nature of the vision of society of
Little Dorrit. One way of describing Freud's conception of the mind is
to say that it is based upon the primacy of the will, and that the organization of the internal life is in the form, often fantastically parodic,
of a criminal process in which the mind is at once the criminal, the
victim, the police, the judge, and the executioner. And this is a fair
description of Dickens' own view of the mind, as, having received the
social impress, it becomes in turn the matrix of society.

In emphasizing the psychological aspects of the representation of
society of *Little Dorrit* I do not wish to slight those more immediate
institutional aspects of which earlier readers of the novel were chiefly
aware. These are of as great importance now as they ever were in Dickens'

career. Dickens is far from having lost his sense of the cruelty and stupidity of institutions and functionaries, his sense of the general rightness of the people as a whole and of the general wrongness of those who are put in authority over them. He certainly has not moved to that specious position in which all injustice is laid at the door of the original Old Adam in each of us, not to be done away with until we shall all, at the same moment, become the new Adam. The Circumlocution Office is a constraint upon the life of England which nothing can justify. Mr. Dorrit's sufferings and the injustice done to him are not denied or mitigated by his passionate commitment to some of the worst aspects of the society which deals with him so badly.

Yet the emphasis on the internal life and on personal responsibility is very strong in *Little Dorrit*. Thus, to take but one example, in the matter of the Circumlocution Office Dickens is at pains to remind us that the responsibility for its existence lies even with so good a man as Mr. Meagles. In the alliance against the torpor of the Office which he has made with Daniel Doyce, the engineer and inventor, Mr. Meagles has been undeviatingly faithful. Yet Clennam finds occasion to wonder whether there might not be "in the breast of this honest, affectionate, and cordial Mr. Meagles, any microscopic portion of the mustard-seed that had sprung up into the great tree of the Circumlocution Office." He is led to this speculation by his awareness that Mr. Meagles feels "a general superiority to Daniel Doyce, which seemed to be founded, not so much on anything in Doyce's personal character, as on the mere fact of [Doyce's] being an originator and a man out of the beaten track of other men."

Perhaps the single best index of the degree of complexity with which Dickens views society in *Little Dorrit* is afforded by the character of Blandois and his place in the novel. Blandois is wholly wicked, the embodiment of evil; he is, indeed, a devil. One of the effects of his presence in *Little Dorrit* is to complicate our response to the theme of the prison, to deprive us of the comfortable, philanthropic thought that prisons are nothing but instruments of injustice. Because Blandois exists, prisons are necessary. The generation of readers that preceded our own was inclined, I think, to withhold credence from Blandois—they did not believe in his aesthetic actuality because they did not believe in his moral actuality, the less so because they could not account for his existence in specific terms of social causation. But events have required us to believe that there really are people who seem entirely wicked, and almost unaccountably so; the social causes of their badness lie so far back that they can scarcely be reached, and in any case causation pales into irrelevance before the effects of their actions; our effort to "understand" them becomes a mere form of thought.

In this novel about the will and society, the devilish nature of Blandois is confirmed by his maniac insistence upon his gentility, his mad reiteration that it is the right and necessity of his existence to be served by others. He is the exemplification of the line in *Lear:* "The prince of darkness is a gentleman." The influence of Dickens upon Dostoevsky is perhaps nowhere exhibited in a more detailed way than in the similarities between Blandois and the shabby-genteel devil of *The Brothers Karamazov,* and also between him and Smerdyakov of the same novel. It is of consequence to Dickens as to Dostoevsky that the evil of the unmitigated social will should own no country, yet that the flavor of its cosmopolitanism should be "French"—that is, rationalistic and subversive of the very assumption of society. Blandois enfolds himself in the soiled tatters of the revolutionary pathos. So long as he can play the game in his chosen style, he is nature's gentleman dispossessed of his rightful place, he is the natural genius against whom the philistine world closes its dull ranks. And when the disguise, which deceives no one, is off, he makes use of the classic social rationalization. Society has made him what he is; he does in his own person only what society does in its corporate form and with its corporate self-justification. "Society sells itself and sells me: and I sell society." [2]

Around Blandois are grouped certain characters of the novel of whose manner of life he is the pure principle. In these people the social will, the will to status, is the ruling faculty. To be recognized, deferred to, and served—this is their master passion. Money is of course of great consequence in the exercise of this passion, yet in *Little Dorrit* the desire for money is subordinated to the desire for deference. The Midas figure of Mr. Merdle must not mislead us on this point—should, indeed, guide us aright, for Mr. Merdle, despite his destructive power, is an innocent and passive man among those who live by the social will. It is to be noted of all these people that they justify their insensate demand for status by some version of Blandois's pathos; they are confirmed in their lives by self-pity, they rely on the great modern strategy of being

---

[2] This is in effect the doctrine of Balzac's philosophical-anarchist criminal, Vautrin. But in all other respects the difference between Blandois and Vautrin is extreme. Vautrin is a "noble" and justified character; for all his cynicism, he is on the side of virtue and innocence. He is not corrupted by the social injustices he has suffered and perceived, by the self-pity to which they might have given rise; his wholesomeness may be said to be the result of his preference for power as against the status which Blandois desires. The development of Blandois from Vautrin—I do not know whether Dickens' creation was actually influenced by Balzac's—is a literary fact which has considerable social import.

the insulted and injured. Mr. Dorrit is too soft a man for his gentility mania ever to be quite diabolical, but his younger daughter Fanny sells herself to the devil, damns herself entirely, in order to torture the woman who once questioned her social position. Henry Gowan, the cynical, incompetent gentleman-artist who associates himself with Blandois in order to *épater* society, is very nearly as diabolical as his companion. From his mother—who must dismiss once and for all any lingering doubt of Dickens' ability to portray what Chesterton calls the delicate or deadly in human character—he has learned to base his attack on society upon the unquestionable rightness of wronged gentility. Miss Wade lives a life of tortured self-commiseration which gives her license to turn her hatred and her hand against everyone, and she imposes her principle of judgment and conduct upon Tattycoram.

In short, it is part of the complexity of this novel which deals so bitterly with society that those of its characters who share its social bitterness are by that very fact condemned. And yet—so much further does the complexity extend—the subversive pathos of self-pity is by no means wholly dismissed, the devil has not wholly lied. No reader of *Little Dorrit* can possibly conclude that the rage of envy which Tattycoram feels is not justified in some degree, or that Miss Wade is wholly wrong in pointing out to her the insupportable ambiguity of her position as the daughter-servant of Mr. and Mrs. Meagles and the sister-servant of Pet Meagles. Nor is it possible to read Miss Wade's account of her life, "The History of a Self Tormentor," without an understanding that amounts to sympathy. We feel this the more—Dickens meant us to feel it the more—because the two young women have been orphaned from infancy, and are illegitimate. Their bitterness is seen to be the perversion of the desire for love. The self-torture of Miss Wade—who becomes the more interesting if we think of her as the exact inversion of Esther Summerson of *Bleak House*—is the classic maneuver of the child who is unloved, or believes herself to be unloved; she refuses to be lovable, she elects to be hateful. In all of us the sense of injustice precedes the sense of justice by many years. It haunts our infancy, and even the most dearly loved of children may conceive themselves to be oppressed. Such is the nature of the human will, so perplexed is it by the disparity between what it desires and what it is allowed to have. With Dickens as with Blake, the perfect image of injustice is the unhappy child, and, like the historian Burckhardt, he connects the fate of nations with the treatment of children. It is a commonplace of the biography and criticism of Dickens that this reflects his own sense of having been unjustly treated by his parents, specifically in ways which injured his own sense of social status, his own gentility; the general force of Dickens' social feelings derives from their being rooted in childhood experience, and something of the special force of *Little Dorrit* derives from Dickens' having discovered its matter in the depths of his own social will.

At this point we become aware of the remarkable number of false and inadequate parents in *Little Dorrit*. To what pains Dickens goes to represent delinquent parenthood, with what an elaboration of irony he sets it forth! "The Father of the Marshalsea"—this is the title borne by Mr. Dorrit, who, preoccupied by the gratification of being the First Gentleman of a prison, is unable to exercise the simplest paternal function; who corrupts two of his children by his dream of gentility; who will accept any sacrifice from his saintly daughter Amy, Little Dorrit, to whom he is the beloved child to be cherished and forgiven. "The Patriarch"—this is the name bestowed upon Mr. Casby, who stands as a parody of all Dickens' benevolent old gentlemen from Mr. Pickwick through the Cheerybles to John Jarndyce, an astounding unreality of a man who, living only to grip and grind, has convinced the world by the iconography of his dress and mien that he is the repository of all benevolence. The primitive appropriateness of the strange—the un-English!—punishment which Mr. Pancks metes out to this hollow paternity, the cutting off of his long hair and the broad brim of his hat, will be understood by any reader with the least tincture of psychoanalytical knowledge. Then the Meagles, however solicitous of their own daughter, are, as we have seen, but indifferent parents to Tattycoram. Mrs. Gowan's rearing of her son is the root of his corruption. It is Fanny Dorrit's complaint of her enemy, Mrs. Merdle, that she refuses to surrender the appearance of youth, as a mother should. And at the very center of the novel is Mrs. Clennam, a false mother in more ways than one; she does not deny love but she perverts and prevents it by denying all that love feeds on—liberty, demonstrative tenderness, joy, and, what for Dickens is the guardian of love in society, art. It is her harsh rearing of her son that has given him cause to say in his fortieth year, "I have no will."

Some grace—it is, of course, the secret of his birth, of his being really a child of love and art—has kept Arthur Clennam from responding to the will of his mother with a bitter, clenched will of his own. The alternative he has chosen has not, contrary to his declaration, left him no will at all. He has by no means been robbed of his ethical will, he can exert energy to help others, and for the sake of Mr. Dorrit or Daniel Doyce's invention he can haunt the Circumlocution Office with his mild, stubborn, "I want to know. . . ." But the very accent of that phrase seems to forecast the terrible "I prefer not to" of Bartleby the Scrivener in Melville's great story of the will in its ultimate fatigue.

It is impossible, I think, not to find in Arthur Clennam the evidence of Dickens' deep personal involvement in *Little Dorrit*. If we ask what Charles Dickens has to do with poor Clennam, what The Inimitable has to do with this sad depleted failure, the answer must be: nothing, save what is implied by Clennam's consciousness that he has passed the summit of life and that the path from now on leads downward, by his belief that the pleasures of love are not for him, by his "I want to know . . . ," by his wish to negate the will in death. Arthur Clennam is that mode of Dickens' existence at the time of *Little Dorrit* which makes it possible for him to write to his friend Macready, "However strange it is never to be at rest, and never satisfied, and ever trying after something that is never reached, and to be always laden with plot and plan and care and worry, how clear it is that it must be, and that one is driven by an irresistible might until the journey is worked out." And somewhat earlier and with a yet more poignant relevance: "Why is it, that as with poor David, a sense always comes crushing upon me now, when I fall into low spirits, as of one happiness I have missed in life, and one friend and companion I have never made?"

If we become aware of an autobiographical element in *Little Dorrit*, we must of course take notice of the fact that the novel was conceived after the famous incident of Maria Beadnell, who, poor woman, was the original of Arthur Clennam's Flora Finching. She was the first love of Dickens' proud, unfledged youth; she had married what Dickens has taught us to call Another, and now, after twenty years, she had chosen to come back into his life. Familiarity with the story cannot diminish our amazement at it—Dickens was a subtle and worldly man, but his sophistication was not proof against his passionate sentimentality, and he fully expected the past to come back to him, borne in the little hands of the adorable Maria. The actuality had a quite extreme effect upon him, and Flora, fat and foolish, is his monument to the discovered discontinuity between youth and middle age; she is the nonsensical spirit of the anticlimax of the years. And if she is in some degree forgiven, being represented as the kindest of foolish women, yet it is not without meaning that she is everywhere attended by Mr. F's Aunt, one of Dickens' most astonishing ideas, the embodiment of senile rage and spite, flinging to the world the crusts of her buttered toast. "He has a proud stomach, this chap," she cries when poor Arthur hesitates over her dreadful gift. "Give him a meal of chaff!" It is the voice of one of the Parcae.

It did not, of course, need the sad comedy of Maria Beadnell for Dickens to conceive that something in his life had come to an end. It did not even need his growing certainty that, after so many years and so many children, his relations with his wife were insupportable—this realization was as much a consequence as it was a cause of the sense of termination. He was forty-three years old and at the pinnacle of a success unique in the history of letters. The wildest ambitions of his youth could not have comprehended the actuality of his fame. But the last infirmity of noble mind may lead to the first infirmity of noble will. Dickens, to be sure, never lost his love of fame, or of whatever of life's goods his miraculous powers might bring him, but there came a moment when the old primitive motive could no longer serve, when the joy of impressing his powers on the world no longer seemed delightful in itself, and when the first, simple, honest, vulgar energy of desire no longer seemed appropriate to his idea of himself.

We may say of Dickens that at the time of *Little Dorrit* he was at a crisis of the will which is expressed in the characters and forces of the novel, in the extremity of its bitterness against the social will, in its vision of peace and selflessness. This moral crisis is most immediately represented by the condition of Arthur Clennam's will, by his sense of guilt, by his belief that he is unloved and unlovable, by his retirement to the Marshalsea as by an act of choice, by his sickness unto death. We have here the analogy to the familiar elements of a religious crisis. This is not the place to raise the question of Dickens' relation to the Christian religion, which was a complicated one. But we cannot speak of *Little Dorrit* without taking notice of its reference to Christian feeling, if only because this is of considerable importance in its effect upon the aesthetic of the novel.

It has been observed of *Little Dorrit* that certain of Dickens' characteristic delights are not present in their usual force. Something of his gusto is diminished in at least one of its aspects. We do not have the amazing thickness of fact and incident that marks, say, *Bleak House* or *Our Mutual Friend*—not that we do not have sufficient thickness, but we do not have what Dickens usually gives us. We do not have the great population of characters from whom shines the freshness of their autonomous life. Mr. Pancks and Mrs. Plornish and Flora Finching and Flintwinch are interesting and amusing, but they seem to be the fruit of conscious intention rather than of free creation. This is sometimes explained by saying that Dickens was fatigued. Perhaps so, but if we are aware that Dickens is here expending less of one kind of creative energy, we must at the same time be aware that he is expending more than ever before of another kind. The imagination of *Little Dorrit* is marked not so much by its powers of particularization as by its powers of generalization and abstraction. It is an imagination under the dominion of a great articulated idea, a moral idea which tends to find its full development in a religious experience. It is an imagination akin to that which created *Piers Plowman* and *Pilgrim's Progress*. And, indeed, it is akin to the imagination of *The Divine Comedy*. Never before has Dickens made so full, so Dantean, a claim for the virtue of the artist, and there is a Dantean pride and a Dantean reason in what he says of Daniel Doyce, who, although an engineer, stands for the creative mind in general and for its appropriate virtue: "His dismissal of himself [was] remarkable. He never said, I discovered this adaptation or invented that combination; but showed the whole thing as if the Divine Artificer had made it, and he had happened to find it. So modest was he about it, such a pleasant touch of respect was mingled with his quiet admiration of it, and so calmly convinced was he that it was established on irrefragable laws." Like much else that might be pointed to, this confirms us in the sense that the whole energy of the imagination of *Little Dorrit* is directed to the transcending of the personal will, to the search for the Will in which shall be our peace.

We must accept—and we easily do accept, if we do not permit critical cliché to interfere—the aesthetic of such an imagination, which will inevitably tend toward a certain formality of pattern and toward the generalization and the abstraction we have remarked. In a novel in which a house falls physically to ruins from the moral collapse of its inhabitants, in which the heavens open over London to show a crown of thorns, in which the devil has something like an actual existence, we quite easily accept characters named nothing else than Bar, Bishop, Physician. And we do not reject, despite our inevitable first impulse to do so, the character of Little Dorrit herself. Her untinctured goodness does not appall us or make us misdoubt her, as we expected it to do. This novel at its best is only incidentally realistic; its finest power of imagination appears in the great general images whose abstractness is their actuality, like Mr. Merdle's dinner parties, or the Circumlocution Office itself, and in such a context we understand Little Dorrit to be the Beatrice of the *Comedy*, the Paraclete in female form. Even the physical littleness of this grown woman, an attribute which is insisted on and which seems likely to repel us, does not do so, for we perceive it to be the sign that she is not only the Child of the Marshalsea, as she is called, but also the Child of the Parable, the negation of the social will.

Great Expectations

by Paul Pickrel

How a critic goes about seeing a novel as a whole doubtless varies
with individuals. I start by trying to see what is at stake in the book—
who loses, who wins, what they lose or win, whose side the author is
on, and how I know which side he is on. You may object that this is
merely to say that I start with the conflict and that not all novels contain a conflict. I am inclined to think that all of them do, though the
conflict need not be between characters, between a hero and a villain.
Often it is not. It may be between two attitudes toward life, or between
the individual sensibility struggling for integrity and the randomness
of experience, or between appearance and reality, and so on. The very
act of writing a novel establishes a kind of conflict, for it is an attempt
to save something—some person or event or attitude or insight—from
the general destructiveness that we see in the world around us. So perhaps it is enough to say that we can start our contemplation of the
novel with the very simple question: what is this book trying to save?

In a novel like *Great Expectations* the answer to that question is not
very difficult, at least until we try to put it into words. The best I can
do is to say that what Dickens is trying to save in *Great Expectations*
is the poetic view of experience. I think that is what all his novels are
trying to do, but in order to make it anything more than a formula of
words we must look at the novel for a little while.

Great Expectations is in the first place a fantasy. It is a fantasy of a
sort that many children have; perhaps all children have it, and certainly
all lonely children, all children who feel too little wanted or appre-
ciated, who feel the powerlessness of childhood. Nor is it a fantasy
limited to children; anyone who buys a chance on a Cadillac or a

"*Great Expectations*" (originally "Teaching the Novel: *Great Expectations*") by
Paul Pickrel. From *Essays in the Teaching of English: Reports of the Yale Con-
ferences on the Teaching of English*, ed. Edward J. Gordon and Edward S. Noyes
(New York: Appleton-Century-Crofts, Inc., 1960). Copyright © 1960 by The National
Council of Teachers of English. Reprinted by permission of the author and The
National Council of Teachers of English. The opening pages have been omitted with
the author's permission.

sweepstakes ticket shares it, and probably it plays a larger part in the fantasy life of adults than most of us would care to admit. It is a fantasy of sudden translation or sudden transformation, the fantasy of arrival at a point where yearning is magically fulfilled, commonly expressed in such phrases as "when I get rich" or "when my ship comes in." It is a fantasy of a beneficent if unpredictable universe that will someday shower us with gold without any effort or indeed any merit on our part.

Pip, the main character and the narrator in *Great Expectations,* is a little boy at the beginning of the novel. He is an orphan who has been "brought up by hand" by his much older sister, the harsh and loveless Mrs. Joe Gargery. In the normal course of events he will be apprenticed to his brother-in-law, the blacksmith of Joe Gargery; he will learn blacksmithing, and he will live out his days working beside Joe at the forge, perhaps someday marrying Biddy, an unkempt little girl who helps her old grandmother run a miserable evening school for the children of the village.

But two powerful, fantastic figures come into Pip's life and change its course. One is Magwitch, the criminal. He erupts in the first chapter, when Pip is out in a graveyard on the marshes one cold Christmas Eve. Magwitch is a convict escaped from the prison ship, the Hulks, "the wicked Noah's ark." He is in leg irons, cold, hungry, desperate. He is everything that a weak and passive child fears in the adult world: its capacity for wickedness, the brutality of its emotions, its strength and violence and consummate egoism, the threat of being utterly outcast and utterly alone. Magwitch demands that Pip steal food for him from Mrs. Joe Gargery's larder and a file for his leg irons from Joe's forge, and in terror of his life Pip does both. That is apparently the end of the incident, but the first encounter with the convict on the marshes that cold winter twilight leaves a slimy trail across Pip's life—a trail of prisons and criminals and crime—until years later when Magwitch erupts again.

The other fantastic figure in Pip's world is Miss Havisham, a rich old woman who represents the promise of adulthood as much as Magwitch represents its threat. At first glance, this is an extraordinary role for her to play, for her whole life has been sacrificed to memorializing the frustration of her own hopes, in commemorating the moment when the man who was supposed to marry her failed to show up for the wedding. Her clocks stand stopped at that hour, she has never since seen the light of day, she sits in her ruined wedding dress, one ruined white satin slipper still in her hand, the ruined wedding feast spread in the room across the hall, the only guests coming unbidden from behind the plaster. The very name of her once fine house is a mockery: it is "Satis House"—"enough house"—so called in boast by the ancestor who built it because he vainly supposed that whoever had such a house could never want for more, although Miss Havisham, the last of her family, has lived out her years there in testimony to the corrosion of all great expectations, whether based upon the love of man or the seeming certitude of stone.

The reason Miss Havisham can represent the promise of adulthood, in spite of her own ruin, comes partly from the fact that she is rich and partly because she is not alone. She has an adopted daughter, Estella, a little girl as beautiful and coldly distant as the star whose name she bears. Like many people who have made one great self-denying gesture, Miss Havisham is abandonedly self-indulgent, giving a free reign to her whims and self-pity. Adopting Estella was an act of indulgence on her part: bored and foolish, she keeps the child as a plaything, and rears her on a principle of vengeance, carefully cultivating Estella's beauty so that she can grow up to break the hearts of men.

Out of her impatience to see what effect Estella will have on a representative of the male sex, Miss Havisham sends down word that she wants a little boy to come and play in her rooms, and the boy who lives at the blacksmith's, Pip, is the one hit upon. When he appears at Satis House Miss Havisham has reason to congratulate herself: Pip is hopelessly smitten by Estella's beauty; in the presence of her superior manners he realizes the crudity of his own upbringing and the vast difference that stretches between Joe Gargery's forge and the polite world. He and Estella play a card game called "Beggar Your Neighbor," and while Miss Havisham croaks out in the background, "Beggar him, beggar him," Estella proceeds to do just that.

Pip dares not speak of Magwitch to anyone, and he cannot tell the truth about what happens at Miss Havisham's. When pressed for details he lies outrageously: Miss Havisham and Estella belong too much to the world of fantasy to be shared with his companions in everyday reality. In their dark, candlelit rooms, they are fairy godmother and the beautiful princess of a fairy tale, and the thick-fingered, badly dressed, ill-mannered boy from the forge must defend them against any suggestion that they might belong to the daylight world.

A few years pass. Pip is apprentice to Joe Gargery, and Miss Havisham pays his premium as an apprentice, in this way rewarding him for past services, and indicating that his relationship with Satis House is at an end. He was good enough for Estella to practice heartbreak on when she was a child, but now Estella is being trained for bigger game.

Cut off from the figures who have nourished his fantasy, no longer content with the humble expectations Joe Gargery had foreseen for his 'prentice days—those larks they were going to have together—Pip sees in the very landscape of the village a token of his lost hopes: he sees himself like the lowly marshes, while Estella is more distant than ever.

Then comes the most fantastic stroke of all. Suddenly from London the lawyer, Mr. Jaggers, appears at Joe's with the information that Pip has expectations—great expectations—after all. An anonymous bene-factor has decided to lavish luxury and education on the boy, to turn him into a "gentleman." The translation that will put Pip on an equal footing with Estella is to take place; the shower of gold begins to fall. Someone—can it be anyone other than the fairy godmother?—has waved a wand; surely the boy from the forge is destined for the glitter-ing princess.

The story is, then, a fairy tale, with a terrible ogre, Magwitch, a wildly eccentric fairy godmother, an exquisite princess, and a sudden magical transformation. But it is not only a fairy tale, for it is set in a moral universe. One beauty of the life of fantasy, and one reason some of us devote so much time to it, is that it is free from considera-tions of good and evil. In fantasy we kill off our friends and relatives with impunity; we grow rich without effort; we bestow lavish pres-ents without impoverishing ourselves; we live in immense houses with-out concern for the servant problem. The moral universe is quite dif-ferent from that: there our acts have consequences, our choices matter, our privileges entail responsibilities.

Now, just as Dickens defines the world of fantasy by two charac-ters, or groups of characters, Magwitch on the one hand, and Miss Havisham and Estella on the other, so he defines the moral universe by two groups of characters, one group centered on Pip's brother-in-law, the blacksmith Joe Gargery, and the other centered on the London lawyer, Mr. Jaggers, who brings Pip word of his great expectations. Or perhaps that is not quite accurate: Dickens uses Joe and Mr. Jaggers not to define the moral universe—that is done by the plot—but rather to personify or embody two different attitudes toward it.

Joe lives by truth to feeling and Mr. Jaggers lives by truth to fact. Joe characteristically looks at a situation as a whole and relates him-self to it as his heart bids him. Mr. Jaggers characteristically breaks the situation down into "evidence" and disposes of the evidence in what-ever way his mind tells him is appropriate. Joe holds a poetic or sym-bolic view of experience; Mr. Jaggers holds an analytical. If Joe, for example, had come across Christina Rossetti's line, "My heart is like a singing bird," he would have known just what she meant, because he would have recognized its truth to feeling; but if Mr. Jaggers had come across the line he would have asked with a snort, "Tell me, Miss Rossetti, precisely what color are the feathers on your heart?" because the evidence that the chief organ of the circulatory system in fact resembles a singing fowl is extremely meagre.

At the bottom the difference between the two men lies in a difference in their sense of how things are related in the universe and, consequently, in their sense of how an individual can relate himself to them. This comes out most strikingly when we look at the way the two men have behaved in roughly parallel situations. Before the novel opens each man has come across a mother and baby, and each man has responded to the situation in a highly characteristic manner. Joe Gargery came across Pip and his older sister, who was attempting to bring the baby up singlehanded. Joe wanted to help the child, and he did so by embracing the situation as a whole. Though the sister was a termagant with little in her nature to bring the idea of matrimony to a man's mind, Joe married her and so became a kind of father to the baby. Mr. Jaggers, on the other hand, came across a young woman with a baby girl, and his method of dealing with the situation was to separate them. The child he put out for adoption where she would never know who her mother was, and the mother he took into his own house, not on terms of affection but as a servant kept in place by terror. The situations are not strictly parallel, because the future Mrs. Joe Gargery was only a shrew, whereas Mr. Jaggers' future servant was actually a criminal and her baby daughter the child of another criminal, but there is enough similarity to indicate the moral points of view of the two men.

Another way that the difference is dramatized is in the way the two men relate themselves to Pip. Joe's relationship is based upon feeling for the boy, and he allows nothing to cloud the purity of that feeling. This is brilliantly dramatized in the scene where Miss Havisham insists on paying Pip's premium as an apprentice. Joe had never expected such a premium, of course; he expected to take Pip as an apprentice because he loved him. So when Miss Havisham summons them to Satis House, Joe addresses all his remarks to Pip; the money he cannot decline, but he flatly refuses to turn a relationship based on love into a commercial transaction. In speaking to Miss Havisham only through Pip he asserts that nothing she does on this occasion can change their love. Mr. Jaggers, on the other hand, never tires of telling Pip that in their relationship he is acting purely as a businessman. Mr. Jaggers does not approve of the unknown benefactor's scheme and says so; he has no confidence that Pip will profit by his expectations and says so; he is simply carrying out instructions.

Life for Joe is a perpetual marrying and giving in marriage. He constantly gives his heart and accepts the mixed consequences of his generosity. Mr. Jaggers is the purest bachelor, the completely disassociated man. For him the world is a dungheap with an occasional jewel in it. The shrewd man rescues the jewels when he can; otherwise he tries to stay at a distance from the dungheap, and when he must touch it, as a criminal lawyer like Mr. Jaggers frequently must, he will constantly wash his hands with strong soap, as Mr. Jaggers does after each interview.

There are several curious things Dickens does with the characters of Joe and Mr. Jaggers. For one thing, they are both men, and for another they are both good men. More recent English novelists who have tried to defend the poetic view of experience ordinarily use a woman to embody it, and ordinarily make her superior to those who represent another view. Virginia Woolf, for instance, in *To the Lighthouse,* uses Mrs. Ramsay for this purpose, and Mrs. Ramsay is in every way a more appealing character than her analytical philosopher-husband. E. M. Forster usually gives us a middle-aged woman who defends the wisdom of the heart, the wisdom that "connects" person with person, or race with race. She is clearly a better person than the callous males whose wisdom only divides.

But Dickens uses men to embody both the poetic and the analytic view of experience. Perhaps by the time he wrote *Great Expectations* he no longer had much confidence in women as an embodiment of the poetic view; at least there are only two rather minor female characters in the whole book who are not cold and heartless. But, whatever the reason, by using male characters to embody both views, Dickens avoided the danger of allowing a question of truth to become a question of sex.

And it is testimony to Dickens' fairness that Mr. Jaggers is so powerful a character and so good a man. Some readers have not thought so well of him, but he seems to me to be admirable—honest, trustworthy, devoted to duty. In the end his way of looking at experience is mistaken, but he remains a good as well as a brilliant man, and in one wonderful scene he drops a hint that he knows his own mistake.

Another testimony to Dickens' fairness is the fact that he does not allow these two characters to stand alone, but surrounds them with other characters who serve the purpose of modifying the argument.

Around Joe are grouped Mrs. Joe, Uncle Pumblechook, and a few other residents of the village, and they are all dreadful people. They show that the poetic view of experience, so noble when held by one of nature's noblemen like Joe, can easily go a little askew and become the blackest of all tyrannies, the tyranny of the heart. Love with the slightest sign of a price tag is emotional blackmail, and Mrs. Joe is an accomplished emotional blackmailer, a tyrant of the affections. She believes that her act of generosity in taking care of little Pip entitles her to a lifetime of adulation, and whenever the adulation grows faint she issues a cutting reminder of her due. Beside such sharp trafficking in emotions Mr. Jaggers' reliance on facts seems honest and dignified.

Mr. Jaggers does not stand alone on his side of the argument either, for he has a clerk, one Wemmick, who manages to combine the analytical view of experience with the poetic. At the office Wemmick is as closemouthed, as adamant for facts, as Mr. Jaggers himself. His constant advice is to accumulate "portable property." But when we see him at home we discover that his property is anything but portable: he has a little house, a tiny Gothic castle surrounded by a moat. He has an Aged Parent, his deaf old father, whom he somewhat lightly calls "the A.P." but whom he cherishes. He has a pig, and a cannon he shoots off, and a ladyfriend, Miss Skiffins. He is as much married to life as Joe Gargery himself—outside the office.

Probably a student of nineteenth century thought would call Wemmick the Victorian compromise at the level of whimsey. He is also the most modern man in the book, living part of his life in accordance with one view of experience and part of it in accordance with another.

Behind *Great Expectations* and behind most of nineteenth century and twentieth century literature lies a fact that was becoming increasingly apparent throughout Dickens' lifetime and is even more apparent today: the fact that in practical matters the analytic approach to problems is vastly more successful than the poetic. Science and technology provide the outstanding examples of the triumph of analysis, but it is difficult to think of any field of human endeavor in which the introduction of analytic techniques has not had a remarkable effect; it has even influenced those undertakings in which traditionally a sense of wholeness has been sought—philosophy, poetry, religion.

Often it seems that what I have called the poetic view of life—the feeling that things somehow hang together and make sense, that we can somehow relate ourselves as a whole to experience—often it seems that the only argument in favor of that view of life is our profound need of it. But Dickens saw a stronger argument, and in *Great Ex-*

pectations he advances it as a novelist ought to advance his arguments
—by the plot.

The plot of *Great Expectations* is a good one; it holds the reader's
interest; it is full of surprises and odd turns; its complexities all come
out neatly in the end. But more than that, it is a symbolic representation of Dickens' vision of the moral universe, and the chief characteristic of that vision is that good and evil, what we most desire and what
we most loathe, are inextricably intertwined, involved with one another
in such a way that no human hand can sort them out.

The plot is resolved through the discovery of a series of surprising
relationships, and each of these is a relationship between something
loathsome and something desirable. The first of these is the discovery
that Pip does not owe his great expectations to the fairy godmother,
Miss Havisham, but to the ogre, Magwitch. Magwitch has been transported to Australia; there he has prospered as a sheep rancher, and he
has decided to use his wealth to make a gentleman of the little boy
who stole the food and file for him on the marshes long ago. Pip's
rise in the world has not been an act of magic; it has actually been a
reward for theft, for what he has regarded as the most shameful deed
of his life.

The second great discovery is that Estella, whom Pip has wasted
his life in loving, is far from being a princess; she is in fact the illegitimate daughter of Magwitch by the criminal who now serves as Mr.
Jaggers' servant. Miss Havisham is no fairy godmother; she is a foolish
old meddler.

Life is not, Dickens is showing us symbolically by the plot, a dungheap in which one can find an occasional jewel to pluck out, as Mr.
Jaggers supposes. It is an old, old growth; the fairest flower and the
most noxious weed have their roots in the same ancient soil. Joe Gargery's
view of experience is right because he has grasped this fact—not intel-
lectually, for Joe is no intellectual, but by accepting in love the complexity of the moral universe. In Lear's phrase, he has taken upon himself the mystery of things.

Pip himself represents an impure mixture of the easiest parts of both
Joe's and Mr. Jaggers' attitudes toward experience.

Actually it is not altogether fair to compare Pip with Joe and Mr.
Jaggers: they are unchanging, fixed points of reference in the book
—so much so that they seem never to age. But Pip changes. When
first we meet him he is an innocent little boy. When last we see him
he is a man in early middle age, much chastened by experience. The
book is essentially an account of Pip's moral education, and in order

to understand the nature of that education we must see Pip's attitude toward experience clearly—in itself, and in relation to Joe's and Mr. Jaggers'.

Joe and Mr. Jaggers have this in common: they are both in some sense moral realists. To be sure, they differ as fundamentally as two men can about what should be dignified with the label of reality, but they are realists in that both accept the consequences of their own views. For Joe this means that, if to follow the demand of his heart, to love and cherish little Pip involves marrying a shrew, then he is ready to pay the price, and he never whines of it afterward. When Joe realizes that the larks that he and Pip were to share are never going to happen, when he realizes that there is no longer any place for him in Pip's life after Pip has gone to London, he recognizes the situation for what it is; his love takes on a tragic cast, but it remains love. Mr. Jaggers is equally steadfast in facing the worst that his own attitude toward life entails: he is a man isolated, cut off from other human beings—respected and feared but unloved. But Mr. Jaggers can face the worst, unflinching, and recognize it for what it is.

Pip differs from both men. He is not a realist; he is a fantasist. He supposes that he can have the best of both views and the unfavorable consequences of neither. He embraces isolation, as Mr. Jaggers does, but he embraces it selectively—or, in other words, he becomes a terrible snob. He cuts himself off from his own past—he neglects Joe, he does not go back to the forge, he is ashamed of his blacksmith's arm among the languid or vicious young bloods whose society he cultivates in London. He isolates himself from those who love him, but he does not accept the natural consequence of his action, which is lovelessness. Love is as necessary to Pip as to Joe Gargery, but Pip wants it on his own terms, the terms of fantasy. He can only love the fairy-tale princess, the coldly glittering distant star, Estella.

Now Pip is not entirely to be blamed in all this. His early life *was* fantastic; his contacts with creatures like Magwitch and Miss Havisham could only encourage the habit of fantasy in him; and then in adolescence to have his wildest dreams realized, to be suddenly transformed from a humble village apprentice to a young Londoner with great expectations—what result could all this have except to make the boy suppose that the world is indeed whatever his fancy would like it to be? How could he avoid supposing that he was one singularly excused by the gods from facing consequences?

Dickens understood the life of the fantasist because he had lived it, and no one who is familiar with the recent scholarship dealing with

Dickens' life can doubt that *Great Expectations* is a kind of symbolic autobiography. *David Copperfield* is closer to the facts of Dickens' life, but *Great Expectations* is closer to its spirit. For Dickens, as for Pip, life had "come true" to an extent that even his wild fantasy could hardly have suggested in childhood. As a boy Dickens knew poverty and limitation and social disgrace—his father in debtors' prison, his own experience in the blacking factory. He knew what it was to be "cut off from all the luxury of the world." But he was extraordinarily successful, extraordinarily young, and with the possible exception of Mark Twain, there has probably never been another writer to know such fame in his own lifetime. The world was at his feet, yet he was afflicted with a passion for a woman who almost certainly did not return his feeling and probably found him simply distasteful. It is useless to speculate how close Estella in *Great Expectations* is to the woman Dickens loved in the last years of his tempestuous, fame-soaked, unfulfilled life; the point is simply that in writing the novel Dickens is not "talking down"; in creating Joe Gargery and Joe Gargery's attitude toward life, he was struggling to save something he needed as much as we do.

The novel ends with Pip and Estella reunited at the gate of the ruined Satis House. As you probably know, Dickens originally had them simply meet and part, presumably forever; but his friend Bulwer Lytton prevailed upon him to supply the "happier" ending. Some readers have deplored the alteration; to me it seems not to matter, for by this point Estella has been so thoroughly discredited as a creature of fantasy and Pip so thoroughly discredited as a fantasist that they are hardly the same people they once were; they are at most a middle-aged couple who have failed.

The healing touch at the end of the novel is not the reunion of Pip and Estella, but Pip's return to the forge. By the time he goes back, his sister, Mrs. Joe Gargery, has long since died, and the ageless Joe has married Biddy, the girl whom Pip might once have married had he been free of the myth of his own life. They have a child, a little boy, and they have named him Pip. "And there was I again!" the old Pip cries to himself. Another generation has come along; another branch of that ancient vine, the human race, has sprung forth. Its roots are in the tangled dark, as ours are; they will have to learn to live with that fact, as we must; but perhaps, acknowledging the dark, they will do a better job of seeking the light.

In the century since his career was at its zenith, there have been many Dickenses. There was, for instance, Dickens the defender of hearth and home. That Dickens is not very popular today, partly because of the sentimentality that marks the more domestic aspect of his work, and partly because increased knowledge of his private life gives the role a doubtful appropriateness. Then there was Dickens the reformer, the social thinker, the radical. As recently as twenty years ago he was something of a favorite of the Marxist critics, who saw him as very nearly one of their own. Dickens certainly did take a marked interest in the social problems of his time, and he attacked injustice where he found it and as he saw it, bitterly and brilliantly. He was also profoundly conservative; he loved the old England before the railroads, and was the last great chronicler of the stagecoach, the country inn, the roast beef of Old England. As for any program of reform he might have envisioned, as George Orwell has pointed out, it hardly amounted to more than this: that we should all behave better, as indeed we should.

The Dickens I have tried to sketch is a kind of symbolist poet, a man with a sweeping vision of the fundamental relatedness that underlies the surface fragmentation of human life, a man with the insight to see the moral and psychological consequence of that vision, and a man with the power of imagination to set it forth in a vivid, wildly fantastic, yet deeply controlled narrative.

Our Mutual Friend

by J. Hillis Miller

Our Mutual Friend is about "money, money, money, and what money can make of life." This theme plays an important part in Dickens' earlier fiction, too, but never does Dickens so concentrate his attention on the power of money as in this last of his completed novels. The central intrigue of the Harmon murder shows the inheritance of a great fortune apparently corrupting its inheritors, Noddy Boffin, and his ward, Bella Wilfer, just as the desire to "become respectable in the scale of society" corrupts Lizzie Hexam's brother, Charley. Money, one source of each character's station in life, separates Eugene Wrayburn and Lizzie Hexam. In this part of the story, as in others, Dickens is acutely conscious of the difference in people made by class distinctions. "How can I think of you as being on equal terms with me?" asks Lizzie of Eugene. "If my mind could put you on equal terms with me, you could not be yourself." Eugene's class status is an inextricable part of himself and stands between him and Lizzie as an almost palpable barrier. Class distinctions are shown in *Our Mutual Friend* to be closely intertwined with the power of money. The opposition of the "Voice of Society" to Eugene's marriage is as much based on the fact that Lizzie has no money as on the fact that she is "a female waterman, turned factory girl." In the England of *Our Mutual Friend* inherited rank is in the process of giving way to the universal solvent of money, and most of the characters set their hearts on "money, money, money."

Mr. Podsnap's value in Mr. Podsnap's eyes is exactly determined by the amount of money he has, just as his possessions are valuable to him only because they are worth so much cash. Greed motivates Silas Wegg and Rogue Riderhood, characters from the bottom of society, as much as it motivates the Veneerings, the Lammles, Fascination Fledgeby, and other characters near the top of society. A minor character like Twemlow has been rendered ineffectual for life by the gift of a small annuity from his cousin, Lord Snigsworth, and another character, Mortimer Lightwood, says, "My own small income . . . has been an effective Something, in the way of preventing me from turning to at Anything."

The good characters are obsessed with money, too. John Harmon's purpose in life is to find some way to take the curse from the Harmon fortune, and the same desire secretly motivates Mr. Boffin. Old Riah suffers in the false position of being taken as the miserly head of Pubsey and Co. Even Betty Higden concentrates her waning energy on avoiding the workhouse and on protecting the burial money she has sewn in her dress. Her central aim is a desire for financial independence. From the top to the bottom of society most of the characters in *Our Mutual Friend* have their lives determined in one way or another by money, and think of little else.

What *is* money, for Dickens, and what has it "made of life"? Money, he sees, is the attribution of value to what is without value in itself: paper, gold, dust, earth, mud. The Harmon fortune has come from dust, the dust that rises in manmade geological formations around Boffin's Bower. Noddy Boffin is "the Golden Dustman." In one remarkable passage dust, the material source of money, is shown to be present everywhere in the city, along with a kindred mystery, the paper which is the basis of another form of currency:

> The grating wind sawed rather than blew; and as it sawed, the sawdust whirled about the sawpit. Every street was a sawpit, and there were no top-sawyers; every passenger was an under-sawyer, with the sawdust blinding him and choking him.
> That mysterious paper currency which circulates in London when the wind blows gyrated here and there and everywhere. Whence can it come, whither can it go? It hangs on every bush, flutters in every tree, is caught flying by the electric wires, haunts every enclosure, drinks at every pump, cowers at every grating, shudders upon every plot of grass, seeks rest in vain behind the legions of iron rails.

If money is the ascribing of value to valueless matter, the basis of its power for evil over man is his forgetting of this fact. *Our Mutual Friend* is about a whole society which has forgotten. Instead of seeing that man has made money of dust and is the source of its value, this society takes money as the ultimate value-in-itself, the measure and source of all other value. As one of the Voices of Society says, "A man may do anything lawful for money. But for no money! Bosh!" The novel is a brilliant revelation of the results of this false worship of money.

When money is detached both from its material basis and from its human origin, it takes on a power of infinite self-multiplication. Cut off from reality and yet treated by men as the final criterion of worth, its infinity is like that reached when any number is divided by zero. "Money makes money," says Mr. Boffin, "as well as makes everything else." Such a false absolute are those "Shares," which, in their inexhaustible power to duplicate themselves and make everything of nothing, Dickens describes as the virtual god of a moneyed society. Like the mysterious paper currency blown everywhere in London, Shares pervade every corner of the nation's life and determine its nature:

> As is well known to the wise in their generation, traffic in Shares is the one thing to have to do with in this world. Have no antecedents, no established character, no cultivation, no ideas, no manners; have Shares. Have Shares enough to be on Boards of Direction in capital letters, oscillate on mysterious business between London and Paris, and be great. Where does he come from? Shares. Where is he going to? Shares. What are his tastes? Shares. Has he any principles? Shares. What squeezes him into Parliament? Shares. Perhaps he never of himself achieved success in anything, never originated anything, never produced anything! Sufficient answer to all; Shares. O mighty Shares!

Money in its proliferation is hopelessly separated from any authentic human value. Its infinity is nothingness. The human beings who measure themselves and one another by such a yardstick become nothing themselves.

This emptying out of human beings as they become more and more alienated from reality can be seen everywhere in *Our Mutual Friend*.

Most obvious is the hollowness of society people like the Veneerings, the Lammles, and their "friends" the "Fathers of the Scrip-Church." As the Veneerings' name suggests, such people are a false surface with nothing beneath it. If people in "Society" are worth exactly the amount of money (or Shares) they possess, and if money is a human fiction, then the appearance of money is as good as really possessing it, as long as one is not found out. The real possession of money is nothing in itself, and the pretended possession of money is a nothing to the second power, which is neither worse nor better. The Veneering dinner parties are an elaborate theatrical ceremony resting on nothing, and the people who come to these parties have been so dehumanized by their submission to money that they exist not as individuals, but as their abstract roles, "Boots," "Brewer," and so on.

In one sense it is true to say that Dickens shows people turned into objects by money. Instead of being a unique and therefore infinitely valuable individual, each person becomes his monetary worth, an object interchangeable with others. To Mr. Podsnap it seems that his daughter can "be exactly put away like the plate, brought out like the plate, polished like the plate, counted, weighed, and valued like the plate." One of the potentates of Society describes Lizzie Hexam as a mere engine, fueled by so many pounds of beefsteak and so many pints of porter, and deriving therefrom power to row her boat. Bella Wilfer has been "willed away, like a horse, or a dog, or a bird," or "like a dozen of spoons." She suspects John Rokesmith of "speculating" in her. Her involvement in the Harmon mystery has alienated her from herself, and "made [her] the property of strangers."

Such objectifying is not the end of the malign magic performed on men by money. Money turns people into objects which are, like the Podsnap plate, valued only according to the money they are worth. This monetary measure of man might more properly be called a subjectifying. Money is an absolute value which has been generated by people in their living together. Another way to put this is to say that its value is entirely subjective. This value lies only in the collective hallucination of an existence where nothing exists, like the emperor's clothes. A piece of paper currency is worthless scrip. Its value is entirely *mediated,* that is, it is valued not for what it is in itself, but only as it is valued by others. In *Our Mutual Friend* all things and people have the mediated worth of a piece of paper money.

The title of the novel may be taken as an allusion to one form of this mediation. John Rokesmith exists not only for himself, but as he appears in the eyes of other people, and Bella Wilfer is guided at first in her response to him not by her own honest reaction, but by what other people think. Many characters in *Our Mutual Friend* are powerless to confront another person or thing directly. Like the unregenerate Bella, they can see others only through the haze which money casts over everything. This means that they value other people only as society values them, according to their worth in pounds, shillings, and pence. But money has reality only when it is based on some solid human or material reality. The characters in *Our Mutual Friend,* in their failure to see this and in their acceptance of money as intrinsically valuable, have come to live in a collective mirage. This mirage is a closed circuit in which nothing is reflected by nothing. Veneering's election to Parliament is a good example of this. The Veneerings, who are nothing in themselves, give value to the Lammles, Lady Tippins, and the rest, who are nothing in themselves, the Lammles give value to the Veneerings, and so back and forth, in a vain mirroring of nothing by nothing.

The motif of a literal mirroring occurs at crucial points in *Our Mutual Friend*. Poor little Miss Podsnap has derived her early views of life from "the reflections of it in her father's boots, and in the walnut and rosewood tables of the dim drawing-rooms, and in their swarthy giants of looking-glasses." She confronts life indirectly, as it is mediated by the massive presence of her father and his possessions. To see a Veneering dinner party reflected in "the great looking-glass above the sideboard," to see the vain Bella admiring herself in her mirror, or to see Fledgeby secretly watching Riah's reflection in the chimney-glass is to witness a concrete revelation of the way the lives of such people are self-mirroring. The reflection in the mirror is emptied of its solidity and presented as a thin surface of appearance hiding fathomless depths of nullity. Mirroring brings to light the vacuity of people whose lives are determined by money. Each such character is reflected in the blankness of the glass, and can see others only as they are mediated by a reflected image.

When this detachment from solidity is complete, human beings have only one opening for their energies: the attempt to dominate others by rising in the unreal scale which is generated in a society dominated by money. The image of a vertical scale permeates *Our Mutual Friend*. The characters feel themselves higher or lower on this scale as they possess more or less money, or as they can cheat others out of money in the perpetual poker game which society sustains. Mr. Boffin invokes the primary law of an acquisitive society in his defense of miserliness: "Scrunch or be scrunched." The Lammles, when they find that each has married the other under the mistaken impression that he is rich, decide to cooperate in fleecing society. Fascination Fledgeby seeks the secret control of others money gives, and Silas Wegg, exulting in the power he thinks the Harmon will gives him, declares he is one hundred, no, five hundred times the man Noddy Boffin is. The unrecognized emptiness of money makes it an unlimited instrument of man's will to power.

A society in which personal relations reduce themselves to a struggle for dominance develops that drama of *looks* and *faces* which is so important in *Our Mutual Friend*. Scenes in the novel are frequently presented as a conflict of masks. Each person tries to hide his own secret and to probe behind a misleading surface and find the secrets of others. The prize of a successful uncovering is the power that goes with knowing and not being known. Bella Wilfer finds that the Boffin household has become a confrontation of stealthy faces: "What with taking heed of these two faces, and what with feeling conscious that the stealthy occupation must set some mark on her own, Bella soon began to think that there was not a candid or a natural face among them all but Mrs. Boffin's." In the same way the Lammles exchange hidden looks over the heads of their unconscious victim, Georgiana Podsnap, and Silas Wegg and Mr. Venus trade glances as Wegg reads stories about misers to Mr. Boffin. In this case, as in the others, the master of the situation is the man whose face is an opaque nonreflector and remains unread.

In *Our Mutual Friend* the unreality of money has spread out to define the lives of most of the characters and to dissolve them in its emptiness. Master or slave, high on the scale or low, such characters float free in an unsubstantial realm of subjective fantasy. This quality is the chief source of the comedy of the novel. As in Dickens' earlier fiction, this comedy has its source in the incongruity of a mind enclosed in its own grotesque vision of things. In *Our Mutual Friend* this detachment has a special linguistic expression, partly a matter of the language used by the characters themselves and partly a matter of the way the narrator describes them. Both narrator and characters speak in metaphors which have separated themselves from their material basis, and hover in a verbal realm, a realm which perfectly defines the deracinated existence of the characters. What begins as a *jeu d'esprit,* a vivid way of describing a character or event, undermines the human reality it names and infects it parasitically with its own inane unreality. The Veneerings' butler is first *"like* a gloomy Analytical Chemist," but the figure of speech soon displaces the reality, and the butler becomes simply "the Analytical." In the same way Mrs. Podsnap is a rocking horse, Gaffer Hexam is a bird of prey, Mr. Wilfer is a cherub, and so on. Sometimes a whole scene is pervaded by a figure of speech and is transformed into a surrealistic nightmare, as in the case of a Podsnap soirée which is described as a steam bath of dinner smells:

> And now the haunch of mutton vapour-bath, having received a gamey infusion and a few last touches of sweets and coffee, was quite ready, and the bathers came. . . . Bald bathers folded their arms and talked to Mr. Podsnap on the hearth-rug; sleek-whiskered bathers, with hats in their hands, lunged at Mrs. Podsnap and retreated; prowling bathers went about looking into ornamental boxes and bowls as if they had suspicions of larceny on the part of the Podsnaps and expected to find something they had lost at the bottom; bathers of the gentler sex sat silently comparing ivory shoulders.

In such passages Dickens admirably exposes the hollowness of his people by describing them in language which affirms that a fantastic metaphor is as real here as anything else. The characters themselves use

language which is hilariously detached from reality, like the poetry
Wegg ludicrously misapplies to any situation. Dickens' characters, even
stupid ones, have an extraordinary gift of speech. The comic characters
in *Our Mutual Friend* unwittingly use this power to reveal their own
vacuity. The weird scenes between Wegg and Venus, or the gammon
and spinach of the Voices of Society, or the gorgeous nonsense of the
colloquies between Mrs. Wilfer and Lavinia are triumphs of this mode
of comedy. Such characters are cut off from any anchor of substantial
feeling and release a splendid linguistic energy which expands inex-
haustibly in the void. Speech, like money, has become in *Our Mutual
Friend* a traffic in counterfeit coin.

If the novel demonstrates what money can make of life, it also shows
what lies behind money, and it shows characters who escape from the
collective dream it creates. If the personages are mostly bewitched by
a false god, the novel as a whole is a work of demystification.

This is accomplished first through the language of the narrator. The
voice the reader hears is cool and detached, very different, for example,
from the emotionally involved voice of David Copperfield as he tells
his own story. This is especially apparent in the scenes of the Veneering
dinner parties. These are described in the present tense, in language
that is cold and withdrawn, terse, with an elliptical economy new in
Dickens. Sometimes verbs and articles are omitted, and the reader confronts a series of nouns with modifiers which produces the scene before
his mind's eye as if by magical incantation: "Dining-room no less
magnificent than drawing-room; tables superb; all the camels out, and
all laden. Splendid cake, covered with Cupids, silver, and true-lovers'
knots. Splendid bracelet, produced by Veneering before going down,
and clasped upon the arm of bride." The ironic detachment of such
language makes the consciousness of the narrator (and of the reader)
into a mirror uncovering the emptiness of the characters. The reader
himself becomes the great looking-glass above the sideboard which shows
what money has made of life. This mirrorlike detachment to a greater
or lesser degree is the narrative perspective of the entire novel. It allows
the reader to escape from the enchantment which holds the characters.

Escape to what? What waking reality, for Dickens, lies behind the
dream? Dickens gives unusual attention in this novel to elemental matter. If money is in one sense unreal, in another sense the paper or metal
of which it is made has a solidity which mediated subjectives can never
possess. Mr. Podsnap's hideous epergne reflects no value on its owner,
but his desire not to have beautiful things on his table has inadvertently
made it possible to see in his silver and plate the sheer, massive inertia
of matter—heavy, impenetrable, meaningless, alien to man:

Hideous solidity was the characteristic of the Podsnap plate. Everything was made to look as heavy as it could and to take up as much room as possible. Everything said boastfully, "Here you have as much of me in my ugliness as if I were only lead; but I am so many ounces of precious metal worth so much an ounce—wouldn't you like to melt me down?" A corpulent straddling epergne, blotched all over as if it had broken out in an eruption rather than been ornamented, delivered this address from an unsightly silver platform in the centre of the table.

The otherness of elemental matter, brought to the surface in this passage, is kept constantly before the reader throughout *Our Mutual Friend*. It is the substance which lies behind or beneath the hollowness of an avaricious society. This substance is there on the literal level of the novel: in the fire where Lizzie Hexam sees pictures of her life, in the wind which blows the dust through the streets, creating a wild disorder in the clouds, and making the pitiful little tumults in the streets of no account. Elemental matter is present in the dust of the Harmon Mounds, in the mud of the river, in the dunghills where Noddy Boffin's misers hid their gold, in the gold itself in the Bank of England —in which Bella would like to have "an hour's gardening, with a bright copper shovel." Elemental matter is present in the river which flows through all the novel and is the scene of much of its action. All four elements are unobtrusively gathered together when Charley Hexam says of a glow in burning coal: "That's gas, that is, coming out of a bit of a forest that's been under the mud that was under the water in the days of Noah's Ark."

These material elements are not "symbols," if that means expressions of some reality which transcends them, and for which they stand. The river, the dust, the wind, and the fire are what they are: mere matter. *Our Mutual Friend* differs in this from Dickens' earlier novels. In *Dombey and Son* or *David Copperfield* the sea is a symbol of transcendent spiritual reality. The river of *Our Mutual Friend* is, in most of the passages describing it, only water, but, like the other material elements, it has a substantiality which the Voice of Society lacks. The narrator keeps this reality before the reader throughout the novel, not only in the literal scene, but in metaphors, overt and covert, in a thousand subtle linguistic touches which refer back to it, as the mutton vapor bath links the Podsnap drawing rooms to the Thames, or as Fascination Fledgeby, after his thrashing by Lammle, is shown "plunging and gambolling all over his bed, like a porpoise or dolphin in its native element."

The various dramatic actions of the novel show characters breaking through illusion to confront material reality. Such a confrontation takes two forms. There is first the literal descent into matter, Silas Wegg's plunge into a garbage cart, the drownings or near drownings of John Harmon, George Radfoot, Gaffer Hexam, Rogue Riderhood, Bradley Headstone, and Eugene Wrayburn. These entries into matter are also encounters with death, and dispersion into dust to which we shall all come at last. In addition, a human and inward form of substantial reality plays an important role in *Our Mutual Friend:* emotions, the affective depths of the self. Alienated, unreal people are incapable of authentic feeling. Their emotions are falsified or betrayed by their conscious behavior. The story of Bradley Headstone shows a man of strong repressed emotions destroyed when these feelings rise from his inner depths. Bradley's feelings are explicitly associated with the sea, those outer depths of water. "No man knows till the time comes, what depths are within him," Bradley tells Lizzie. "To me you brought it; on me, you forced it; and the bottom of this raging sea . . . has been heaved up ever since."

Only the characters who confront material and emotional depths, and then return to live their surface lives in terms of those depths can reconcile "Society" and reality. Eugene Wrayburn returns from his near death in the river to reject class distinctions, marry Lizzie Hexam, and conquer the boredom which has undermined his life, making him "like one cast away, for the want of something to trust in, and care for, and think well of." Bella Wilfer, who, like Eugene, has been "giddy for want of the weight of some sustaining purpose," renounces her desire for money and chooses to become the "Mendicant's Bride." This proves that "she's the true golden gold at heart." Gold does not measure the value of man. Man's heart, golden or empty, gives value to money and makes it a force for good or for evil. In the hands of Bella and John Harmon the Harmon fortune "turns bright again, after a long, long rust in the dark, and at last begins to sparkle in the sunlight." Just as Mr. Boffin's change to a miser is only apparent, just as Rogue Riderhood is not changed by his near death in the Thames, and just as Eugene Wrayburn has been a good fellow all along, so Bella Wilfer does not really change. Her true nature is brought to the surface. Even in this last of his finished novels, a novel with so many apparent transformations of character, Dickens remains true to his feeling that each man or woman has a fixed nature, a selfhood which may be obscured or distorted but never essentially altered.

Chronology of Important Dates

1812	February 7. Born at 387 Mile End Terrace, Landport, Portsea.
1824	Father imprisoned in the Marshalsea for debt. Dickens works several months in a blacking warehouse.
1824-26	School at Wellington House Academy, London.
1827-28	Clerk in attorney's office, studies shorthand.
1829-31	Shorthand-writer (law-reporter) in Doctors' Commons. Reading at the British Museum.
1832	Reporter for the *True Sun* and the *Mirror of Parliament*.
1833	First publication in the *Monthly Magazine,* December.
1834	Reporter for the *Morning Chronicle*.
1836	February 7. *Sketches by Boz* published in volume illustrated by George Cruikshank. April. Engaged to undertake *The Pickwick Papers* in monthly numbers. Sales reach 40,000 in later parts (to November 1837). April 2. Marries Catherine Hogarth. December 25. Meets John Forster.
1837	Charles, first of ten children, born January 6. February. *Oliver Twist* (to March 1839).
1838	April. *Nicholas Nickleby* (to October 1839).
1840-41	*The Old Curiosity Shop* and *Barnaby Rudge* appear in weekly parts in *Master Humphrey's Clock*.
1842	January-June. Tour of the United States. October. *American Notes*.
1843	January. *Martin Chuzzlewit* (to July 1844).
1844-45	Dickens and family in Genoa; tour of Italy and France.
1846	*Pictures from Italy*. October. *Dombey and Son* (to April 1848).
1849	May. *David Copperfield* (to November 1850).
1850	March. Starts periodical, *Household Words*.

1851   May. Performs with amateur company of actors before Queen Victoria.

1852   March. *Bleak House* (to September 1853).

1854   April 1. *Hard Times* (to August 12).

1855   December. *Little Dorrit* (to June 1857).

1857   June 30. First public reading from his works, London.

1858   June 10. Public declaration of separation from his wife.

1859   April 20. *A Tale of Two Cities* (to November 26) in new periodical, *All the Year Round*.

1860   December 1. *Great Expectations* (to August 3, 1861).

1864   May. *Our Mutual Friend* (to November 1865).

1867   November 9. Leaves for tour of public readings in the United States (to April 22, 1868).

1869-70   Public readings in England.

1870   June 9. Dies at Gad's Hill Place, Rochester. Buried, June 14, in Westminster Abbey. *The Mystery of Edwin Drood* published posthumously.

Notes on the Editor and Authors

MARTIN PRICE, editor of this volume, is Professor of English at Yale University. He has written *Swift's Rhetorical Art* and *To the Palace of Wisdom: Studies in Order and Energy from Dryden to Blake,* and he is completing a study of character in the novel since Jane Austen.

ANGUS WILSON, the distinguished author of novels, short stories, and criticism, has published, among other works, *Hemlock and After, Anglo-Saxon Attitudes, The Middle Age of Mrs. Eliot,* and *Late Call.* He has also written a study of Zola and a book on his own writing, *The Wild Garden.*

DOROTHY VAN GHENT, late Professor of English at the University of Buffalo, was the author of *The English Novel: Form and Function.*

BARBARA HARDY, Professor of English at Royal Holloway College, University of London, is the author of *The Novels of George Eliot* and a more general critical study of the novel, *The Appropriate Form.*

GEORGE H. FORD, Professor and Chairman of English at the University of Rochester, has published *Keats and the Victorians* and a critical study of D. H. Lawrence's novels, *Double Measure.* In addition to *David Copperfield,* he has edited (with Lauriat Lane) *The Dickens Critics* and (with Sylvère Monod) the Norton Critical Edition of *Hard Times.*

W. H. AUDEN, the distinguished poet, has also published two notable volumes of criticism, *The Enchafèd Flood* and *The Dyer's Hand.*

JOHN BAYLEY, critic and novelist, is a Fellow of New College, Oxford, and the author of the novel, *In Another Country,* and of three critical studies, *The Romantic Survival, The Characters of Love,* and *Tolstoy and the Novel.*

STEVEN MARCUS, Associate Professor of English at Columbia University, has published *The Other Victorians* and plans a second volume of his critical study of Dickens.

KATHLEEN TILLOTSON, Professor of English at Bedford College, University of London, has published (with John Butt) *Dickens at Work* and (with Geoffrey Tillotson) *Mid-Victorian Studies.* She has prepared *Oliver Twist* for the new edition of Dickens published by Oxford University Press.

W. J. HARVEY, Professor of English at Queen's University, Belfast, is the author of *The Art of George Eliot* and *Character and the Novel.*

LIONEL TRILLING, Professor of English at Columbia University, is the author of a novel, *The Middle of the Journey*, and several distinguished volumes of criticism, including *The Liberal Imagination, The Opposing Self*, and *Beyond Culture*.

PAUL PICKREL, Professor of English at Smith College, has published a novel, *The Moving Stairs*, edited *The Yale Review* for many years, and has reviewed books in many periodicals.

J. HILLIS MILLER, Professor of English at The Johns Hopkins University, is the editor of *William Carlos Williams* in the Twentieth Century Views series, and author of *The Disappearance of God* and *Poets of Reality*, as well as a forthcoming book on Thomas Hardy.

Selected Bibliography

Editions

There is not yet a standard edition of Dickens' novels; a new one has begun to appear under the sponsorship of the Oxford University Press as the Clarendon Dickens. The most useful complete editions are the New Oxford Illustrated Dickens and the Nonesuch Edition, which includes three volumes of letters edited by Walter Dexter (London, 1937-38). The letters have begun to appear in the new Pilgrim Edition, ed. Madeline House and Graham Storey; the first of twelve projected volumes was published by the Oxford University Press in 1965. *The Speeches of Charles Dickens* were edited by K. J. Fielding, Oxford, 1960.

Biography

The best biography is now Edgar Johnson, *Charles Dickens: His Tragedy and Triumph,* New York, 1952 (2 vols.). The *Life* by John Forster, 1872-74, has been usefully edited by J. W. T. Ley, London and New York, 1926; and more recently by A. J. Hoppé (Everyman's Library), London and New York, 1966 (2 vols.). Of more special interest is Arthur A. Adrian, *Georgina Hogarth and the Dickens Circle,* London and New York, 1957. There is also a pictorial biography with text by J. B. Priestley, *Charles Dickens,* London and New York, 1961.

Criticism

The most useful list of Dickens criticism appears in *The Dickens Critics,* ed. George H. Ford and Lauriat Lane, Ithaca, N. Y., 1961; paperback, 1966 (a collection of criticism). There is an extensive review of Dickens studies by Ada B. Nisbet in *Victorian Fiction,* ed. Lionel Stevenson, Cambridge, Mass., 1964. Current annual bibliographies appear in *Victorian Studies,* Bloomington, Indiana.

Axton, William F., *Circle of Fire: Dickens' Theatrical Vision and Style and the Popular Victorian Theater,* University of Kentucky Press, 1966.

Butt, John, and Kathleen Tillotson, *Dickens at Work*, London, 1957.

Chesterton, Gilbert K., *Appreciations and Criticisms of the Works of Charles Dickens*, London and New York, 1911.

Clark, William R., ed., *Discussions of Charles Dickens*, Boston, 1961 (a collection of criticism).

Cockshut, A. O. J., *The Imagination of Charles Dickens*, London, 1961; New York, 1962.

Collins, Philip A. W., *Dickens and Crime*, London and New York, 1962, 1964; *Dickens and Education*, London and New York, 1963.

Dabney, Ross H., *Love and Property in the Novels of Dickens*, University of California Press, 1967.

Davis, Earle R., *The Flint and the Flame: The Artistry of Charles Dickens*, University of Missouri Press, 1963.

Engel, Monroe, *The Maturity of Dickens*, Cambridge, Mass., 1959.

Fanger, Donald, *Dostoevsky and Romantic Realism: A Study of Dostoevsky in Relation to Balzac, Dickens, and Gogol*, Cambridge, Mass., 1965.

Fielding, K. J., *Charles Dickens: A Critical Introduction*, Boston, 1965.

Ford, George H., *Dickens & His Readers: Aspects of Novel-Criticism since 1836*, Princeton, 1965; paperback, New York, 1965.

Garis, Robert, *The Dickens Theatre: A Reassessment of the Novels*, Oxford, 1965.

Gissing, George, *Charles Dickens*, Port Washington, N. Y., 1966 (originally published in 1924).

Gross, John, and Gabriel Pearson, eds., *Dickens and the Twentieth Century*, London and Toronto, 1962.

House, Humphry, *The Dickens World*, London, 1941; paperback, 1960; *All in Due Time*, Part III, London, 1955.

Jackson, Thomas A., *Charles Dickens: The Progress of a Radical*, London and New York, 1938.

Leavis, F. R., *The Great Tradition*, London, 1948; "Dombey and Son," *Sewanee Review*, LXX (1962) 177-201.

Lindsay, Jack, *Charles Dickens: A Biographical and Critical Study*, London, 1950.

Manning, John, *Dickens and Education*, Toronto, 1959.

Marcus, Steven, *Dickens: from Pickwick to Dombey*, London and New York, 1964.

Miller, J. Hillis, *Charles Dickens: The World of His Novels*, Cambridge, Mass., 1958.

Monod, Sylvère, *Dickens, Romancier*, Paris, 1953.

Peyrouton, N., ed., *Dickens Criticism: A Symposium* (with George H. Ford, J. Hillis Miller, Edgar Johnson, and Sylvère Monod), Boston, 1962.

Orwell, George, "Charles Dickens," *Inside the Whale,* London, 1941 (reprinted in later collections of Orwell essays).

Shaw, George Bernard, Introduction to *Hard Times,* London, 1912; to *Great Expectations,* Edinburgh, 1937; London (Novel Library), 1947. See also House, *All in Due Time,* for "G. B. S. on *Great Expectations,*" a commentary.

Spilka, Mark, *Dickens and Kafka: A Mutual Interpretation,* University of Indiana Press, 1963.

Stoehr, Taylor, *Dickens: The Dreamer's Stance,* Ithaca, N. Y., 1965.

Tillotson, Kathleen, *Novels of the Eighteen-Forties,* Oxford, 1954; paperback, 1961.

Wilson, Edmund, "Dickens: The Two Scrooges," *The Wound and the Bow,* Boston, 1941; New York, 1947.

Zabel, Morton Dauwen, *Craft and Character in Modern Fiction,* New York, 1957.